SALVATION AND PROTEST

Roy Wallis

Studies of Social and Religious Movements

St. Martin's Press   New York

Printed in Great Britain

First Published in the United States of America in 1979

ISBN 0-312-69834-8

Library of Congress Cataloging in Publication Data

Wallis, Roy.
   Salvation and protest.

   Bibliography: p.
   Includes index.
   1. Cults—Addresses, essays, lectures.
2. Sects—Addresses, essays, lectures. 3. Social
movements—Addresses, essays, lectures. I. Title.
BP603.W34 1979   301.5'8   78-22008
ISBN 0-312-69834-8

Contents

Acknowledgements

This book has grown from over six years of research and writing on new religious and social movements. Most of the chapters have been 'tried out' on various audiences during that time. A number have been published although sometimes in rather obscure locations.

Chapter 2 was delivered at the 12th International Conference on the Sociology of Religion, The Hague, Netherlands, August 1973, and included in the Conference Acts (available from CISR Secretariat, 39 Rue de la Monnaie, 59042 Lille Cedex, France.) Chapter 3 appeared in *The Zetetic*, 4, 1, 1975, pp. 9-14. Chapter 4 was first published in *The Sociological Review*, 24, 4, November 1976, pp. 807-29. Part of Chapter 6 was published in *The Scottish Journal of Sociology*, 1, 2, April 1977, pp. 195-203. Chapter 7 appeared in *Sociology*, 10, 2, May 1976, pp. 271-95. Chapter 8 was also published in *The Scottish Journal of Sociology*, 1, 1, November 1976, pp. 81-93. Chapter 11 first appeared in Colin Bell and Howard Newby, editors, *Doing Sociological Research*, George Allen & Unwin, London, 1977. I am grateful to all the editors and publishers involved for permission to include previously published material here.

The research and writing of these essays have been greatly facilitated by various awards and grants. I am grateful to the Social Science Research Council whose generous funding made possible many of these studies. The awards of a Morris Ginsberg Fellowship at the London School of Economics and a Lever-hulme Research Fellowship made possible individual chapters. Stirling University generously granted me sabbatical leave.

For helpful comments on particular aspects of the various

Acknowledgements

researches included here I am grateful to Vic Hanby, Stewart Butts and Richard Barron. Richard Bland has been a boon companion during all the studies and writing which have led to this book. A better colleague and more amiable friend one could not wish for. I am grateful to him for his enduring kindness to an irascible neighbour; for his willingness to share of his time; and for his assistance with the study on which Chapter 9 is based. Dr. Bryan Wilson has been a major stimulus and my principal commentator on half-thought-out ideas and ill-formulated prose for several years. He has read most of the chapters in one form or another, and patiently but trenchantly criticised all he has seen. Had I followed his model and advice more closely this book would, I cannot doubt, be better than it is. Dorothy Buchan is the final member of this trio of paragons. Her typing and gently caustic asides have often enabled me more clearly to see where I had quite failed to convey even a modicum of sense. My wife and children have, to my utter amazement, continued to love me regardless.

For my mother, Constance Rose

Introduction

The essays in this volume display a considerable diversity of style, focus and method. The movements discussed in the following chapters are themselves very diverse, including moral crusades, citizens' action movements and religious groups, and it may well be asked whether these collectivities share any significant common features; whether, indeed, they are *movements* at all. I take the domain of social movements (of which, perhaps *religious* movements are a sub-class; and while the addition is useful as a descriptive distinction its continued repetition would be monotonous, and it will therefore often be omitted) to inhabit a vague realm bounded on one side by almost entirely *un*institutionalised collective behaviour like crazes, 'cultural trends' such as hippy dress and speech, or panics, in which interaction is largely informal, and where organisation is almost entirely absent. On the other side, the boundaries are marked by *highly* institutionalised forms of collective behaviour in which modes of procedure are thoroughly routinised, established means are employed for the implementation of ends, and interaction is largely formalised. Social movements, then, I shall define as relatively sustained collective efforts to change, maintain, or restore some feature(s) of society or of its members, which employ relatively uninstitutionalised means to promote those ends. There are undoubtedly limitations to this definition, but I shall not give these any attention here, since the issue of precisely how social movements are to be defined is simply not consequential for my enterprise. I do not propose to offer *a* theory of social movements. The term merely marks off in a loose and flexible way a range of phenomena which interest me.

1

Any theories expounded in the course of discussing these various movements aspire to nothing so general as a theory of social movements, and indeed to borrow an analogy from Alasdair MacIntyre (1971), the effort to produce such a theory seems as likely to succeed as the effort — should anyone be so foolhardy as to undertake it — to produce a theory of holes. Social movements are so very diverse that it seems altogether implausible that any convincing theory could accommodate them all. My own programme is much more modest. Social movements define an area of interest within which there are phenomena to be explained. Why do people join together to restore moral standards in a society which seems no longer to desire standards of that kind? Why do efforts to create a social movement founder? What conditions favour the emergence of schisms within religious groups, or alternatively, the development of highly cohesive collectivities? It is issues of this kind which are addressed in these studies. In so far as theories and explanations are offered, they should not be understood as attempts to generalise about *all* social movements on the one hand, nor as always restricted to social movements on the other. Social organisation most probably has common features wherever it is found, and explanations for some characteristics of social movements may well have application beyond them. On the other hand, social movements are also highly situated in cultural and historical contexts from which arise differing aims, methods and composition. Hence explaining some features of these movements will similarly require the elucidation of particular aspects of history and cultural context.

Not all the essays have an explanatory purpose. In some cases the motivation has been rather (perhaps 'merely') to develop an intelligible analytical description of the movement concerned, to provide an interpretative understanding of some aspect of its form or development, or in the case of the final essay, to make some sense out of my own relationship with one such movement (as well as telling a cautionary tale).

The essays therefore seek to generate explanation and generalisation on the basis of a relatively (although variably) close acquaintance with particular movements. In part the reason for this is the conviction that it is usually better to get to know one or a few movements well and in the richness of their context, than to know many movements fragmentarily. The investigator who adopts a surveying approach, directing few questions at many cases, inevitably loses much of the context

2

from which the answers come and within which they derive their meaning (which is not to say that on occasion surveys may not be useful tools). The issue of meaning is, indeed, a crucial one. Favouring as I do, a metaphysic of free will, my inclination is to seek to understand social phenomena as an outcome of the interpretation of the world and their situation within it by human agents who attempt to formulate the most rational strategies they can to contend with life's vicissitudes. Hence the understanding and explanation of their actions demands close attention to the agents' interpretations, their beliefs and motives, as well as to the wider structural circumstances which provided the occasions for and the resources within which, this interpreting, reasoning and deciding takes place.

I leave entirely open the question of whether a social science can be developed following the (alleged) model of the natural sciences, with abstract theories and a nomological-deductive mode of explanation. I believe that a quite reasonable ground for not pursuing such a programme myself is that the results available to date in sociology at least have often been unconvincing, uninteresting, or both, particularly in the field of social and religious movements. If eschewing that programme means that my researches are not 'science', then so much the worse for science.

The aim to incorporate the subjective meaning of human agents into explanation is no new endeavour. Unfortunately its implementation often founders on a residual positivism among sociologists which assumes that such meaning can quite adequately be derived from an analysis of the objective situation of the actors concerned, or even worse, that some guess about subjective meaning can be introduced in explanation as a last resort when correlations indicate only weak relationships between objective variables. An interesting case is th use of the concept of *relative deprivation*. Glock and Stark (1965), Aberle (1966), and Hine (1974) are among the numerous sociologists who look to some form of relative deprivation to provide an explanation for features of social and religious movements. The term, pointing to some disparity between the actual and the desirable, indicates a state of affairs which all men must experience at some time or another. Hence it readily enables us to identify with the condition of those of whom it is alleged this frustrating experience provided the motivation for joining or founding a social movement. But the very generality of the condition provides the first stumbling-

3

block. The class of those one might presume to be experiencing some degree of relative deprivation of some kind or another greatly exceeds in size the class of those who join social or religious movements. A theory of movement origins or affiliation must therefore do more than point to a group we might suppose to be experiencing deprivation.

One solution to this has been the proposal that various *types* of relative deprivation can be distinguished. Glock and Stark, for example, list five such types: economic, social, organismic, ethical and psychic. David Aberle lists four types: relative deprivation of possessions, status, behaviour and worth. Graham Allan (1974) adds yet another with the notion of 'relative deprivation of *total* worth'. These efforts would seem to add greater precision to the task of relating particular types of deprivation to affiliation with particular types of social or religious movement, were it not for the fact that the types are so ill-defined that the researcher can have little confidence that he can unambiguously allocate cases to the types. Moreover, even here it will generally prove to be the case that the class of those who may be said to suffer such deprivation will considerably exceed the class of those joining a particular type of social movement. It is often implied that those who do join experience the postulated type of relative deprivation more chronically or acutely than the rest, but without clear means of identifying the characteristics of each type or measures of their strength, this argument lacks any great force. The suspicion also arises that a plausible 'type' of relative deprivation can be invented for any particular movement. Indeed, the procedure seems to take the following form: the observer examines the movement's belief system and concludes that it offers a resolution to frustrations of status, to ethical dilemmas, or to physical handicap and concludes that this is what its members seek. Hence, they must have been deprived of that to begin with. Apart from the very substantial problem that those who join the movement may not see what is offered in this way — and indeed may see it in very diverse ways — this procedure risks tautology. A movement offers x, hence the recruit is deprived of x (perhaps under some slightly more sociological description). How do we know? By looking at the amount of stress on x in the movement's belief system. I do not assume that this procedure may never give us any insight. A close acquaintance with the beliefs of those one is studying is always a good way to begin trying to explain their behaviour. But statements of doctrine or programme, and actual beliefs of members may differ widely, particularly in the weighting and ordering of issues and priorities, if not always in actual substance. The sociologist who takes Clause Four of the Labour Party Constitution concerning sweeping nationalisation as an important motivating factor in the recruitment and behaviour of Labour Party members, merely because it continues to play a prominent role in official programmatic statements would simply not have understood the Labour Party.

This raises a further problem. The notion of relative deprivation refers to a *felt* or *experienced* disparity between aspirations or expectations and reality, i.e. to a subjective experience. Curiously, however, exponents of this view tend to look for their evidence, on the one hand to the objective circumstances affecting groups and strata and, on the other, to the ideology of the movement itself. This is perhaps the crucial criticism of the way the concept is employed. Relative deprivation is descriptive of actors' interpretations of the situation, of the meanings with which they endow social circumstances and a movement's message. It is applied, however, in an essentially positivistic way by seeking evidence in factors *external* to the actor. While paying lip-service to the individual's interpretation of his environment and social circumstances, the thesis of relative deprivation is applied in such a way as to disallow any interpretative role in the understanding of the character of the movement joined. The movement and its ideology are seen as unambiguous stimulus objects with precisely the same impact on all those deprived in the appropriate way and with similar background beliefs. But this scarcely meets the demands of voluntarism. If human agents are capable of interpreting the same social conditions in different ways they are capable of interpreting the same social movement and its message in different ways.

Moreover, it is clearly mistaken merely to take the objective circumstances of social groups and (our interpretation of) the movement's ideology as the basis of a claim that the actors concerned are experiencing relative deprivation. However plausible the alleged connection, it provides no convincing ground for the belief that (a) the relevant category from which the movement recruited actually did *experience* the circumstances in which they found themselves as depriving; (b) that it was those who experienced the objective circumstances in this way who formed or joined the movement; or (c) that it

5

was not some entirely different aspect of the movement which attracted them to it, other than its supposed provision of resources for resolving deprivation of this type. The failure to locate evidence relevant to the *experience* of members leads the deprivation theorists into the speculative psychology described by Evans-Pritchard as the 'If I were a horse fallacy'. If I had lived under those conditions I might well have experienced relative deprivation of a particular type and have joined the relevant social movement to alleviate it. Hence those who *did* join must have felt the same way. Again, this may be a very reasonable way to begin, but it is hardly conclusive. Appropriate and convincing evidence must be based on some account of relevant actors' experiences, and it seems reasonable wherever possible to seek such accounts from the actors themselves. While an explanation of why people form or join a social movement cannot end with their accounts it must at least take these into consideration.

This poses, however, the issue of how much *reliance* can be placed on participants' accounts of their own motives in explanation of their behaviour. The question of the extent to which these can be taken 'at face value', or should be discounted as justificatory rather than explanatory, has exercised many commentators on social movements (see for example, the dialogue between Neil J. Smelser, 1970, and Currie and Skolnick, 1970). There does not seem to me any general rule to be followed here, rather the problem is one of practical method, and it is one with which anthropologists and historians have perhaps grappled more adequately than sociologists. The statements of participants and informants must be evaluated in the light of their role in the structure of the situation (Do they have a position to defend?); their biographical experience (Do they have an axe to grind?); their conception of the audience (Do they have something to hide, someone to impress?); their proximity to the circumstances discussed (Did they see it happen?); their reliability and consistency (Do they produce different accounts in different circumstances?); etc. The fact that these checks on sources may often be difficult to make hardly entails that the accounts should simply be ignored as inevitably suspect. As Bryan Wilson has argued concerning the analysis of institutions (1967b:111)

To know from whom in an institution certain policies and pronouncements originated, in what circumstances they

6

were put forward, to what public directed, and what contradictions, retractations, or deviations from previous policy they involved, is the beginning of a living understanding of an organisation.

Moreover, of course, investigation does not cease with a questioning of participants, informants, or documentary resources. Wherever possible it can be supplemented by observation of the operation of the collectivities concerned to determine to what degree information gleaned at second hand accords with action.

These essays, then, take the view that social events are constituted by human activity of a meaningful kind. The essential prior step to *explaining* that activity is *understanding* it, learning the language, interpreting the symbols, and acquainting oneself with the reasons people have for engaging in it. It is in this sense, I think, that sociology has a useful social, and even moral purpose. We are most readily able to treat inhumanely those who, because their beliefs, practises, or mode of life differs radically from our own, we can construe as less than entirely human or rational. By displaying the meaningful human character of diverse social worlds, the sociologist may hope to eliminate one major element of intolerance, the element of ignorance; or at least to temper the more de-humanising aspects of what is taken to be 'common knowledge'.

I
ASPECTS OF NEW SOCIAL AND
RELIGIOUS MOVEMENTS

CHAPTER 1

Movement, context and decline: A study of two incipient social movements

The study of social movements is, almost inevitably, founded upon a biased sample. Sociological research is often oriented by extra-theoretic considerations such as alleged social relevance which deflect attention from the brief and ephemeral, the *outré*, and the unsuccessful, towards those forms of social action and organisation which persist, articulate with wider interests and values, and which succeed, or if they fail, do so after at least some period of worthwhile history to make the research effort look respectable. Moreover, sociological research has become highly routinised and bureaucratised and the activation of the sometimes cumbersome superstructure of grant-funding bodies renders it difficult to capture social forms which appear and decline almost before the ink dries on the grant application.

The enduring social movement thus presents a more viable research target and hence while we have various studies of movements which, after recruiting a broad following and initiating programmes of action, lost their way, ossifying or disappearing, studies of social movements which made a sudden bid for prominence and then as suddenly disappeared, are rare indeed in the sociological literature. I have been able to locate only one study explicitly concerned with the failure of an incipient social movement in an advanced industrial society, the study of a Los Angeles County tax protest movement (Jackson *et al.*, 1960). Sadly, otherwise excellent studies, perfectly placed to describe the decline of ephemeral movements, have stopped short at some earlier point. For example, we never do learn what happened to Mrs. Keech and her followers except in the broadest terms from the otherwise fascinating ethnography of Festinger and his associates (Festinger *et al.*, 1956)* *(Notes can be found at the end of each chapter)*.

Hence, although much theorising in this area is concerned with how and why social movements are able to develop a stable institutional and recruitment base, the comparable materials on movements which *fail* to develop such a base are extremely limited.

Research on such movements *is* extremely difficult to conduct. They do not survive long enough to institutionalise the routine production of documentation, providing therefore few records for examination. In cases where the movement's demise has not been at all glorious, leaders and participants may be loath to expose themselves to any intensive post-mortem on the vilified or ridiculed remains. The quality of data that results from such studies is, therefore, likely to be poorer than could be expected of movements which have a longer history. Fortified by the coviction that a little knowledge is better than none at all, and the plea of Jackson *et al.* (1960:40) that 'more studies of unsuccessful social movements are needed in order to compare them with successful ones so that the conditions essential for the success of social movements can be more rigorously specified', I present an account of two movements, 'Civil Assistance' and 'GB 75' which briefly emerged on to the British public scene in 1974 only to disappear again almost as quickly. I preface my account with a discussion of the one relevant prior study which addressed the issue of incipient movement disappearance.

The tax-protest movement

In November 1957 county tax bills were issued in Los Angeles County which contained an appreciable increase in taxation. A number of taxpayers' meetings took place. Three meetings were reported to have drawn respectively 800, 1800, and 8000 people. The protest seems to have emanated particularly from suburban residential property owners, and 'was chiefly a result of the sudden rise in the value of property in new tract areas where persons were already burdened with maximum financing' (Jackson *et al.*, 1960:36). Numerous spontaneous local organisations formed, 'seldom co-operating and often working at cross purposes' (*ibid.*) but the emerging trans-local movement rapidly disappeared. The county tax assessor was re-elected and despite further increases the following year, there was no reactivation of the attempt to establish a protest movement.

Jackson *et al.* argue that support for a social movement 'ordinarily cannot be maintained unless there is a welding of spontaneous groups into some stable organisation which will supply effective communication, leadership, an ideology and plan of action, and a viable public image' (Jackson *et al.*, 1960:37). The emerging protest movement received widespread newspaper coverage which was not directed to the discrediting of the movement or its leaders. However, the incipient movement lacked any pre-existing network of organisations and personal contacts between suburbs through which enduring communication and mobilisation could be effected. Nor was it able to gain the support of organisations which already possessed such a communications network. An emerging supralocal leader, moreover, refused to incorporate many local leaders into his group, eliminating one means by which the local efforts could be welded into a community-wide movement. No long-term programme developed around which the incipient movement could coalesce, and the public image of the movement suffered when a mass meeting in the Los Angeles Coliseum with a seating capacity of 100,000 was attended by an audience of an estimated 6000-10,000 persons, conveying an impression of failure.

The case discussed above displays a clear failure of the social movement concerned. It disappeared without achieving the immediate aims which it had set, and without establishing any enduring form of movement organisation to continue pursuit of those aims. A similar pattern marks the history of two 'citizens' action' movements, Civil Assistance and GB 75, which developed in Britain in 1974. The effective disappearance of these two movements can, however, be traced to a rather different set of circumstances. We shall analyse these after first describing the context in which the movements arose and the major details of their brief histories.

Things fall apart, the centre cannot hold

The two 'citizens' action' movements to be analysed grew out of an impending sense of anarchy and chaos felt by some to be the inevitable outcome of conditions and circumstances developing in the early and mid 1970s. The relative ebullience and optimism of the 1960s gave way before rapidly rising inflation. From an average of 4% per annum during the 1960s, the cost of living was increasing at over 9% per annum by 1972-73. Attempts to control inflation had lead to increasing militancy from many of the more powerful unions. Prominent among them had been the National Union of Miners whose industrial action had led to the declaration of a State of Emergency in February 1972 and a three-day working week (Jackson, 1974:137). Their position was strengthened by the rapid rise in the price of oil as part of the long-term economic policy of the OPEC countries. Substantial oil price rises occurred each year from 1972 and was doubled in 1973 and again in 1974.

On May Day 1973, the Trades Union Congress supported by the Labour Party organised a one-day stoppage which brought to a standstill the railways, motor and aero-engineering and shipbuilding industries, coal-mining and the docks, and national newspapers.

Late in 1973 the NUM again initiated industrial action leading to a further State of Emergency. The problem on this occasion was compounded by the overtime ban being enforced by the power engineers of the Central Electricity Generating Board in pursuit of their own wage claim, and in December 1973, the railway union ASLEF decided to take industrial action leading to a fear that even coal which was mined could not be transported to the power stations (Jackson, 1974:151), and the Government announced a three-day week and drastic restrictions in electricity supply to commence on 30 December.

The Conservative Leader of the House of Commons, James Prior, ominously warned 'that if the government had not taken action the country might have faced a situation in which we could not get fresh water and we could have sewage floating in the streets of London and in other big cities' (*The Times*, 31 December 1973, cited in Jackson, 1974:154). Battle lines were being drawn between the Government and the miners' union supported by the TUC. In January the union executive secured a mandate from its members in favour of a national strike, and the Conservative Government announced a General Election making it clear that the dispute was a major reason, and amid accusations of communist influence on the miners. This theme of an 'extremist' threat was taken up in the Conservative Party election manifesto which criticised the Labour Party on the grounds that the latter 'today faces the nation committed to a left-wing programme more dangerous and more extreme than ever before in its history'. The rhetoric of extremism, subversion and anarchy found readier ears in some quarters as a consequence of the worsening situation in Northern Ireland, and the initiation of an IRA bombing campaign in London and elsewhere in England from late December 1973 and into 1974.

The election resulted in an ambiguous situation with a Labour majority over the Conservatives, but no absolute majority. When the Conservatives were unable to form a coalition with the Liberal Party, the Government resigned and Labour formed a minority Government.

In May 1974, an *ad hoc* body of Northern Ireland Protestant trade unionists, under the name Ulster Workers' Council, determined to defeat constitutional proposals for the Province which they feared would lead to possible ultimate union with the Republic of Ireland, and declared a general strike. On 15 May workers were called out of the power stations and output reduced to 60%. A State of Emergency was declared in the Province on 19 May, but the UWC tightened bans on the distribution of petrol and oil, and the Northern Ireland Executive finally collapsed on 28 May, after which the UWC recommended a return to work.

The period preceding the emergence of Civil Assistance and GB 75 in 1974, was then, a period the events of which provided ample grounds for interpretation as heralding the imminent collapse of Britain under the weight of foreign economic pressure, internal subversion, the growing menace of trade union militancy, political extremism, and the manifest power of left-wing 'extremists' in key industrial and political positions. For many, the revolution in Portugal and the events in Chile preceding the military coup provided object lessons in the course which they saw as almost inevitably about to overtake Britain. A General Election was necessarily to take place soon and if the conciliatory Labour Government was ousted by a Conservative victory at the polls, confrontation and chaos it seemed to many, could scarcely be avoided.

Many groups formed in the beleagured middle classes to fight specific or diffuse threats created by these circumstances. The National Association of Ratepayers Action Groups (NARAG) was one manifestation of the sense of threat. Formed in June 1974 in the face of substantial rate increases it was alleged to have a membership of between 300,000-400,000 by late 1975. The National Federation of the Self-Employed emerged soon after, claiming 30,000 members by April 1975. A number of smaller groups also appeared, including the Middle Class Association, formed by John Gorst, MP, in the autumn of 1974. Some, like the 'friendly society' unnamed in press reports, organised by Major Alexander Greenwood, appeared to be based around a network of former military officers. Set up in 1973, Greenwood's group was said to have recruited more than 900 volunteers by 'word of mouth'. Its members were described as principally 'members of the professional classes who are desperately concerned about the way things are going' (*The Times*, 29 July 1974).

The two citizens' action groups which we now discuss were not, therefore, isolated eccentricities, but part of a substantial and widespread feeling that the middle classes in British society, if not the very structure and indeed existence of British society had been sorely threatened and even damaged, and that further catastrophe loomed on the horizon.

Civil Assistance

General Sir Walter Walker was a recently retired Allied Commander-in-Chief, Northern Europe, whose hostility to communism was widely known, and who had received considerable publicity in April 1974 for his 'hawkish' comments on the Northern Ireland situation. In an interview in the *Daily Express* he advocated capital punishment for armed opposition to the security forces, and the delegation of complete autonomy and authority in the Province to the army. His interview included highly derogatory remarks about the capabilities of both Commons front benches. In letters to the press he voiced what he felt to be the country's disillusionment with existing leading politicians and its yearning for a leader capable of rousing the people to 'determination and valour as Churchill did during the war' (*Evening Standard*, 11 July 1974). In subsequent interviews he indicated a belief that Enoch Powell might be an appropriate candidate. His views are reported to have included a claim that 'First this Government is in the hands of the Left-Wing, and secondly, the country is in the hands of the trade unions – Hugh Scanlon is running this country' (*ibid.*). He is reported not to have ruled out the possibility of a military take-over in Britain, and saw his primary duty at the present as that of trying to 'waken the country' to the danger facing it (*ibid.*).

His public statements led individuals and the leaders of

various ex-service men's organisations to make contact with Walker. Since the activities of most of these groups are hedged in secrecy very little information is available about them. One such group formed early in 1973, called Unison, had developed to offer its services in the event of 'a collapse of law and order'. Unison's leaders contacted Sir Walter, and this appears to have been the main group through which he initially worked and to which he sought to recruit on a broader scale. In August he is reported to have circulated a letter to six hundred people describing the work of Unison (*Guardian,* 12 August 1974). In interviews he explained its purpose as follows: 'There are a growing number of people in this country who are becoming impatient with the lack of effective leadership. They appreciate the real dangers that face us from within and have taken their own initiative to do something about them' (*The Times,* 29 July 1974). However, after a short period as a member of Unison's executive, General Walker came to view it as too extreme and differences of opinion led him to found a separate organisation, Civil Assistance (letter from Noel Currer-Briggs, former General Secretary of CA).

The leader of the National Association of Ratepayers' Action Groups, Mr David Petri, also engaged in discussions with Sir Walter but thereby precipitated a crisis of leadership within his own organisation (*Daily Telegraph,* 13 August 1974). Prominent members of NARAG were disquietened at the possibility of an alliance with Civil Assistance, an alliance which they believed could prove an embarrassment. Yet another group to affiliate with Sir Walter was known as the British Military Volunteer Force. This group claiming over 2000 members subsequently broke with Civil Assistance apparently feeling some antagonism towards the 'officer-type members belonging to the general's movement', and expressing opposition to involving themselves with strike-breaking efforts (*Daily Telegraph,* 3 January 1975; Press Association Bulletin, 31 December 1974). Offers of assistance also came from smaller bodies such as the Sunderland Flying Club (*Daily Telegraph,* 14 August 1974).

The General's message was founded on an appeal to the rhetoric of patriotism, 'loyalty to the Crown', 'the imminence of the Communist threat', 'extremism' in the trade unions, and a belief in the inadequacy of existing police and security forces to cope with threatened disorder. In a pamphlet circulated to enquirers, Sir Walter warned against infiltration in education and the media. Ten per cent of officials in major industrial unions were alleged to be 'communists or far left revolutionary marxists'. Such men have 'made it impossible for the Conservative Party to govern; it will not be long before the Labour Government finds itself in the same predicament'. He warned against further strikes in key industries which would bring 'disaster to the country and the total collapse of our economy. Such a situation would create the right climate for an eruption of violence and civil disturbance on a country-wide scale. There are many anarchist organisations formed and waiting to exploit just this situation'. The forces of law and order, are seen as so seriously stretched that 'there can be no question that, if there were to be a serious outbreak of violence in Britain today, our present resources would be hopelessly inadequate', and 'Russia will have achieved her aim without herself firing a shot'. The General's clarion call was that: 'Time is desperately short, perhaps no more than a few months. It is becoming daily more urgent that those who do not seek the spoils of anarchy should band together to resist the threat to freedom and democracy in this country.'

The programme of the movement was therefore to alert the British public to the dangers; to encourage volunteers to join auxiliary services such as the Special Constabulary, armed forces reserves, the Fire Service, etc.; to band together in a national organisation prepared to resist anarchy; and to offer their services to the 'recognised authorities'. Sir Walter encouraged as many as possible to join Civil Assistance, and thereby 'swell the number of sympathisers who are prepared to stand up and be counted'. While in newspaper interviews the General had kept his estimates of the movement's ultimate following to three million (*Daily Telegraph*, 12 August 1974), a letter to sympathisers circulated later in 1974 estimated its potential at nearer fourteen million, although it is doubtful if, at its peak, the following of the movement ever exceeded about three thousand.

Despite all the sound and fury in 1974, Civil Assistance never became more than a network of local organisers, predominantly retired senior military officers, with local coteries of assistants recruited from similar circles. By early 1975 it was evident that the campaign of mass recruitment envisaged by Walker was merely a chimera. Sir Walter had engaged in negotiations with a number of other patriotic and law-and-order organisations. In particular he had sought a merger with the new umbrella organisation the National Association for Freedom. This organisation, while eager to secure new members, was cautious of the public image associated with Civil assistance as a 'private army' and was concerned not to attract similarly adverse publicity to NAFF in the event of a merger.

During 1976 there emerged a growing feeling among many members of CA that it could no longer play a very effective role because of its de-legitimation through the 'private army' labelling. NAFF was becoming, they felt, a more viable focus of right-wing activism. In response to this growing feeling, Sir Walter seems to have seen the need to purge CA's ranks. In a circular to his followers he recommended that all who wished to do so should shift their allegiance to NAFF and indicated his willingness to withdraw from the leadership of CA if this would help the assmilation of those wishing to join NAFF (letters from Noel Currer-Briggs formerly General Secretary of CA and from General Sir Walter Walker; *Guardian*, 2 March 1977). While the purged and re-organised CA continues to exist, it clearly now commands the support of no more than a tiny fraction of the mass following to which it originally aspired.

GB 75

Colonel David Stirling had also had a distinguished military career in the course of which he had founded the Special Air Service. He had thereafter achieved a certain fame when his organisation Watchguard, which offered training in security and intelligence work, and bodyguards to the heads of emerging nations, became involved in a (subsequently abandoned) scheme to rescue a number of individuals from Colonel Quadhafi's Libyan jails (*Observer*, 13 May 1973). Stirling had become increasingly concerned about the power of the unions, led by what seemed to him men of extreme left-wing views, and their potential for politically motivated action designed 'to achieve power and destroy Parliament' (Colonel Stirling, interview with author early 1975).

During May, June and July, 1974, Colonel Stirling began to prepare and circulate his diagnosis and proposals to individuals upon whose sympathy he thought he might rely. These documents, published dramatically in a *Peace News* scoop (*Peace News*, 23 August 1974), reveal that Stirling viewed his movement, Great Britain 1975 (GB 75) at least in the immediate future as a resource to cope with the crisis engendered by a general strike or a strike involving power and communications workers. He argued that the Government had no plans to cope with such a contingency but believed his movement would be viewed with sympathy and turned to with alacrity should such a situation develop. He even argued that a government which failed to call upon the aid of GB 75 in a widespread strike situation would receive a parliamentary vote of no confidence, and the new government would immediately call upon them.

The movement aimed to prepare its members to assist in the maintenance of major public utilities. He envisaged the possibility that it might be necessary to 'round up' strikers occupying key buildings and to resist the efforts of pickets to re-occupy. The members of GB 75 were to be motivated 'not by politics but by pure objective patriotism' and Stirling stressed the need to ensure that it did not become identified with, nor a haven for, 'the extreme right wing and neo-fascists already appearing on the scene'. GB 75 'must be seen to be giving "teeth" and credibility to the centre'. The documents express the heightened sense of urgency precipitated by the action of the Ulster Workers Council in Northern Ireland, and a sense of disappointment and dissatisfaction at the failure of government and Parliament to curb 'the Trades Union militants'. One item circulated by his organisation expressed this sense of failure and incapacitation of the political institutions:

> The long continuing crisis in Britain is so grave and multi-dimensional, the Government and Opposition so clearly lacking the will to tackle its root causes, and Parliament itself so enfeebled that we believe fundamental and creative solutions must be initiated from outside Parliament.

While GB 75 was presented as a movement with pragmatic and tactical aims in a potential situation of near chaos, Stirling also proposed the formation of a 'Greater Britain League' (later renamed the Better Britain Society) which would: (1) help to arouse mass support for GB 75; (2) 'define and propagate a re-statement of what constitutes patriotism today'; (3) define a set of constitutional precepts for democracy; and (4) plan a compulsory national citizenship service which 15-16 year-olds would undergo for one year.

With the publication of the documents Stirling had been circulating, in August 1974, enquiries began to descend on his offices and in reply, interested persons were asked to indicate their skills and capabilities and also invited to join the 'Better

Britain Society'. They were advised that after the forthcoming General Election training courses would be held: 'These courses will relate solely to our aims of sustaining the essential services and will not have a military flavour.' Colonel Stirling claimed in August 1974 that GB 75 had 'hundreds of members' (*The Times,* 23 August 1974) and that it aimed to have a few thousand. Offers of financial support from a Jersey arms dealer were publicised, and full-time officials were recruited to organise the movement's headquarters.

Although membership may have increased to 1500 by September 1974, and some publicity continued into October, thereafter it almost entirely disappeared from view until it was disbanded in April 1975. During late 1974 and early 1975, Colonel Stirling appears to have concluded that what might be viewed as 'strike breaking' and counter-action in the face of widespread crippling strikes was less pressing or practical a task than reform of the trades unions from within. He became associated with a trades unionist, Frank Nodes, who had begun the formation of a Movement for True Industrial Democracy (TRUEMID) which aimed to combat union left-wing militancy from within. Nodes was prepared to combine his efforts with those of Stirling and the Better Britain Society on the condition that all connection with GB 75 be severed. As joint membership of the Better Britain Society and GB 75 was extensive, Stirling decided to disband the latter.

Although the Better Britain Society in association with TRUEMID still voiced an intention 'to enrol a massive membership' and to 'generate massive support from the grass roots of the country', there is no evidence that it was able to create any extensive interest or following.

The failure of the citizens' action movements

It is impossible to do more than speculate about what Civil Assistance and GB 75 might have become if they had secured the massive support to which they aspired. The possible scenarios are numerous. What *is* evident is that both movements entirely failed to achieve any substantial level of membership. They were able to gain combined support from no more than about 5000 people and within a few months had both all but disappeared. Why did they fail?

I shall argue that their failure resulted primarily from an inability to achieve a level of *legitimacy* essential to their purpose. To a lesser extent their failure resulted from changed circumstances which rendered their aims largely irrelevant, and from a failure to establish new aims to which the existing movements could viably be adapted.

(i) *Legitimacy*

From their first appearance, both groups were subjected to mass media coverage which often slighted the leaders and impugned their motives and political aspirations; ridiculed the movements they had formed; or drew uncomplimentary parallels with the Weimar Republic, or Greek and Chilean colonels. Trade union leaders described General Walker and Colonel Stirling as 'silly fanatics' who should 'go back to their pink gins in their clubs' (*Daily Mirror,* 24 August 1974). Members of the Labour Government were understandably hostile, and Mr. Roy Mason is reported to have attacked the two movements as 'anti-democratic endeavours to assert their extreme views beyond and outside our recognised democratic and parliamentary procedures', and assimilated them to a 'near-fascist groundswell of Blimpish reaction' (*The Times,* 23 August 1974). Even otherwise friendly reports tended to describe the leaders in slighting terms (e.g. *Observer,* 25 August 1974). While Labour Party and trade unionist response could have been expected to take a hostile form, no moral support was publicly offered from Conservative sources either. Mr. Geoffrey Rippon, a Conservative front bench spokesman suggested that there were dangers in such groups and recommended them to work through existing political parties and organisations. Other defenders of traditional values and institutions also spoke out against the movements. Lord Longford totally dissociated his own efforts to diagnose the nation's moral and economic ills from those of Walker and Stirling, voicing his opposition 'to anything that remotely resembles a paramilitary force or private army'. The magistrates' journal *Justice of the Peace* inveighed against vigilante forces and private armies (*Daily Telegraph,* 10 September 1974).

The prominence of a rhetoric which characterised the two groups as 'private armies' appears to have been deeply resented by both leaders and the connotation of anti-democratic intent conflicted with the imagery they wished to promote of a defence of national values and institutions. The two movements were widely defined as 'extremist', and combined, these labels must have led to a concern among many followers who wished

21

to cast themselves as moderate supporters of the British way of life rather than as subversive to it, and undoubtedly frightened off or otherwise alienated potential supporters.

Unlike social movements such as, say, Black Power, Gay Lib, or radical left-wing movements and other groups opposing prevailing social structures and cultural values, the citizens' action movements defined themselves as defenders of national institutions. Their claim to legitimacy fundamentally rested on the acceptance of their proclaimed intent to be supporting these institutions and values from unwarranted attack, and thus on an identification of their efforts with the interests of dominant institutions. When that claim was rejected not only by the Labour Government, but also by the Conservative Opposition, and ridiculed antagonistically in the press, it readily collapsed. Led by military men and spread initially through ex-military networks, the 'paramilitary' label could only too easily be applied (whatever the real motives of the movements' leaders), leading to a loss of legitimacy. This paramilitary identification had resulted in the potential link of CA with the National Association of Ratepayers' Action Groups being rapidly severed, and evidently provoked concern even in Colonel Stirling who had early seen the necessity for withdrawing as GB 75's leader in favour of a civilian. This loss of legitimacy occurred so early in the growth of both movements that neither had time to develop a substantial enough following to rest its legitimation on the size of its support. They remained tiny and hence rather deviant phenomena on the fringe of the political scene.

(ii) *Relevancy*

The two movements might none the less have overcome these problems if their prognosis of confrontation, chaos and collapse had come to pass. Legitimacy might have been regained had their prophecies been proven right. Such a scenario, in which the hitherto vilified 'paramilitarists' were recognised as the only clear-thinking patriotic group with the forethought and preparation to handle the situation, could only have developed if the Labour Government had been defeated in the October 1974 election, a Conservative majority returned, and an escalating confrontation between Government and unions taken place. In the event, the Conservatives lost the election, the Labour Government was returned with a slightly increased parliamentary majority and the possibility of confrontation became ever less likely.

The citizens' action groups had simply become an irrelevancy. Their primary immediate purpose had disappeared. In this situation, since neither movement had ever drawn upon the discontents of any very specific constituency, they were unable, saddled as they had become with the 'paramilitary' label, to appeal to any such constituency as the vehicle for longer-term reforms. Movements already existed like NARAG, the National Federation of the Self-Employed, etc., with long-term aims, and directed towards a clear and specific constituency. By and large these movements refused to co-operate with the citizens' action groups. Hence, the latter were unable to shift their goals and methods in the context of the imagery with which they had become associated. Stirling was obliged to disband his movement before the Better Britain Society could merge with TRUEMID.

Moreover, not only were Civil Assistance and GB 75 unable to link effectively with other middle-class protest movements, they were unable to co-operate or merge with each other. Talks were begun to consider the possibility of collaboration, but documents leaked to the press from Stirling's office indicate that he was 'uneasy about the apparently highly militaristic and very Right-wing nature' of the group around General Walker (*Daily Telegraph,* 5 September 1974; *Guardian,* 4 September 1974).

Conclusion

The analysis of the rise and fall of two citizens' action movements has suggested that although they emerged on the basis of a widespread sense of threat to middle-class British society, their conceptualisation of the problems it faced was too broad to appeal effectively to any particular constituency, and their remedy too specific in that it was rapidly rendered irrelevant to the circumstances. Public labelling of these movements as 'extremist' and 'paramilitary' effectively undermined their legitimacy and rendered them unattractive as partners in coalition to other movements based upon middle-class grievances. Mutual suspicion limited the possibility for collaboration between them, and opposition even from conservation sectors of the *status quo* drastically inhibited their potential for growth.

Zald and Ash argue that a social movement organization may

fail "because its legitimacy as an instrument may be discredited . . . central to the discreditation process is the [movement organization's] inability to maintain legitimacy even in the eyes of its supporters" (1966). They suggest that organizational tactics which the movement employs lie at the root of such discreditation. For example, a moderate organization may lose support if it appears "to accept support from extremist groups". However, the study reported here suggests that of equal importance is the loss of legitimacy in the eyes of *potential* supporters. Discreditation may also have much to do with the ideological rhetoric of the movement, the nature of its leadership, and the characterization of these by the mass media. In the case of GB 75 and Civil Assistance a hostile mass media and opposed politicans were readily able to utilize the fact of the military backgrounds of the leaders, and the apparent intention of the movements to train members to provide services cut off by strikers, in ways which severely undermined members' self-conceptions as supporters of British institutions and of moderation in political life. One can readily conceive of social climates and milieux in which the characterization of these movements might have issued in quite different consequences.

* One study of some relevance to this concern is Brill's acutely perceptive account of a public housing rent strike in a US city (Brill, 1971). Although Brill's study is a fascinating and insightful one, I do not discuss it here because the group concerned made little serious attempt to recruit a broad following, and the specificity of its concern perhaps entitles it to be characterised as a pressure-group rather than a social movement. I realise, however, that the distinction between the two can only be a matter of degree.

CHAPTER II

Coping with institutional fragility: An analysis of Christian Science and Scientology

The tendency for some sectarian groups to undergo a gradual process of modification in organisation and ideology towards a more denominational form, has been extensively explored (see, for example, Niebuhr, 1957; Pope, 1942; Wilson, 1961, 1967a). A somewhat neglected area of concern, however, has been the prior processes sometimes involved marking the transition from loosely organised cults to cohesive, authoritarian sects.

Ideal typically, the cult is generally presented as a loosely structured, ephemeral, individualistic group with little effective cohesion, prone to disintegration and disappearance unless the transition to sectarianism is successfully negotiated (Becker, 1932; Yinger, 1970; Eister, 1950; Nelson, 1968; Mann, 1955). Two manipulationist movements which began in this way have been outstandingly successful in developing a highly cohesive sectarian form: Christian Science and Scientology (for the concept of manipulationism, see Wilson, 1970b). After a brief introduction of these two movements the analysis will be organised in terms of three distinct problems acutely faced by manipulationist movements: the problem of ideological precariousness, the problem of authority, and the problem of commitment.

Christian Science

Mary Baker Eddy began her career as healer and teacher after herself receiving treatment from Phineas P. Quimby in 1862. Originally practising Quimby's methods of mental healing, she later claimed (after an accident around the time of his death)

25

to have experienced a 'spiritual awakening', which enabled her to recover, and led her to develop a method of healing different in many respects from that of Quimby. Her method, originally called Moral Science drew a small following in Lynn where she set up practice with Richard Kennedy.

The publication in 1875 of her textbook, *Science and Health*, brough notice from farther afield and led to gradual expansion. A formal organisation began to emerge in June 1875, when several of her students pledged themselves to pay her a small salary to speak to them regularly each Sunday, but this arrangement proved unsatisfactory and in 1876 the Christian Scientist Association was formed.

The incorporation of the Church of Christ (Scientist) in Boston in 1879 marked both a shift from the earlier largely secular mode of organisation, and an interest in wider fields of endeavour than that provided by her small following at Lynn. The Massachussetts Metaphysical College was also chartered in Boston in 1881. This decision to expand farther afield was precipitated by a crisis among the Lynn students. Eight of her core disciples resigned from the Church and Association amid complaints about Mrs. Eddy's leadership, her 'frequent ebullitions of temper, love of money, and the appearance of hypocrisy' (Bates and Dittemore, 1933). The rebellion and subsequent events at Lynn attracted much attention in the press, with the result that Mrs. Eddy became aware of the need for a more effective means of communication among the following generated by the distribution of her book and the migration of her students. The *Journal of Christian Science* was founded in 1883.

As the movement grew, the notice of other former patients of Quimby was attracted by the publicity attendant on the growth of Christian Science and they began to defend his claim to priority in the press. Succcessful practitioners within Science were eager to challenge Mrs. Eddy's sole right to teach and expound the doctrine, and were sometimes resistant to her claim of complete authority over their actions. Some of her students, who had established Colleges and Institutes farther afield seemed to be developing ideas at variance with her own. Heretical ideals appeared to be a danger even among her closest following, and altogether outside her control were a growing number of teachers of 'Christian Science', often defectors from or expelled members of her own movement, now teaching very much their own ideas.

The followers of Quimby were attacked in the press, those with heretical or independent leanings within the movement were expelled and followers forbidden to write on Science or read other metaphysical literature than her own.

The need for radical reorganisation became more evident as her students took an increasingly independent line. To prevent the possibility of her followers subverting her authority, Mrs. Eddy acquired ownership of the property which they were purchasing in order to erect a church building. In 1889 she closed the Massachussetts Metaphysical College, and later dissolved the Boston Church, and directed the National Christian Scientist Association to disband.

These steps were designed to demolish the haphazardly developed structure of the movement and cleared the way for the creation of a highly centralised bureaucratic organisation administered by Mrs. Eddy through a personally appointed Board of Directors. (On Christian Science see: Bates and Dittemore, 1933; Dakin, 1929; Wilson, 1961; Braden, 1958; Studdert-Kennedy, 1947; Zweig, 1933; Beasley, 1953; Pfautz, 1964, 1956; England 1954.)

Scientology

L. Ron Hubbard's career effectively began in 1950 with the publication in a science fiction periodical of an article on Dianetics shortly followed by the appearance of his book *Dianetics: The Modern Science of Mental Health*. Hubbard's ideas of a simple lay psychotherapy which could be practised by any two people to relieve psychosomatic illness and psychological disturbance, had an enormous appeal. Small groups of 'auditors' (practitioners) sprang up throughout the United States and individuals practised the technique (called 'auditing' or 'processing') on family and friends.

The Hubbard Dianetic Research Foundation had been chartered in New Jersey shortly before these publications appeared, but as Dianetics experienced a brief boom, dissension began to develop at the centre. The other directors of the Foundation became alienated by Hubbard's authoritarianism and resigned. The Foundation moved into debt and was subjected to attacks by medical agencies.

A businessman offered to help the Foundation financially and it was moved to Wichita only to be pursued by its creditors. In Wichita, Hubbard found himself increasingly constrained.

Whilst having been president of the New Jersey Foundation he was only vice-president of that at Wichita. Disagreements between Hubbard and his fellow directors again emerged and Hubbard resigned, moving to Phoenix. There Scientology was launched and the Hubbard Association of Scientologists International (HASI) was formed.

The early Foundations had attempted to organise the loose, widely diffused following of Dianetics by promoting auditor groups in local areas, with the Foundation acting as a central clearing-house, research, training and professional therapy establishment. Association with the Foundation was purely voluntary, no attempt being made to coerce affiliation. Under this *laissez-faire* system, local groups and leaders had a high degree of autonomy and several established independent and competing Institutes and Foundations, offering to do all that Hubbard could and more, refusing to be directed by him, and introducing their own theory and techniques, or compounding Dianetics with other practices. The following of the movement was split between these competing schools.

Hubbard early saw the need to curtail this tendency to fragmentation, dilution of doctrine and financial competition. After establishing himself in Phoenix he attempted to assert control over the autonomous groups and to eliminate his competitors. Competing practices and independent journals were severely attacked in Scientology publications and their sponsors accused of practising 'Black Dianetics'. Certification of professional auditors was centralised in the HASI, and all earlier certificates declared revoked unless their owners became members of Hubbard's organisation. Subsidiary organisations, from 1953, were denied the right of certifying auditors except at the most elementary levels. A major step in gaining control over the autonomous groups and individuals was through the ability of the HASI to withhold from non-affiliated groups the new information that Hubbard was generating.

Groups were not however, an effective means of organising his following. Independent amateur groups were therefore progressively dropped in favour of locally established professional auditors franchised by the HASI (and later Missions, franchised by the Church) which ran introductory courses and low-level auditing. On completing the introductory courses or for advanced auditing, the student would be sent on to one of the central organisations (the Franchise receiving a commission payment).

An attempt was made to secure conformity from trained auditors engaged in practising Scientology by requiring them to post a bond of $5000 as a guarantee of good behaviour. From the late 1950s, however, a fully articulated system of internal social control began to emerge, described as a Code of Ethics, and enforced by Ethics Officers.

Scientology embraced a very much wider metaphysical domain than Dianetics and although Hubbard presented his followers with a more pragmatic rationale, there were certainly strong arguments for declaring Scientology a religion broadly conceived. A Church of American Science was incorporated in 1953 and practitioners began using the style 'Reverend'. It was not until 1954, however, and the incorporation of the Church of Scientology of California that Hubbard widely announced that Scientology was a religion.

From 1955 to 1959, Hubbard was mainly established in Washington, where the success of the Church of Scientology of Washington came to the attention of tax authorities concerned about the three-quarters of a million dollars earned during this period by the tax-exempt Church. In 1959, Hubbard moved the centre of his operations to England. By this time the organisation had several small branches in other English-speaking countries. During the ensuing few years, Scientologists were to find themselves 'the people everywhere spoken against' as in each of these countries Scientology was attacked in the press and official enquiries into its activities were instigated.

As as result of the widespread attacks on Scientology through the 1960s Hubbard declared in 1966 that he was resigning all directorships of Scientology organisations and withdrawing from the movement. As the Foster Report indicates, however, Hubbard clearly remains in active control of the movement (Foster, 1971). Its policy is still issued by him. All its literature is copyrighted in his name. His wife is the Guardian World Wide of Scientology and on his death control over the movement is vested in an International Council headed by his wife and appointed by Hubbard. The most advanced courses of Scientology are taught only on the 'Sea Org', a fleet of nine vessels owned by a corporation independent of the Church and the HASI, which effectively forms the international headquarters of the movement. 'Missions' despatched by the Sea Org have full powers to take over other organisations of the Church and HASI temporarily in order to straighten out their administration, processing or training. At such times, they may impose what Hubbard himself has referred to as 'martial law'. (On Scientology see, Cooper, 1971; Malko, 1970; Vosper 1971; Kaufman, 1972; Foster, 1971; Anderson 1965; Jackson, 1966; Jackson and Jobling, 1968; Lee, 1970; Wilson, 1970b; White-head, 1974; Wallis, 1976.)

Doctrinal precariousness

Doctrinally, manipulationism frequently emerges as a synthesis of prevailing theories and practices available in the surrounding cultic milieu (Campbell, 1972). Christian Science originally emerged as a primarily secular healing system, Moral Science, in which Mrs. Eddy saw herself as mainly expounding the ideas on healing she had learned from Quimby. Quimby's own ideas had developed out of Mesmerism into a method of suggestive treatment based on the theory:

> that health was man's natural state; that only man's false ideas, suggesting impotence and misfortune to his whole self from earliest childhood were responsible for holding the race in the thrall of disease . . . he maintained that a beneficent God could and would not have created disease and suffering — only man himself was to blame because of the falsity and error in his concepts (Dakin, 1929:42).

Disease for Quimby was a matter of false thinking. Thus to eradicate the false thought was to cure the diease, and in his practice therefore he would sit opposite his patient and explain to him this theory in the expectation that the patient's acceptance of it would produce the desired improvement in his physical condition.

Mrs. Eddy's developing system drew heavily on Quimby's work as well as owing a lesser debt to other currents of thought then prevalent in New England: Transcendentalism, Swedenborgianism, Spiritualism and possibly Hegel's Subjective Idealism (Wilson, 1959b). Her early following was in large part drawn from Mesmerism, Spiritualism and the healing cults such as hydropathy and homeopathy then prevalent.

Scientology emerged originally as a form of lay psychotherapy. Whilst its intellectual antecedents are less well established than is the case for Christian Science, Dianetics clearly also reflects the intellectual milieu from which it emerged. In Dianetics, the mind was conceived as embodying two parts; The *Analytical Mind* which controlled man's conscious, logical reasoning, and the *Reactive Mind* which came into operation in moments of emotional stresss, pain or unconsciousness, recording all the perceptual details involved in this situation. These recordings, or engrams, it was argued, reactivated in situations having some perceptual similarity to the original situation, and caused individuals to behave in aberrated ways.

The earlier the engram has been formed the stronger its effect. Consequently the technique of therapy directed the patient (pre-clear) in Dianetic 'reverie' to earlier and earlier periods in search of the first engram, or 'basic-basic'. This was held to occur typically shortly after conception. This theory published in 1950 appears to have drawn on a number of trends in mainstream and marginal psychotherapy then current.

Hubbard's notion of the Analytical and Reactive Mind parallels the Freudian conception of the Conscious and Unconscious Mind, and the process of engram formation is analogical to the mechanism of repression. Psychoanalysis had, in some of its less orthodox forms, envinced an interest in progressively earlier periods of individual development (Wallis, 1976). Otto Rank and his followers had directed their attention to the 'Birth-trauma' as a vital episode and Phyllis Greenacre and Nandor Fodor had published works on the pre-natal period and its influence on psychological development (Greenacre, 1941; Fodor, 1949). The deconditioning techniques developed to handle war neuroses are strikingly similar to Dianetic auditing. Another fairly clear influence on Hubbard's formative thought was the work of Alfred Korzybski in General Semantics. Many of Hubbard's early followers were former adherents of Korzybski, whilst others had engaged in the practice of hypnotherapy, chiropractic, or various healing and self-improvement cults.

Christian Science and Scientology in their emergent forms did not differ radically from the cultic background from which they were derived. They were essentially a modern form of magic offering a metaphysical means of compelling the cosmos in lawlike ways, their founders magical healers able to collect a sufficiently stable following to institutionalise their mystagoguery. Unlike the ethical prophet, the mystagogues who lead manipulationist movements rarely call for a radical break with the prevailing social order. The theories and techniques they offer, are primarily means of achieving the valued goals of this world rather than new salvational goals. The world is tacitly accepted (even if it is held not to exist) and the adherent seeks new means of attaining the good things it has to offer. As Bryan Wilson has argued

Manipulationist sects are secularised sects, for which only the means to salvation are religious: the goals are largely those of secular hedonism (Wilson, 1970b: 141).

Since the manipulationist movement offers no radical break with the world and is founded on a doctrine syncretically derived from current, if marginal or deviant, thought, it suffers from doctrinal precariousness. There exists a danger that under the impact of a membership recruited from cultic groups with which its doctrine has affinities, it will be dedifferentiated into the component parts to which its adherents are attracted, becoming reabsorbed into the cultic milieu as it is, in turn, subjected to synthesis and mixing with other cultic doctrines. Some of Mrs. Eddy's early apostate students accused her of teaching 'mere mesmerism', threatening the reassimilation of Moral Science to its origins. Later, others were to practise or argue for the combination of Christian Science with hypnotism, theosophy, or even with orthodox medical practice, threatening a loss of doctrinal distinctiveness.

Many of the early students of Dianetics similarly argued that its theories and practices could be combined with psycho-analysis, chiropractic, or Yoga. Followers of both movements were heard to argue that although their founders had taken a significant step forward there was no reason why others should not develop their ideas further. In short there existed a problem of controlling the distinctiveness of the doctrine and its development to prevent its disappearance as a result of modification and compounding. Both movements evolved a number of mechanisms to handle this problem and thereby create a cognitive space between themselves and their surroundings.

One such step was the development of a transcendental theology or metaphysics to provide a wider framework and a theodicy within which the healing practice could be located and legitimised. The early elaboration of a transcendental doctrine had a number of advantages. It effectively distinguished the movements from competing secular systems. It also facilitated the abandonment of elements of theory and practice which most closely linked them to the alternatives then current. Mrs. Eddy developed a systematic theology of a radically Idealist kind. Her theory passed from Quimby's acceptance of the physical world and the causal priority of thought, to a sweeping monism in which God alone exists, and the material world and evil are mere errors of thought. She dropped the practice of manipulation and that of arguing the disease away, which had been associated with Quimby. Instead silent affirmation and denials became all that was required. Her textbook was persistently modified until all the more obvious traces of its origins were obliterated.

Mrs. Eddy claimed that her writings, in particular *Science and Health* were inspired revelations whose profundity and true impact could be understood only by constant study. Some aspects of the teaching became hidden doctrine available only to those undergoing special instruction, thereby protecting and elevating the ideology by surrounding it with an aura of mystery and secrecy. A 'hierarchy of sanctification' developed based on knowledge of the more esoteric teachings, the Normal Course being taught only to selected students vetted for their loyalty to the Church and forbidden to take notes.

Hubbard was able to achieve a more radical break with his early derivative system. While it could claim to be a revolutionary development of Dianetics, Scientology had much less obvious links with the surrounding cultic milieu and current psychotherapeutic practices. From a 'do-it-yourself' psychotherapy Scientology evolved a systematic metaphysics based on a theory of reincarnation. The notion of the 'Operating Thetan', a spiritual entity, the essential persistent element of the individual which transmigrated at death, emerged. The goal of the practice therefore shifted from that of resolving the impediments to full human potential, to 'rehabilitating the Thetan', restoring the individual to his full capacities as a spiritual being 'at cause over Matter, Energy, Space and Time'. This movement towards increasing esotericism did not cease, however, with the invention of Scientology. Its theory and practice underwent continual modification over the years following its inception. From a relatively simple theory and technique that could be practised by the layman, it became extremely complex with its own highly technical language and literature, and required lengthily acquired skills in handling the E-meter, an electropsychogalvanometer, in order to practise. Higher level courses were made available only to those of proven loyalty to the movement, after 'security checking', and these courses remain a closely guarded secret.

Transcendentalisation permitted the founders to claim the doctrine as a direct personal revelation, and thereby to establish themselves uniquely as the source of doctrinal innovation and adaption or even doctrinal interpretation. Until the establishment of the Board of Education, only Mrs. Eddy could claim to teach the advanced levels of Christian Science. Students were required not to indulge in writing on Christian Science or reading other metaphysical literature, and heretical teachers not responsive to excommunication were pursued by Mrs. Eddy in the press and the law courts for infringements of her copyrights. There had to be a clear ideological boundary between Christian Science and any other metaphysical system, and this boundary was heightened by the fear instilled into her students of malicious animal magnetism held to be particularly the domain of heretics, apostates and imitators. On her death, the Board of Directors took over as the authoritive interpreters of Christian Science. In Scientology, ideological boundary-maintenance was enhanced by Hubbard's attacks on heretics and imitators in his publications, threatening legal action for infringement of his copyrights, and describing their activities as 'Black Dianetics' or 'suppressive'. Hubbard remains the sole permitted interpreter of Scientology.

Both movements have a common antagonism towards presentation of their doctrine by outsiders — whether former members or not — believing that only an officially approved and practising Christian Scientist or Scientologist could accurately portray these movements and their beliefs. Christian Science and Scientology have exerted themselves strenuously to discourage the publication of accounts of their activities by non-approved writers. The Board of Directors of the Mother Church has acquired copyrights and the plates of various books on Science and Mrs. Eddy which do not meet their approval, and the Church of Scientology has been extremely active in litigating against the authors and publishers of books and newspapers which published commentary on Scientology.

The problem of authority

Both Mrs. Eddy and Hubbard have had to face challenges to their authority, indeed in the early years of both movements such challenges were frequent and present a problem common to many manipulationist movements. Since these movements have largely instrumental goals for whose attainment techniques are offered, the purveying of such techniques through practice and teaching usually has a much higher priority than any devotional activities. Individual practitioners and teachers thus acquire a clientele whose loyalties are directed primarily towards the practitioner rather than the wider collectivity. Practitioner-based movements tend to disperse charisma to the lower echelons and therefore to suffer from schism as local practitioners assert their autonomy from the movement leadership (see, for example, Nelson 1969). The leadership may also be challenged by aspiring practitioners who believe themselves able to advance the doctrine beyond the pioneer work of the founder, or who feel that their own following is sufficient to permit them to challenge the leader's decisions on questions of policy. A variety of mechanisms for centralising authority are likely to be invoked in such contingencies.

As we have seen, an early step taken by the leaders of both movements was that of securing transcendental legitimation for their authority. In Mrs. Eddy's case, *Science and Health,* and indeed all her writings, were claimed as divine revelations, and although her position on this seems to have changed periodically, she was certainly indentified by some of her followers as the 'woman clothed in the sun' prophesied in Revelations. Hubbard, on shifting Dianetics to a more occult level identified himself as the discoverer of the 'source of life energy', and the transcendental realm of the Operating Thetans, whose origins only he had plumbed. Scientology publications have also suggested that Hubbard might be the Maitreya Buddha, believed to be due to follow the Gautama Buddha, and to offer a new path to Enlightenment. These developments appear to have enhanced the charismatic authority of the founders.

The personalities of these leaders became all pervasive in the movements they founded. Mrs. Eddy's name was to be mentioned before each church service and at each reading from her *Science and Health.* Christian Science lecturers are required to refer to the exemplary life of the founder in their lectures, and the Church Manual still bears her name as the Pastor Emeritus and the head of the Church. Only her writings and a limited range of further works are thoroughly approved reading for members. Hubbard's presence is felt throughout Scientology. Virtually all the literature of the movement is written by him. All internal policy directives bear his name. His photograph, larger than life dominates Scientology offices. But while omnipresent as persona, both Mrs. Eddy and Ron Hubbard became increasingly distant as real people. Mrs. Eddy gradually withdrew from day-to-day contact with more than a tiny nucleus of trusted followers in her home. Ron Hubbard did likewise aboard the Flag Ship of the Sea Org. By thus secluding themselves the leaders enhanced their charisma by adding to the mystery surrounding them. By creating social and ecological boundaries they also protected their charisma from defilement particularly through seepage of information concerning their health and behaviour as they became elderly, information which would contrast with the elevated expectations of followers.

The authority of the leader was also heightened by undermining alternative loci of power within the organisation, and its centralisation in the hands of a personally appointed executive. Branch Churches and societies in Christian Science are subordinated to the central organisation by the requirement that the Readers of the Branch Churches be approved by the Mother Church Board of Directors. In Scientology there is a strict organisational hierarchy. Franchises (i.e. the semi-independent subsidiaries) are licensed only for members in good standing with the HASI or Church of Scientology, and subsidiary Churches and branches of the Church and HASI are controlled by direct appointment of leaders as well as the presence within each organisation of offices responsible directly to Hubbard and his wife. Missions of the Sea Org have full authority to take control of organisations to which they are despatched by Hubbard. Communications are also highly centralised and controlled by the organisation. Only authorised literature is permitted and publication of non-approved materials in the case of either movement is liable to lead to exclusion. Whilst approved, loyal members may be permitted to publish works on Christian Science or Scientology, these will be suppressed if the writer subsequently apostasises, such suppression being facilitated in the case of the latter by the fact that the copyrights on their works are almost invariably held in Hubbard's name.

The authority of local teachers is further undermined by constraints on teaching beyond the preliminary levels of doctrine. Whilst little is taught at the Normal class with which a student of the Primary class would be unfamiliar, and in the case of Scientology most of the advanced materials are available in various of Hubbard's books, advanced training remains an essential requirement for teaching and mobility within either Church, and carries a mystique endowing its graduates with high prestige. Subsidiary organisations of Scientology are permitted to train and process only through the lower levels, higher levels of professional processing and training can be acquired only through the central Advanced Orgs.

Two further developments have vastly increased the power and authority of the leader at the expense of practitioners and teachers. The first of these is the progressive impersonalisation and standardisation of practice and teaching. After 1895 the only pastors permitted in Christian Science churches were *Science and Health* and the Bible, preachers were reduced to Readers whose performance was controlled to the extent of standardising the emphasis with which passages were read. Their expository task was taken over by a Board of Lecturers, appointed by the Directors and obliged to submit the text of their lectures, in advance, to the Mother Church. The technique of healing had long been standardised in Mrs. Eddy's textbook. The annual re-election of Lecturers by the Directors and the requirement that Readers could hold office for three years only precluded the development of these offices as a source of independent authority that could be directed against the Church leadership. Teachers were brought under increased control by permitting them to hold a class only once a year, for no more than thirty students, and forbidding gatherings of teachers and their students on other occasions.

In Scientology, the shift from Dianetics, the practice of which had been something of an art, with a growing reliance on the E-meter, led to a complete standardisation of training and processing. Both are organised around texts produced by Hubbard. Teaching is entirely based on duplicated course materials written by Hubbard, from which no deviation is permitted. No interpretation of training material is allowed to instructors who are required simply to direct the student to the appropriate location in the materials written by Hubbard for the answer to any difficulties. Processing is based on standard lists of auditing commands and questions issued in a trained stereotypic fashion. No lectures above the most elementary level are given other than by Hubbard, and these are heard by students from tape-recordings.

Finally, both movements employ effective mechanisms for isolating disaffected teachers and practitioners. In Christian Science this mechanism takes the form of placing a teacher whose loyalty is suspect on probation in the Church. While on probation he may practise but not teach, and may not convene his student association. Since his readmittance as a full member is dependent upon his good behaviour he must strive to conform to the requirements of the Board of

37

Directors, and probation is therefore a means of sanctioning the dissident and isolating him from his followers, whilst not fully alienating him from the Church. Excommunication of a teacher brings with it the furthur consequence that all his students are required to retake the Primary class under another teacher, and thus incurring the disapproval of the Board puts the standing of the teacher's students in jeopardy as well as his own. Practitioners can be controlled by the threat of having their names dropped from the *Journal* with the result that loyal members will no longer seek their services.

Scientology here, as elsewhere, employs a more differentiated procedure. A hierarchy of Conditions is available, ranging from Power to Treason, in which a member can be located. Being assigned a 'lower condition' incurs a range of penalties, out of which the individual must work himself, again sactioning the deviant whilst making him work harder to retain his standing. Committing a 'High Crime' against Scientology* results in the assignment of a Condition of Enemy and a declaration that the individual concerned is a Suppressive Person.

At least until 1966 it was a requirement that all members who had any association with a Suppressive Person were obliged to cut off all connection with him. It remains the case that they are regarded as Potential Trouble Sources and are required to signify and demostrate their continued loyalty to Scientology. The penalties of probation and the Conditions serve to undermine the influence of the individual penalised with other members whilst often maintaining his loyalty.

The members of the Christian Science and Scientology movements have no official voice in policy and decision-making, and little basis for united opposition to the leadership. In Scientology even meetings 'to protest the order of a superior' are forbidden. Since the highest officials hold office only on sufferance of the leadership, it is hardly to be expected that lower echelon members will have any effective influence.

The problem of commitment

Manipulationist sects are faced with a further major problem, that of maintaining membership commitment. This problem exists principally because they arise in secularised societies in which the domain of religion is highly restricted, and in which religious institutions are obliged to compete with secular agencies as sources of knowledge and technique to control the world. As the natural world has been rendered more explicable by natural science the concern of new religious movements has been directed towards the less predictable and less well explicated areas of human relationships, psychology, health and social achievement. Their solutions to these problems are offered as a service purveyed on a quasi-commercial basis and it is this service-orientation that provides the rationale for affiliation.

While sometimes including as part of their doctrine and ritual the traditional, communal, features of religious institutions, these typically have no central role in the ideology or practice of the movement. Congregational and devotional aspects of both Christian Science and Scientology are relatively peripheral. In the case of Scientology particularly there is complete absence of devotional elements, and attendance at church services is in no way a requirement of church membership. These services principally involve an exposition of some very basic element of doctrine directed towards those unfamiliar with Scientology rather than the initiated.

In highly differentiated societies such movements emerge to supply a relatively specific need and typically employ the modes of organisation and communication utilised by successful commercial organisations. Presenting themselves as service agencies, albeit of a peculiar kind, the involvement of their adherents is, as Bryan Wilson (1970b) has indicated, often occasional or of limited duration and segmental. Retaining, enhancing and institutionalising membership commitment under these circumstances thus presents a not inconsiderable problem. Failure to find an effective solution to this problem may lead to the typically very limited involvement and declining adherence characteristic of Spiritualism, and many movements in New Thought.

Christian Science and Scientology have generated a number of mechanisms for maintaining cohesion and heightening involvement among the general membership. Not only do they offer services of a highly specific kind as does contemporary spiritualism, but foster a wider theoretical and doctrinal concern. Adherents are expected to grow in knowledge of the gnosis through extensive study of the movement's literature. Greater returns can be expected from movement practices the higher the level of understanding of the exponent. Impersonalisation and standardisation facilitate involvement with the movement on an entirely solitary basis. They also generate loyalty to a wider social unit than the practitioner-client relationship. The leader particularly offers a focus of loyalty transcending the purely local, and membership in the wider corporate collectivity (the Mother Church, the HASI or Church of Scientology) is encouraged, fostering a commitment to the movement as a whole rather than any particular unit. Instruction in the highly articulated doctrine is also differentiated, only the more elementary components being provided by the local subidiaries or semi-independent practitioners, whilst advanced instruction can be received only from the central organisation. A desire to progress in the doctrine thus carries as an almost automatic concomitant a growing identification with the central organisation.

Christian Science and Scientology also require greater commitment in both time and financial resources than many similar movements, e.g. Spiritualism. While the cost of treatment or processing may not be excessive in comparison with private medical or psychiatric attention, there is also the cost of class instruction and training, as well as the cost of literature, which makes the financial commitment involved more extensive than would be the case for members of most other denominations, although considerably less than for many utopian or millennialist sects (Kanter, 1972). Similarly a thorough understanding of the literature will require a considerable investment of time. Resource commitment is fostered among some adherents by the opportunity available and aspiration to become practitioners or teachers of the technique on a professional basis.

Commitment is further enhanced by ideological insulation, the prohibition or denigration of alternative sources of opinion, ideology or involvement. Christian Science frowns upon other metaphysical literature, officially prohibits membership in other groups or movements outside the Church, and even forbids private meetings of members in which Science may be discussed. Involvement with alternative occult ideologies is regarded as 'suppressive' in Scientology and doctrine is regarded as finally and conclusively given in Hubbard's writings. Interpretation beyond the very preliminary levels is regarded as 'invalidating the data of Scientology'. Only Hubbard's voice may be heard as authoritative.

Although eschatology plays a negligible role in manipulationism in comparison with millennialism, Christian Science and Scientology have a sense of mission which seems lacking in most other manipulationist movements and commitment is enhanced by a conviction of historical inevitability. Christian Scientists see themselves as part of a progression towards the time when error and false belief will be eliminated and the material world with all its powerful apparency will yield to a purely spiritual order in which illness and death can have no place. Scientologists see themselves as engaged upon a mission to 'clear the planet', to clear the Reactive Minds of the world's population and rehabilitate man to his full potential as Operating Thetan, a mission whose urgency is enhanced by Hubbard's oft-voiced prophecy that it is a race between Scientology and the atom bomb.

As Simmel long since indicated conflict may have adaptive consequences, tending to enhance group integration. The ideologies of Christian Science and Scientology have led them into conflict with the wider society. Their engagement in healing — or what has been construed as the practice of healing in the face of disclaimers from both movements — has tended to generate institutional opposition from both the state and medical agencies. Scientology has also caused antagonism through the practice of 'disconnection' when members were encouraged, and sometimes ordered, to cut off relationships with family or friends regarded as 'suppressive'. While such conflicts have sometimes caused defections they have also tended to heighten the solidarity and commitment of those who remain, viewing themselves as a beleagured band bravely proclaiming the truth in the face of intolerance and prejudice.

Finally, both Christian Science and Scientology exhibit an acute preoccupation with an enemy and offer a conspiracy theory of its activities. This enemy provides an opportunity to heighten solidarity through vilification. As Orrin Klapp has indicated,

> Vilification is a kind of symbol-making that groups engage in . . . in order to repair and defend the social structure and to build consensus and morale . . . (Klapp 1959).

The enemy of Christian Science is, of course, malicious animal magnetism. Originally practised by apostates but now by the Catholic Church, its activities form the basis of every threat to Christian Science. The former enemy of Scientology, 'Black Dianetics', has now largely been replaced by the activities of the 'psycho-politicians', the psychiatrists who provoke every attack on Scientology through 'front groups' such as the British

Government, the World Federation for Mental Health, etc. The adherent of Christian Science or Scientology is sensitised to the fact that the world outside the safety of the movement is a place full of dangers whose existence he never suspected prior to affiliation.

A note on differences

Drawing attention to parallels between Christian Science and Scientology in order to illuminate the processes leading to sectarianisation inevitably blurs the differences between the two movements. Apart from the obvious differences in beliefs and practices, Christian Science is much closer to the traditional model of the religious association. While highly centralised, it is very much more dependent on the personal charisma of practitioners and teachers. Its religious services have a more important role and retain some of the communal features of more traditional Christian collectivities.

The more extensive *Gesellschaftlich* pattern of Scientology, its more thoroughgoing centralisation, standardisation and social control, and the more extensive commitment encouraged through the differentiated ladder of courses and their consider-able cost, clearly reflect features of the period and social environment from which this movement emerged. The more prominent secularism of Scientology reflects the greater secular-ism of Western society in the formative years of this movement in at least two respects. Scientology has had a wider range of organisational styles from which to choose. The existence of models of highly bureaucratised business corporations, institu-tions for the mass distribution of higher education, and totali-tarian political parties, has clearly been an important influence on the development of Scientology organisational structure. Moreover, these models do not simply exist, but flourish, and enjoy higher prestige than the earlier more typically adopted model for voluntary associations, the Church. Secondly in a more secular age, its potential clients are less likely to require their philosophies of life and theories of the mind and human behaviour to assume a religious form.

Conclusions

This chapter has argued the view that manipulationist move-ments face a number of common problems which tend to inhibit the development of a cohesive collectivity. Their ideologies, derived from movements of thought common in their cultic milieux, tend to be precarious and liable to dedifferentiation; authority tends to be widely dispersed in practitioner-based movements leading to factionalism or schism; and extensive commitment among the following is difficult to generate owing to the specific service-orientated basis of affiliation and segmental and occasional involvement of members.

A survey of Christian Science and Scientology suggests the development of a cohesive collectivity may be enhanced by the elaboration of a transcendental ideology legitimising authoritarian centralisation and rigorous control. Impersonalisation and standardisation facilitate the undermining of alternative sources of authority. The focusing of commitment upon the leader and central organisation, and engagement in conflict with the wider society and competing belief systems, tend to enhance the integration of the movement and more clearly define its ideological boundaries. Thus pursuing a strategy of *sectarianisation* is one viable and attractive mode of adaption for the leadership of fragile ideological movements.

* See for example, Hubbard (1968). Such High Crimes included: making 'Public Statements against Scientology or Scientologists . . .'; 'publicly resigning staff or executive position in protest or with intent to suppress'; 'seeking to resign or leave courses or sessions and refusing to return despite normal efforts'; 'continued adherence to a group pronounced a suppressive group . . .'; 'dependency on other mental or philosophic procedures than Scientology (except medical or surgical) after certification, classification or award'.

CHAPTER III

Reflections on
When Prophecy Fails

When Prophecy Fails has been the object of reflection both in terms of its status as evidence for the theory of cognitive dissonance and, more controversially, in terms of the ethics of social research. My concern is not with either of these issues. Re-reading this book after several years, it occurred to me that taken as a piece of ethnography *When Prophecy Fails* provides remarkably good support for an account of the characteristics and dynamics of cults which I have outlined in a number of papers (Wallis, 1974, 1975b, 1975c). Remissly, I did not turn to the study of Festinger *et al.*, when formulating my account, hence I feel justified in utilising it now as independent supporting evidence.

The emergence of cults

Colin Campbell (1972) has proposed the very suggestive notion of a *cultic milieu.* By this he means to refer to the network of individuals, groups, practices, institutions, means of communication and beliefs which embody what we might term 'rejected knowledge'. Ideas which have not been accepted and incorporated into the legitimate operation of any 'respectable' institutions of a society tend to percolate down to a kind of underground typified by the occult bookstore.

Cults emerge around a synthesis of ideas current in this underground supplemented and refined by the researches or insights of their founders. They are essentially precarious collectivities. This precariousness derives from two central features of the cultic milieu (which Campbell does not mention).

First, there prevails in the milieu an attitude of 'epistemological individualism', that is, a belief that the individual is the ultimate locus for the determination of truth. Secondly, there prevails an ideology of 'revelational indeterminacy', that is, a belief that the truth may be revealed in diverse ways and through diverse agents. No individual or collectivity possesses a monopoly of the truth.

The characteristics of cults are greatly constrained by these features of the cultic milieu, as they are incorporated into the background assumptions of the seekers recruited to it from that milieu. Since they see many groups and doctrines as embodying some aspects of the truth, no particular cult can command their loyalty totally. Since the loyalties of members are shared with other ideological collectivities, the cult leadership cannot afford to offend by intolerance of other organisations and faiths, and hence can draw no firm boundary around the beliefs of the movement which anyway overlap with the beliefs of other groups. Since only the individual member is the ultimate authority for what is true for him, there can be no overriding authority beyond the individual member for determining what is or is not heresy. Hence the boundaries of the group are fluid and open both in terms of belief and membership. The membership will tend to change rapidly as seekers move on from one group to another. Dissension may arise due to the relatively limited basis of shared belief, or due to claims arising from the membership that they possess an equally authoritative access to the truth or revelation.

These characteristics of the membership pose a problem for the leadership of a cult. Unless that leadership accepts these background assumptions fully and thereby accepts that their own beliefs and practices are of merely partial and relative truth, they will typically seek to secure some priority in matters of interpretation. Proposing that one has a distinctive set of beliefs and practices at all tends to imply that one believes it is *more* true than its competitors in the cultic milieu; and a desire to preserve that truth and institutionalise the collectivity formed around it may inspire the leader to claim a more unique authority. This, in turn, may alienate some of the following. However, if successfully accomplished, the arrogation of authority provides the basis for a process of *sectarianisation,* and hence, a solution to the problems of the institutional fragility of the cult.

Mrs. Keech's cult

Mrs. Keech is the archetypal *seeker* (note that the church-based group organised by Dr. Armstrong in Collegeville is referred to by Festinger *et al.,* as 'The Seekers'. When written with a lower-case s, I am using the term to refer to an individual who has entered and journeyed through some sectors of the cultic milieu, in search of truth). She had attended lectures on Theosophy, had read the writings of the I AM movement and much other occult literature. She had become involved with Dianetics and Scientology, and shortly prior to her revelations had become interested in the controversy concerning flying saucers. Her revelation initially took the form of automatic writing, a phenomenon which has played a part of some prominence in the spiritualist movement, and indeed her first message was identified as emanating from her father. Later she received messages from more elevated spiritual beings, and ultimately from Sananda, the contemporary identity of the historical Jesus. Sananda advised her that she was being prepared for a task of liaison in preparation for his coming.

Mrs. Keech's experiences remarkably parallel those of the founder of another flying saucer group which I have studied, the Aetherius Society (Wallis, 1975a). (I should perhaps add that despite the fact that a reviewer of my paper on the Aetherius Society complained that I had not cited the study by Festinger *et al.,* I did not even *then* read the work, since I had the impression that it was concerned with the matter of cognitive dissonance and therefore not of sufficient relevance to merit the time at that point!) George King, himself a seeker of some standing, heard a voice commanding him to prepare himself to become an intermediary between spiritual beings in space, and people on earth. Later, while in a trance, King was visited by a yoga adept who gave him secret yogic practices to equip himself for his role. Later still, he was contacted by the Master Aetherius a Venusian, whose messages formed a large part of what he was to convey to the people of Earth. Like Sananda, Aetherius was greatly exercised by the dangers of the atomic bomb, beginning to be a major source of anxiety for many humans also during the early 1950s. I shall identify some important differences between these two flying saucer cults later.

Mrs. Keech's revelations were principally circulated by word of mouth, prior to the development of any newspaper publicity.

Through networks of personal contacts, Mrs. Keech's experiences were passed on to other individuals, or to the contiguous institutions of the cultic milieu. An acquaintance of Mrs. Keech who was assisting in the typing of copies of the messages introduced her 'to a small, informal circle of housewives who met in various Highvale homes to discuss dianetics, scientology, metaphysics, and occult topics' (Festinger *et al.*, 1956:39). A lecturer on flying saucers whose talks she had attended and to whom she spoke of her messages, mentioned her in turn at the Steel City Flying Saucer Club, and brought her to the attention of Dr. Armstrong, who was to prove her mainstay in the months to come. Dr. Armstrong and his wife were also paradigm-case seekers studying the writings of oriental religions, mysticism, occultism and metaphysics. They believed in spiritual communication, reincarnation and flying saucers, and had organised a group at the church which they attended to discuss such matters.

Mrs. Keech was later to give readings from her messages at the Metaphysical Bookstore in Lake City. Although Mrs. Keech did not proselytise actively, knowledge of her revelations was spreading and followers were being drawn to her. Dr. Armstrong distributed copies of the messages via a mailing list of individuals and organisations interested in the study of flying saucers and metaphysics. The bulk of those drawn to the movement (other than Festinger and his associates and the occasional prankster) were also seekers. A number were attracted through The Seekers run by Dr. Armstrong, and some had prior involvements in the activities of the cultic milieu, although in many cases insufficient information is provided to secure any detailed cultic biography. Bob Eastman had been a member of the Steel City Flying Saucer Club (*ibid.* 77). Hal Fischer 'had had considerable experience with occult matters' (*ibid.* 83). A 'middle-aged woman' had 'a long series of involvement in mystical activities' (*ibid.* 85). Among those who participated in Lake City, Mrs. Keech's home town, Edna Post 'had a history of participation in quasi-mystical groups with an intellectual orientation', including Dianetics and Scientology (*ibid.* 87). Bertha Blatsky was 'another member of the scientology group' (*ibid.* 88). Mary Novick was or had been a Dianetics or Scientology 'auditor' (practitioner) (*ibid.* 90). Clyde Wilton 'had had a long-standing interest in flying saucers' (*ibid.* 91).

The ideology of the group, Festinger *et al.*, tell us, was an eclectic synthesis. Flying saucer lore mingled with theosophy, lost continents and spiritualist practice. A message of immediate pessimism based on man's evil and incompetence in managing his affairs combined with long-term optimism. Higher spiritual beings are watching over us and will rescue the worthy from their fate.

> True, Mrs. Keech put together a rather unusual combination of ideas — a combination peculiarly well adapted to our contemporary, anxious age — but scarcely a single one of her ideas can be said to be unique, novel, or lacking in popular (though not, for the most part, majority) support (*ibid.* 55).

That epistemological individualism characterised the attitude of most of those associated with the group is evident. While the commitment of some of the adherents to the validity of Mrs. Keech's message came to be near total, resulting in the abandonment of job or career, the alienation of friends and relations, the group displayed a considerable fluidity in its composition. Individuals drifted into the group, and drifted out, sometimes accepting some components of the belief system, or the authenticity of some aspects of Mrs. Keech's revelation, but rejecting others. The individual member was the sole arbiter of what constituted the truth. This attitude was reinforced by some of the messages that were transmitted from beyond. Bertha advised everyone at one stage to 'follow your inner knowing' and to at least one member she said: 'Accept no authority, not even the authority of the Creator'. The content of the messages received were often referred to the 'inner knowing' of leaders, or self-referred by members for confirmation of their validity.

The absence of any unique source of ideological authority within this cult is exemplified in a number of ways. Mrs. Keech and other leading figures constantly sought further guidance and direction from visitors, investigators or telephone callers. Even the most committed believers, the Armstrongs and Mrs. Keech herself, had recourse to alternative channels of communication with the transcendent, particularly in the form of Ella Lowell the spiritualist medium. The clearest support for a belief in revelation indeterminacy, however, is the possession of Bertha Blatsky by Sananda and then by the Creator. Bertha briefly challenged Mrs. Keech's priority in ideological revelation when the Creator revealed that she (Bertha) had been chosen as 'the greatest prophet' (*ibid.* 99). The Creator's messages diverged considerably from those of Sananda through Mrs. Keech. The Creator mocked Sananda's knowledge and the language of Mrs. Keech's lessons (*ibid.* 111). New ideological elements were introduced and the vegetarianism of the group was ended. After her most dramatic revelation that she was to be 'the Mother of Christ', a thaumaturgical act which she drastically failed to accomplish, Bertha ceased to challenge in any radical way Mrs. Keech's authority. She re-emphasized the doctrine of 'inner knowing', and the Creator declared that all members of the group were now capable of receiving messages (*ibid.* 113) thereby threatening the devaluation of revelation as a source of authority, although the task of instruction and hence a slight priority were retained for Mrs. Keech and Bertha. Thereafter the Creator largely confirmed the messages of Sananda via Mrs. Keech.

It is most significant that throughout these events, Mrs. Keech made no attempt to constrain Bertha, nor did she challenge her messages and their authenticity, even when some of her fundamental tenets were attacked and a favoured acquaintance of Mrs. Keech was turned away from the group by the Creator. Along with the Armstrongs, however, Mrs. Keech did abstain from eating meat when the Creator legitimised its consumption (*ibid.* 111). Mrs. Keech was too committed to the cultic milieu's assumptions of epistemological individualism and revelational indeterminancy to attempt to maintain the purity of the group's belief-system and buttress her position by a strategy of securing a monopoly over the means of revelation, arrogating authority and leading the group in the direction of sectarianism.

Comparisons with the Aetherius Society

George King, founder of the Aetherius Society, also became a channel for the messages of transcendental beings connected with the operation of flying saucers. Unlike that of Mrs. Keech, the doctrine conveyed through King has no millennialist orientation. King is less a *prophet* than a *mystagogue*. His messages designated no apocalyptic end to humanity. Rather they described the threat mankind was under from a variety of forces of evil which these supernatural beings, aided by King, sought to combat on man's behalf. King was to become a prominent combatant in this cosmic war, and he sought to mobilise his following to undertake with him various ritual acts of magic designed to strengthen the forces of good against the forces of evil.

King differed from Mrs. Keech in another important respect. He did not eschew publicity. Rather he actively sought it throughout. His early following was gathered by the expedient of giving public performances of his thaumaturgy, by going into a trance on the platform of a public hall, and relaying messages from the Space Masters, for the edification of his audience. He later toured America speaking to metaphysical and flying saucer groups to publicise his revelation.

Most important of all, however, King, unlike Mrs. Keech, actively pursued a policy of monopolising access to the means of revelation. The Space Masters designated him as 'Primary Terrestrial Channel' between themselves and the earth. King, in the Society's publications, defended the legitimacy of his contact with space people and sought to refute other published contact claims on the basis of his superior knowledge. The only report of a contact with the space people, other than his own, which has ever appeared in the Society's magazine, was one involving his mother, the content of which further supported his own primacy.

King exercises clear ultimate authority within the movement, and brooks no challenge to the validity of his revelations from within the movement. His priority has since received further legitimation when one of the Space Masters, the Master Jesus, conveyed that King had also become a Master, 'one of Us'. King has therefore accomplished what Mrs. Keech, with her commitment to the norms of the cultic milieu did not even attempt. He had established an authoritarian epistemological base to the movement's doctrine which endowed him with a unique authority, and thereby undermined the validity of alternative agencies of revelation. By these steps he institutionalised the movement which he had founded and enhanced its stability and probability of survival. By these means, King loosened the relationship between his group and the cultic milieu, and shifted it towards a sectarian rather than cultic character.

CHAPTER IV

Millennialism and community: Observations on the Children of God

Introduction

The spirit of Durkheim is not dead. Incorporeal and insubstantial his ghost is conjured yet to awe the superstitious. This now somewhat enfeebled apparition flitted, not long ago, through two recent works on millennial movements. Rosabeth Moss Kanter toys in a recent paper with the notion that '. . . millennial ideas are secondary to the social act of mobilisation and formation of a new community . . . millennial ideas provide the justification for engagement in the worship of an emergent group' (Kanter, 1972:221). But, that this is little more than a flirtation is shortly revealed as Kanter spells out the implications of this claim in terms of a functional account in which millennial ideas merely serve to support and maintain the community. Nevertheless, there remains the implication that the formation of the community is a prime imperative for which millennialism merely provides a justification. Social structure causes belief and appropriate beliefs will be called forth by structural needs. Once more the natives dance not as they declare, in order to make rain, but to create social solidarity, and their beliefs are merely the quaint stories of simple, childlike minds rationalising what they do despite themselves.

James Beckford similarly adopts a position stressing the priority of the organisational collectivity over the beliefs of its members. In a discussion of Jehovah's Witnesses, he claims that 'the nature of the millennial message is so highly ambiguous that it is largely determined by the organisational form . . .'' (Beckford, 1975:119). Commenting on the Christadelphians,

51

the Shakers, and the Oneida Community, he also observes that 'their goals and imposed organisational design were heavily determinant of their respective, and widely differing, ways of embodying millenarian doctrines' (*ibid.*). These statements are not themselves without considerable ambiguity, but in general they would seem to concur with Kanter that the structure of the organisation or collectivity has some independent causal priority in the generation of beliefs.

Kanter's account is based not only on historical communitarian groups, but also on the contemporary commune movement. Doubtless there are contemporary or recent cases in which youthful middle-class enthusiasts romanticising the utopian way of life have determined to form communes and then cast about for an appropriate integrating ideology. Some may have hit upon a millennial vision which met their need. But to erect this into a general principle concerning millennialism seems to me profoundly mistaken. Kanter has been rather too much impressed by the playful antics of contemporary communards and too little by the serious efforts of historical millennialists. Historically, the evidence surely points to the prior existence of millennial ideas around which a movement formed in the case of such groups as the Doukhobors, Hutterites, Millerites, Jehovah's Witnesses and numerous others. The formation of a community in the sense of any communal enterprise typically occurred in the face of persecution or environmental exigencies. Communitarianism was, if anything, entirely secondary in the case of Hutterians, Doukhobors and Shakers, being grafted onto the millennialist hope in the face of social and economic conditions in which communitarianism promised the best hope of survival of their distinctive beliefs and way of life.

Kanter suggests in a not altogether unambiguous passage that: 'Whether the idea or the incipient community came first in time, *development* of the movement can be viewed as *supported* by, rather than *defined* by, the existence and further specification of a millennial vision' (Kanter, 1972:222). I should like, in rebuttal of this view, to present a case in which the development of the movement as a social structure has been altogether defined and directed by the leader's specification of his millennial revelation, and in which it seems clear that the community itself will be readily eliminated by the leader should it fail adequately to fulfil the demands set by his millennial beliefs.

The present paper represents a first attempt to summarise material on various aspects of the development of a new religious group, the Children of God (or the 'Family' as members refer to it), which I have gathered through the analysis of extensive documentary materials; through interviews with existing and former Children of God and parents of committed members; and through participation in various activities in communes or 'colonies' and coffee-bars of the Family. Providing a coherent analysis of the Children of God is made difficult by a number of factors. First, the group is less than 10 years old and only in recent years has any extensive documentation been published by it. Secondly, th group has regarded itself as continually liable to persecution by the outside 'system'. It therefore adopts a rather secretive stance *vis-a-vis* the outside world. Thirdly, the Children of God have been a topic of controversy in the mass media, even giving rise to an oppositional group, FREECOG, Free Our Children from the Children of God, composed primarily of parents hostile to the Children of God, whose offspring have joined it. FREECOG possess and promote their own theory and analysis of the movement, which has been adopted, albeit not monolithically, by the mass media. Finally, my impression is that the beliefs, organisational practices and orientation to the world of this group have fluctuated considerably over the course of time and vary between different colonies of the Children of God. That is, my feeling is that the leader of the movement have often modified their views regarding these matters, and it is perhaps still too soon to be confident that any firm set of beliefs and practices have crystallised in some particulars. Here we focus on general developments up to 1974, turning later to specific subsequent innovations.

A brief history of the Children of God

The Children of God was founded by David Brandt Berg who regards himself as a prophet chosen by God to convey a warning of the coming end of time, and new revelations of God's plan and purpose for the current age. (Information on the origin and development of the Children of God can also be found in Enroth, Ericson and Peters, 1972; Berg, 1972a.) As Berg occupies such a dominant status within the Children of God it is important to understand something of his biography, since features of his life and background seem to have had a marked influence on the ideology and structure of the movement.

Berg was born into a second-generation evangelical family. His maternal grandfather had been a prominent evangelist in the Disciples of Christ, and his father also became a minister for this denomination, and his mother a prominent radio evangelist. His parents later left the Disciples to affiliate with the Christian and Missionary Alliance. Berg, born in 1919, spent many of his early years travelling with his parents engaged upon evangelism. This period seems to have instilled in him a love for the wandering life and a nostalgia for the pre-war rural *Gemeinschaft* of the many small towns in which his parents must have preached. After the Second World War, Berg himself became a minister of the Christian and Missionary Alliance but seems shortly to have fallen into dispute with the board of his Arizona church leading to an acrimonious parting. This experience seems to have been the beginning in Berg of a fierce contempt and dislike for the organised churches of America. After a period at college on the GI Bill, he became a school teacher, finding time also to spend three months on Fred Jordan's 'Soul Clinic Personal Witnessing Course'. Jordan, a fundamentalist Southern evangelist, also produced a radio and television show called Church in the Home, and Berg later worked for him for thirteen years, arranging bookings for his show on local radio and television stations.

Berg had for some time regarded himself as the subject of prophetic revelations through which God had indicated that he had been chosen for a task of some importance. In 1965 his mother received what came to be called the 'Warning Prophecy' concerning the imminence of the Great Confusion and the rise of the Anti-Christ.

In the summer of 1967, Berg left Jordan's employ and set out with his family apparently as a travelling evangelist. In this enterprise he seems to have had little concrete success, and when his mother, who had settled in Huntington Beach, California, wrote to tell them of the hippie drop-outs flooding to the west coast, and of the failure of the established denominational facilities to reach them, Berg hurried to Huntington Beach in 1968, believing that he had at last found the ministry he sought.

David Wilkerson's Teen Challenge had established a coffee-house, the Huntington Beach Light Club, to try to minister to the hippie population, but had made little impact. Berg and his family at first aided Teen Challenge, and then took over the coffee-house from them. There he, his wife, his children and their spouses established themselves as Teens for Christ. Using the language of the hippie community, wearing long hair and informal clothes, and providing free food, music and a welcoming atmosphere for youthful drop-outs, open until 2 o'clock in the morning, Berg and his family ministered to the young street people, surfers and drug-addicts of Huntingdon Beach (Huntington Beach *Daily Pilot,* various issues). In common with a number of other groups and individuals in various part of California and elsewhere in the United States, Berg had begun a fundamentalistically-based ministry directed at the young drifters and drop-outs of the late 1960s, which came to be known generically as the Jesus Pople.

From these early days of the Light Club, Berg appears to have preached a message of total commitment and the imminence of the millennium. Converts were encouraged to move into the club and other houses later made available to them. They 'forsook all' their wordly possessions, having all things in common on the pattern of the early Church in Acts 1-5. They engaged in intense Bible study under Berg's leadership, and their alienation from American society and institutions was intensified by the attacks on the materialistic, individualistic, capitalistic world from which they had dropped out. More concretely, Berg's antipathy to what he saw as the hypocrisy, complacency and lack of spirituality and evangelistic fervour of the established denominations was demonstrated by a series of *en masse* visits to churches in the neighbourhood of the Light Club.

Berg and 30 or 40 of his followers would arrive at respectable middle-class churches attired in hippie garb, troop down to the front of the church, and sit on the floor in front of the pews. Berg was to refer to these later as 'goodwill visitations to local churches to help them get better acquainted with us . . .' (Berg, 1972a:18), but this description is perhaps more than a little self-serving. The hostility felt by the group toward organised religion led its members on occasion to challenge the minister or shout abuse at worshippers. Their radical enthusiasm led them to loud praising and prayer to which the church members were unaccustomed. It seems to have been the case that they were, for their part, met with suspicion and some hostility by church officials faced with this deluge of scruffily-attired zealots, and whether the disruption that often ensued was the fault of Berg and his followers or of the affronted denominationalists seems less clear than that it occurred and resulted in considerable newspaper publicity when they were ejected from various churches.

Berg also felt a strong antipathy towards the institutions of education. Their secularism, rejection of the Bible and acceptance of evolutionism had made them a major focus for Berg's fundamentalist dislike. Six members of his group were arrested for refusing to leave a college campus where they had been handing out leaflets in late 1969. Before their members came to trial, the group received a prophecy confirming their feeling about California and revealing that it would shortly sink into the sea as a result of an earthquake. In consequence Berg and his 50 or so followers left California, settling first in Tucson where their numbers increased to about 75. From there they split into smaller groups and travelled across America, witnessing and demonstrating in various urban centres and gathering a few converts *en route*, eventually collecting together at Laurentide in the Laurentian mountains in Canada, over 100 strong.

Here David Berg, now known as Mo, Moses or Moses David, appears to have formulated some ideas which were to lead to the movement's distinctive organisational structure. In a letter addressed to his disciples early in 1970, Berg shows that he had come to see that this nomadic peregrination had achieved little in terms of concrete new disciples (Berg, 1970a). Nevertheless, he and his followers journeyed again across America, becoming prominent in the news media as they demonstrated, dressed in sackcloth and ashes, wearing yokes and bearing staves at such events as the lying in state of Senator Everett Dirksen in Washington DC (Dirksen had won their favour by his unsuccessful stand for Bible reading in public schools). They also demonstrated in Philadelphia; in New York before the UN Building; in Pittsburgh; in Chicago at the conspiracy trial of Jerry Rubin and the Yippies; and elsewhere. It seems that during the course of press publicity in these wanderings they received the name Children of God. By early 1970 they were back in Texas, and here Berg observes:

. . . we soon began running out of campgrounds as well as patience and endurance with the cold, wet rainy winter weather, some of the poor kids sleeping in leaky tents and soaked bags on flooded ground. So I was inspired to fly to California to request the use of the old Texas Soul

56

Clinic Missionary Ranch near Thurber, from . . . my
former boss, Fred Jordan . . . (Berg, 1972a:21).

They were given permission and during February 1970, about
120 Children of God moved into properties owned by Jordan
at Thurber in Texas, Coachella in California, and in Los Angeles.

Securing a base on Jordan's property fitted well with Berg's
developing organisational ideas. In a letter written shortly after
settling at the Texas Soul Clinic, Berg, who was increasingly
segregating himself from his followers, indicated his disapproval
of Jordan's policy of sending out evangelists and missionaries
on an individual basis, without support, and outlined the plan
God had revealed to him:

> . . . God has given us a plan whereby we're going to set up,
> by the grace of God, bases, strongholds, fortresses of God,
> Colonies. Whole communities . . . we are going to divide
> like the amoeba and then each half divide again. So that
> we can ship a whole colony of maybe a hundred people to
> start a new colony (Acts 13: 2, 5, 13), where everything
> will be there that is needed. Every kind of gift and every
> kind of trade, and every kind of vehicle, and every kind of
> knowledge about how to do it and how to start a new base
> . . . out of which we can send forays, and teams of skirm-
> ishing forces to attack in various ways and accomplish
> their purpose. God's purpose . . . this is an entirely new day,
> a new culture, a new nation, a whole new method of
> operation (Berg, 1970a).

Berg recognised that the travels of his group across the
continent had resulted in only a relatively slight increase in their
numbers. If potential converts heard of the group and were
attracted by it, the Children of God had moved on before they
could locate, and commit themselves to it. Establishing large
colonies or communities with a complete range of needed skills
and personnel would enable them to become 'self-supporting',
independent of the system which they detested, and 'self-
propagating' as a result of converts and offspring.

In this letter, Berg deploys an imagery of rural self-
sufficiency, a frontier independence in alien territory, 'with our
own stock of horses and buggies'. He also reveals the development of tensions between the Family and their patron, Fred
Jordan. Jordan's generosity towards the Children of God had
not been entirely disinterested. The 'youth revolution' and the

Jesus People had become a part of contemporary consciousness and Jordan saw the utility of promoting the Children of God as his protégés to his radio and television audiences to demonstrate that he was reaching this field of evangelism, and that his work continued to merit their donations. The Children of God appeared on his programmes singing and smiling and witnessing to their rescue from drugs and sexual liberty, and presenting themselves as respectable, if slightly unorthodox, upholders of conservative, fundamentalist American values. Jordan promoted and solicited funds for a scheme to establish an elaborate agricultural holding, a citrus fruit farm, for the Children of God at his Coachella property. Their relationship, a marriage of convenience from the outset, inevitably broke down. The occasion of the rupture seems to have been a dispute between the colony leader at that facility and Jordan over why the Children of God were not being permitted to utilise the entire farm when this was supposedly the purpose for which he was soliciting funds. Jordan sought unsuccessfully to get the leader replaced, and then attempted to win over the followers, again without success. He therefore promptly evicted them from the various buildings which he had hitherto made available, in September 1971. By this time the Family had grown to some 500 members.

But already, Berg had decided that his earlier plan of large colonies as bases for guerilla style evangelism needed modification. In a letter dated March 1971, he advocated the establishment of smaller colonies dispersed far more widely in order to reach the world's population more speedily. He had realised that large colonies suffered from 'their cumbersome burdensome machinery, and their impersonal, conglomerate fellowship where leadership loses the personal touch, intimate fellowship and close attention to the individual' (Berg, 1971a). Hence, thereafter, although large headquarter and regional colonies continued to exist, Berg continually exhorted his followers to split up, disperse and found small colonies in groups of no more than a dozen.

In response to Berg's exhortations and his prescience of the imminent collapse of America and the onset of the Great Tribulation, his followers began to disperse themselves throughout North America, and by the end of 1971, they were increasingly abandoning the North American continent and heading out in couples and small groups into South America and to England. From England they began migrating again into

58

Europe, Asia, Australasia and Africa. They now claim more than 600 colonies throughout the world and perhaps comprise over 4000 full-time disciples (recent issues of the Children of God periodical, *New Nation News*).

Organisation

At least by the time of their occupation of Fred Jordan's properties at Thurber, Coachella, and on Los Angeles' Skid Row, an organisational structure had emerged. Members were assigned to particular tribes modelled after those of Israel, but supplemented by new tribes. Division of these tribes was on a functional basis, each being composed of individuals responsible for particular kinds of tasks. Within each colony the members of a tribe would be directed by a tribe leader, responsible to the colony leader and his wife, and collectively comprising the 'elders' of that colony. In overall day-to-day charge of affairs were Berg's daughters Faith and Deborah (and their husbands), his sons, Hosea and Aaron, and one or two trusted intimates of Berg and his wife Eve. Berg himself no longer lived with the following, having departed for Israel and later to Europe, some time in 1970. He continued to direct, interpret and supplement the movement's beliefs and practices, and to direct its policy through letters, some to leaders only, others to all followers, and later increasingly to the public in general. The rank and file following was divided into Babes — those who had only recently joined — and 'older' brothers or sisters, who had passed through the initial period of indoctrination. Some of these older brothers and sisters, particularly those who had married within the group or were about to do so, became 'leadership trainees' in preparation for leadership responsibilities in their own colony. Colony leaders were, wherever possible, married couples.

The early movement also identified another status associated with the movement. This was the 'kings', that is parents or businessmen who while not fully members of the group, provided it with funds or support and defended it against its detractors. Fred Jordan was recognised as such a king, being named 'King Saul' by Berg who in turn construes himself as a latter-day David. The Children classified all others as 'Systemites' who, since they served Mammon, were enemies of the Family. 'There are no neutrals' an early Mo Letter proclaims. Radically separated or proselytising religious groups such as the Amish or

59

the Jehovah's Witnesses merited qualified approval and Berg recognised the existence of a few 'Saints' in the world at large, but the rest, the Jesus People included, were serving Satan, not God. Some were more actively enemies of the Children of God than others. In particular, there were the '10:36ers' (a reference to Matthew 10:36) used to designate parents actively hostile to the Family, who sought to remove their offspring from it, sometimes by force.

Later, when Berg discovered the utility of support from Systemites for his movement, a range of new categories was introduced. An organisation, THANKCOG, was established by parents favourable to the Children of God, to combat the propoganda of FREECOG. Berg decided that there were 'other sheep' than the Children of God, and hence the Jesus People, earlier anathematised as 'false Christians', and as 'nothing but a bunch of System kids and church kids with long hair!' who 'couldn't hold a candle to you!' (Berg, 1971b), were from 1972 to be actively cultivated. Only those who fully accepted direction by Family leadership and forsook all, could become 'disciples' and members of full colonies. Jesus People groups attracted to the movement could become Associate Members, and form Associate Colonies, and fellowship with them. There was even to be a category of 'Friends' who, while remaining Systemites and not forsaking all, were sympathetic towards the Family and assisted it. Berg says:

A lot of these folks have no other church or fellowship and would really like to feel they belong somewhere or to something. So we might even give them some kind of certificate of Membership so they can really feel like they are one of us and a part of the Family, even though they live outside. Systemites are geared to this sort of thing, so they could come to our meetings like going to church and give to us like putting their offering in the plate. We should have at least one special meeting each week for this purpose of these people — a meeting full of music, good positive songs and testimonies and inspirational instruction, but not necessarily any of the heavy stuff. You could even read them the lighter Mo Letters designed for Babes and the general public. You could either have an offering box by the door where they can't miss it as they leave, or pass a plate — they're geared for this! (Berg, 1972b).

As Berg indicates later, 'if you think we don't need their money and you're so damned independent you think you can do without their help, you're mistaken!'

The international structure of the Children of God was presented as a theoracy, with God revealing through King David, i.e. Mo, the directions to be followed by the movement. Berg was supported by his Royal Family of offspring and their spouses, who were the rulers of this New Nation. Members of the Royal Family also occupied positions in the Council of Ministers with overall responsibilities for particular activities and a Prime Minister in general direct charge. Below the Council of Ministers were the Bishops. The world was divided into 12 major areas, with a Bishop responsible for each. Below them were the Regional Shepherds, then the District Shepherds, then the Shepherds for particular colonies.

As the movement dispersed throughout the world, it became essential to establish some central offices to monitor the activities of scattered colonies, provide materials, organise printing and magazine publication, and handle national news media, etc. Regional and international headquarters were set up, and since their personnel were engaged for most of their time in administrative, clerical and production tasks, a problem began to develop of how such headquarter colonies were to be maintained. In 1972 the solution was seen to be one of sending any surplus cash to such offices to help support them, but this later came to be much more firmly institutionalised as the economic basis of the movement shifted.

Leadership within the Family has always been highly authoritarian with enormous stress on the divine appointment of leaders and the need for immediate obedience and complete submission to authority. Berg observes 'I guess you can blame it all on me, because that's the way I ran my own family and our early schools and Colonies to some extent, because you were my sole responsibility, slept under my roof and ate my food and I was your sole support, so I could expect you to do as I said and that was that or get out!' (Berg, 1972c). This authoritarian tradition seems to have been continued by Berg's Children. His daughter Faith is reported in an interview in a Family magazine in 1973 to have responded to a question on how disciples might draw closer together and become more in tune with Moses: 'Obey! Obedience. Do you know what our greatest goal is this year? — UNITY! But there is only one way to have unity, and that is to have total obedience by every member of the body. We must obey the words that God has given our prophet' (*New Nation News* 4, 5, 18 January 1973). Berg himself seems to have sought from time to time, to encourage a less dictatorial and more participatory style of leadership among his subordinates. For example, in 1972 he cautioned

> . . . I don't see how we can have that bossy, dictatorial, tough kind of attitude over other Colonies and their affairs, when they're supposed to be independent and indigenous, a fellowship of the Spirit, merely melted together in love and not just frozen together in formality! (Berg, 1972c).

The consequence of this ambiguity seems to be considerable variability in leadership styles throughout the movement, tending at that time to be more rather than less authoritarian.

Beliefs

The Children of God believe that we are approaching the time of the end prior to the Second Advent of Christ. Although no clear statement of Berg's early views is available, it seems that he may have believed that prior to Christ's return the Jews would be converted and that God's Covenant with the Jews remained in force. There was among the Children of God an early appreciation of things Jewish. They were guided as much by the Old as the New Testament, they divided into tribes, and the Kibbutz provided a model for the communal way of life. They engaged in a form of dance which they described as Jewish.

This regard for the Jews and for Israel did not long survive David Berg's visit there in 1970. He was profoundly disappointed by its materialism; by the predominance of highly individualistic Moshavs, which he saw as 'backsliding' from the communal life of the Kibbutz; and by the dominance of women in Israeli society, which he saw as 'contrary to the Scriptures, and God's Divine Order' (Berg, no date a[1970]). Israel, he discovered was 'becoming more like America every day!' (*ibid.*). He became progressively more hostile to the Jews, particularly because of the State's opposition to Christian missionary activity, and its disinclination to renew the visas of Berg and his party. The Jews he found 'right now are kind of cocky and in a superior position, and not too needy or hungry'

(Berg, 1970b). The Arabs whom he met, he found to be more responsive. Israel had 'become almost a closed nation to the Gospel' (Berg, 1971c). Thereafter Berg's writings are implacable in their hostility to the State of Israel, and increasingly favourable towards the Arabs.

His model for God's New Nation thenceforth was not the nomadic tribes of Israel, or the modern Kibbutz, but the gypsies. In a letter titled 'The Gypsies' written in March 1972 Berg suggests that the gypsies had their origin in Israel, but after the captivity of the Israelites in Babylon, they fled to India, from which they again migrated 'due to persecution for becoming Christians'. Their nomadic way of life in small communities greatly appealed to him. In subsequent letters he indicates that he had actively sought out groups of gypsies, and believed his glossolalic tongue to be 'an ancient Slavic gypsy language' (Berg, no date b[1970]). He saw the gypsies also as independent of, and enemies of, the System, drop-outs persecuted by the surrounding world. The Children of God were to become a latter-day gypsy nation.

The timetable of the end which had been revealed to the Children of God marked their origin in 1968 as the 'End of the time of the Gentiles' and as the time of the 'Restoration of the Remnant of Israel in the Children of God'. The Christian world had failed to carry out God's will, departing from His spirit and becoming obsessed with church buildings rather than God's word. For them being Christian meant attending church for an hour a week, while they continued to store up treasures on earth the rest of the time.

The Children of God have been mandated to gather out those who will commit themselves totally to Christ, forsake all, abandon the Whore of Babylon, the System, and suffer the coming persecution of the saints faithfully. Berg and his followers do not seek to gather just anyone into the fold. They employ the image of the 'new wine'. The older generation (and indeed anyone else who cannot accept the new wine of God's new revelations through Moses) are 'old bottles' which would break under its impact. They seek only the 'new bottles' who can take this new wine, and these they expect to find among the young, and particularly the 'disinherited' and 'dropped-out' young. Rather than gathering all believers the Children of God seek to draw together and train cadres able to face the Great Confusion and the Tribulation, underground if necessary and worthy to be rulers in the post-Adventual Kingdom. They believe that the message must be preached throughout the world to every nation before Christ's Return.

Prior to this Return, however, a number of events are to occur. First, the Children of God expect a progressive worsening of the world situation, rampaging inflation, increased pollution, civil strife, political chaos and economic disaster. Berg believes that the United States, being the national most objectionable to God, will suffer particularly. He believed that Nixon would establish a dictatorship of the radical right, leading in turn to revolution by the left. The time-scale here is not altogether clear, but more or less simultaneously, Berg believed that the Arab-Israeli War would intensify, drawing Russia and America into open conflict, leading to the invasion of Israel by Russia, World War III, and the virtual destruction of America. These times are designated by the movement as the Great Confusion in which they will be persecuted by the right wing.

Out of the Great Confusion, which will probably transpire in the late 1970s and/or the early 1980s, the Anti-Christ would rise to power and world domination on the basis of promises of peace and justice. In 1985 the Covenant would be confirmed by the Anti-Christ, and in 1985 or 1986 the last seven years of world history would be entered. The first three and a half years would be relatively benign as a communistic system was brought into being, but thereafter, the final three and a half years would be the period of the Great Tribulation. During this time the Anti-Christ would demand worship as God, and would persecute the saints — especially the Children of God — and the Jews who remained faithful. The Children of God would have to go underground, and many would be martyred.

About 1993 the Rapture of the Saints would occur, with those who remained faithful rising up to meet Christ for the Marriage Supper. Then Christ would descend to do battle at Armageddon, vanquish the Anti-Christ and his minions and establish His throne in Jerusalem. There would follow the thousand-year dictatorship of Christ. The saints, prominent among them the Children of God, would be the kings, priests and judges of the earth. There would still be time for many of the unrighteous to follow Christ, but not all would take the opportunity. After the thousand years, there would be a battle between the Devil and the Saints at which he would finally be vanquished. The Great White Throne Judgement would take place, followed by the destruction of those who had rebelled. Thereafter, the earth, heaven, hell and death would be

destroyed, the Heavenly City would descend, and there would
be a New Heaven and a New Earth. However, not all would
cease at this point. It seems that some could still be redeemed
even then, and Berg envisages the salvation of beings perhaps
on other planets. There would ultimately be total redemption,
universal reconciliation, and cosmic retribution (Berg, 1973a).

Economics

As the domestic organisation of the movement shifted, so too
necessarily did its economic base. While occupying the
Coachella Ranch the Family could aspire to become a self-
supporting, agriculturally-based, communitarian group living
on its own produce; the 'forsake-all' of converts; and in the
interim support from Jordan's donors. The break with Jordan
and the move towards smaller colonies made this non-viable.
Each colony could not hope with a membership of 12 or fewer,
to possess the range of skills and competence necessary for
independent self-support. The rapid growth in membership
during this period meant that a certain amount of economic
support came from the cash, goods and the sale of goods
brought by new converts, their 'forsake all'. Although a few
notably wealthy converts were secured, however, the bulk
of the new recruits were young, drop-outs or college students,
and in most cases had few economic resources to forsake.
Hence the processes of 'spoiling Egypt' were developed more
extensively. These involved members soliciting funds and
aid in goods from parents and more importantly 'procuring'
or 'provisioning' foodstuffs and necessary items of hardware,
clothing, etc., as well as cash donations, from local businesses
and businessmen. Members would visit food markets to collect
bruised fruit and vegetables, and would arrange with bakeries
to take away day-old bread or with supermarkets to remove
dented cans or damaged cartons of food. On procuring expedi-
tions members would modify their appearance to conform to
the expectations of businessmen. They would cut their hair,
and would, it seems, at least sometimes present themselves somewhat vaguely as Christians trying to get young people off drugs,
or as students of a Bible College. On some occasions at least
they would thoroughly dissemble, using an alternative name
not identifiable in connection with the Children of God, or
claim that they were rehabilitating former drug addicts to
enable them to return to useful jobs in society. In the latter

case the procurers must have realised that what the business-men heard and the speakers meant, were altogether different things. Such 'camouflage' in the face of Systemites was legiti-mised as necessary by the hostility of the System to the Child-ren of God.

At one point, Berg seems briefly to have accepted the idea of a colony working for a printer in return for free printing, but this was perhaps too close to working in the System and the life of the Systemate to be acceptable as a general practice*. After the period at the Coachella Ranch, little serious attempt seems to have been made to return to the idea of rural self-sufficiency and an agrarian life-style. Although farms and rural facilities were sometimes made available to the Family, its members seem not to have been very successful in managing them. Since the bulk of the members are almost certainly drawn from urban backgrounds, they have little acquaintance with farming and after a few failures, such facilities now seem to be maintained largely as rural retreats for the leaders and as sanctuaries for the time of the Great Confusion when the cities will collapse.

Conditions in the colonies seem by and large to have been fairly spartan. Former members stress that while the food was wholesome and adequate nutritionally, it was not elaborate or luxurious. The colonies were usually housed in property made available to them by benefactors, empty houses, warehouses, shops, etc., usually without lavish appointments. Later a num-ber of colonies were to squat in empty property, and sometimes it would seem property is rented. It is never usually purchased, nor even accepted as a gift where this might encumber the Children of God with property taxes, legal obligations and the like. Their clothing was derived from the colony free store of 'forsake-all' goods brought by new members. Consumer dur-ables were not widely available and were usually sold when brought as forsake-all. Personal possessions were minimal: a change of clothes, toilet articles, a rucksack, sleeping bag, Bible, notebook and perhaps a guitar were all that the member typically retained, all else being kept as communal property, or sold by the colony shepherd. They would only have sufficient cash to get back to the colony or to make a telephone call for aid, and goods and money sent by parents to individuals were all turned over to the common fund.

This rather austere existence began to undergo something of a transformaton more recently, as the economic base of the movement shifted yet again. From late 1971 or early 1972, the Children of God have possessed the equipment for printing, and as well as producing for a while a news-sheet, the *New Improved Truth* secured from the Jesus People Army some of whom joined the Family, and later the *New Nation News,* a smaller periodical for publicity purposes, they began to print the Mo Letters formerly only available to a few members in mimeographed form. Initially these letters were distributed free on the streets in the course of witnessing, and a donation might be accepted for the larger, more expensively produced *New Improved Truth.* But gradually the pursuit of 'donations' was encouraged. Members were instructed to ask for donations ('Can you spare a donation for our work', or 'we help young people on drugs, can you spare a donation?') and later a 'suggested donation' was printed boldly on the front of each leaflet. Distributing literature was becoming more important to Moses than gaining converts. In a letter written in June 1973, Mo explained

> We can't possibly reach enough people in our personal witness. So God gave me the answer: literature is the answer! (Berg, 1973b).

He also stressed the shift in the role of the followers:

> It's not the kids' responsibility to preach a sermon and persuade them. Our main job is not soul winning, but witnessing. Our main job is not *their* witnessing, but *my* witnessing *(ibid.).*

Witnessing became 'litnessing', and that Berg saw this as a new economic basis for the movement is evident from the same letter:

> God has provided a means to get out the message, and at the same time a means of support in return by selling it or giving it away for a donation, whatever you want to call it *(ibid.).*

Members were admonished to become 'shiners' who secured the maximum return for literature distributed, rather than 'shamers' who distributed little or brought little back for it. Quotas for literature distribution were introduced, with rewards for shiners and punishments for shamers. While shamers received kitchen duty, or were sent out for extra time and with extra letters to distribute before they were allowed back into the colony, shiners were permitted to take a percentage of their receipts for personal use, take time off after distributing all their materials, or awarded cash prizes or personal tape-recorders in the case of the top distributors.

Literature distribution had become the major source of income for the Children of God to such an extent that new converts need not be sought so actively nor need the colonies procure thrown-out foodstuffs. They could now afford to buy their needs. They could also afford to support their central offices by remitting a proportion of their receipts. A letter to the English Region in January 1974 suggested 2½p per letter distributed should be remitted. It is also suggested that an average of 5p per letter should be secured, and that each member should average 1000 letters a week. The quantities and sums involved can be calculated from various figures in internal documents. For the week prior to this letter, the English Region had distributed 102,044 pieces of literature. At an average of 5p per piece this would be over £5000 per week. Figures for various colonies in North America for four weeks in April and May 1974 showed an income for this region of approximately $15,000 a week. This was raised by between 130 and 145 people each week, and each colony averaged about $1300-1400 a week. There were then perhaps 140 colonies throughout the world. Many of them were in underdeveloped areas, and most were undoubtedly in poorer areas than the Northern States of America and Canada, and the United Kingdom. It is not unreasonable to suppose that a third of these colonies remained in fairly affluent parts of the world, which would suggest an annual income of around $2 million. Such a figure is inevitably rather speculative and it needs, moreover, to be placed in the context of the number of personnel supported by the movement. At about 4000 members, annual income per person would be only about $500, which does not seem excessive. It may be the case that 'forsake-all', contributions from wealthy patrons, and any continuing procuring render these figures a substantial underestimate. Evidently, colonies in the more affluent parts of the world are doing very much better. The North American colonies just discussed are producing an annual income of around $5000 per person. In 1975 the Children of God was distributing around 1.5 million pieces of literature a week. If they average 10c per piece throughout the world, their 'litnessing' income would be something under $8 million per annum or an average of about

$2000 per person. It is, however, unlikely that 10c per piece is realised on average throughout the world. Moreover, the Children of God have, of late, increasingly moved out of the more affluent parts of the world, to the poorer.

A Natural History

It is clear that a profound transformation has occurred in the style and rhetoric of the Children of God during the course of its brief history. With the increased emphasis on colportage and distribution there has developed an acceptance of functional rationality which contrasts sharply with earlier phases of the movement's development. We can, I think, distinguish four such phases up to 1974:

1. *The Children of God as prophetic gathered remnant.* This phase covers the period from the inception of Teens for Christ through the time of wandering prior to settlement on the Texas Soul Clinic Ranch (1968 through 1969). During this period separation from the world, adoption of the life-style of Acts 1-5, and conveying a message of doom and warning of the end were the major features. A clear line existed between the Family and the System.

2. *The New Nation and Subsistence Communitarianism.* This phase covers the period during 1970 and 1971, of settlement at Texas Soul Clinic. While temporising with the world to maintain Jordan's patronage, and to gain converts, the group continued its adamant opposition to the System and other Christians, and sought to found a new collectivity of saints on fundamentalistic lines. The New Nation, modelled after the tribes of Israel and the gypsies was informed by a vision of rural self-sufficiency. Recruitment was fairly rapid during this period.

3. *Evangelical millennialism.* This period covering the ejection from Texas Soul Clinic through 1971 and 1972, was a phase of dispersion. Small colonies were founded throughout America, and from there spread abroad in the wake of the Family's nomadic migrations. Small colonies were favoured. There was an attempt to win support from other churches and church groups, to draw in the Jesus People, and to convert new members on the basis of personal witnessing, and presentation of the happy, loving atmosphere of their way of life through the mass media, in coffee-houses, or on the streets. This was probably the period of most rapid recruitment.

4. *Colportage and routine proselytisation.* This phase, emerging most strongly in 1973 and 1974, marked the vigorous introduction of functional rationality into the movement. There was a return to the cash nexus. Funds were to be secured through the sale of literature; members were encouraged in their sales efforts by cash incentives; rational accounting procedures of a formalised kind were introduced; and the Children of God became greatly concerned with statistics. The face-to-face conversion of new disciples figures less prominently than measurable criteria of success. Sheer bulk of literature distributed became the major emphasis, or getting it into the hands of someone particularly prominent, statemen and pop stars especially. The proselytisation activities became thoroughly routinised. (The notion of routine proselytisation is employed by Beckford, 1975; and Bruce, 1976. O'Toole, 1975, employs the related notion of 'pseudo-proselytisation'). Colonies and evangelism came to be seen as hindrances and Berg even considered hiring hippy non-members to distribute his literature.

Conclusion: belief and social organisation

Millennialist movements often face a pronounced dilemma. They bear the responsibility for gathering the faithful and warning the world, yet the world is viewed as evil and corrupting. There therefore exists a tension between proclaiming the warning of the end of times and evangelism on the one hand, and withdrawal for the preservation of purity on the other.

The Children of God emerged from Berg's background in the evangelical tradition and within the context of a loosely linked evangelistic movement, the conversionist Jesus People. Many of those recruited to the Family became committed as a result of their conversion experience. This experience fired them in turn with evangelistic fervour. They saw the movement as a vehicle for 'winning souls to Christ'. But the introversionist aspects of the movement have also been attractive, its 'uncompromising' separation from the evils of the world. There has, therefore, been a pronounced ambiguity in the character and orientation of the movement. This ambiguity is as evident in the writings of Berg as it is in the practices of his followers, but it seems clear that at different times different orientations have been uppermost in Berg's mind and have informed his

policy. But equally clearly, these did not always coincide with
the orientation uppermost in the minds of his followers and
he has taken pains to criticse leaders and disciples for their
failures to follow his direction promptly enough and their
lingering commitment to an earlier dominant orientation.

His early writings with their execrations upon the System and
its evils, and their obsession with persecution have a pronounced latent introversionism embedded in them, as does his
continuing nostalgia for the simpler, pre-industrial, rural, small-
town life, or the nomadic peregrinations of close-knit gypsy
bands. This attitude predominated in what I have described as
the movement's second phase, that of *subsistence communitarianism.* In a letter written in December 1970, he asserts
'Numbers are not what counts in the Eyes of God!' and continues:

> As long as we're *still small, still poor,* and *still per-
> secuted* we're pretty safe and most likely to be in the Will
> of God! But how can we stay that way? By specialising
> in *quality* rather than *quantity!* And by keeping ourselves
> unspotted from the world — uncompromising with the
> System. . . .

> I'd rather see you establish and ground in the Word a small
> tough colony that endures and stays true and pure and
> continues to make slow, solid, enduring progress and
> growth as the Lord adds daily to the Church — than to
> open the flood gates to every Tom, Dick and Harry that
> wants to come along for the ride! (Berg, 1970a).

Early in 1971 he wrote 'Those looking for the Kingdom of
God on earth will only find it within your own hearts and
fellowship of the saints, the Children of God — Heaven on
earth!' (Berg, 1971c). But by late 1971, Berg is complaining
that '. . . we've lost the Pilgrim spirit, haven't kept up our
campers, tents, and camping equipment, and have settled down
to the ease and luxury of more stationary and conventional
housing in large, expensive Colonies!' (Berg, 1971d). The
following month in December 1971, movement into the phase
of evangelistic millennialism is emphasised in a letter in which
Berg complains that:

> Some get so involved in the massive complicated opera-
> tions of big Colonies that they seem to forget what they
> joined the Army for: not just to demonstrate our way of

71

life, but to save the youth of the world for Jesus! The Colonization method the Lord has given us is merely a means to that end, but if we get so busy with the means that we forget the end, we'll never reach it (Berg, 1971e).

The following months into 1972 were to see the development of a much more active evangelising orientation. This was the period in which 'Other Sheep' were recognised, Associates and Friends became possible statuses, and the Children of God witnessed in the streets and parks singing and dancing and engaging in personal face-to-face evangelism with anyone who would listen. A number of musical groups were formed which received publicity and promotion on radio and television in various nations, and the Children of God made records. There had been a major shift from introversionism to conversionism and the structure of the community followed this drift, breaking into small groups to facilitate dispersion and evangelism.

By mid 1973, Berg's strategy had changed again. Witnessing shifted to 'litnessing' evangelism to colportage. His disciples were no longer to waste time trying to convert others, they were merely, in his words, 'news boys' selling their wares, and were exhorted to be effective salesmen securing a good return. By early 1974, Berg's rhetoric is more pronouncedly commercial in character, referring to his movement as 'a big business', a 'tremendous multinational chain of publishing houses . . . you've got over 200 branches with about 4000 full-time salesmen! I mean it's a big business' (Berg, 1974a). The followers are promised a less austere life henceforth, with 'a few of the little conveniences of comfortable living' and everyone receiving 'a little spending change' as long as they work hard. And working hard meant distributing the words of Moses David. Late in 1974, Berg still has occasion to chastise his followers for being too interested in show-business. This interest they must subordinate to acquainting themselves more closely with his writings and thereby better equipping themselves as convinced salesmen (Berg 1974b). The colony way of life comes under attack during this period. Berg had begun to feel that the mere existence of colonies was a hindrance to distributing his words. All that were really necessary were 'road teams', pairs of disciples with rucksacks and a supply of literature, travelling and distributing, supporting themselves from part of the proceeds and returning only periodically for more literature supplies. That he had considered hiring outsiders to sell the Mo Letters displays the subordination of the community and the communal life to what he believed were the imperatives of his millennial vision.

At each stage, the movement adapted, albeit not without internal opposition and considerable defection each time, to Berg's new strategy as he believed it was revealed to him. The way of life to be pursued was merely a contingency of that vision and never at any point came to dominate it. Of course, a way of life and form of collective organisation can become endowed with enormous ideological and moral value. At such times it will prove resistant to ready change and may motivate changes in other components of the ideology. But it is the perceived moral value or ideological status of the community which is thus resistant, and not, the structure of the community *per se,* nor any mysterious 'system needs' which functionalist sociologists may impose upon it. Beliefs lead rational men to act and in this respect there is no reason to believe that primitive peoples or millennialists are any different from the rest of us.

* At this stage a sharp break with the 'System' was required. Later, around 1978, the idea of working at System jobs was to become more acceptable.

CHAPTER V

Sex, marriage and the Children of God

That religious innovation may bring departures from conventional mores in other aspects of life, even the sexual, is sufficiently well known to have become a commonplace of the polemic directed (and sometimes misdirected) at new religious groups.* This chapter explores further innovations in the life-style of the Children of God (discussed in the last chapter). Specifically it aims to illuminate the structural and motivational facilitators of innovations in the sexual and marital lives of members of this new religious movement.

As we saw in Chapter 4, David Berg became recognised by his young followers as a latter-day prophet of God and, under the stimulus of his revelations, dreams, visions and prophecies, the Children of God began to develop away from their early fundamentalism. Moses David, or Mo, as Berg now became known, imparted a considerable sense of urgency to the witnessing efforts of the Children of God. The rise of the Anti-Christ was to be expected soon, and God's message of love and salvation had therefore to be spread through every nation as speedily as possible. Supporting themselves primarily through 'litnessing' — distribution the writings of Moses David in pamphlet form on the city streets and soliciting a donation — the Family, as the Children of God refer to themselves, spread into Europe, Asia, Africa, South America and the Pacific, forming small communes or 'colonies' of disciples. By May 1977, the Children of God numbered 3835 adult, full-time, 'live-in' disciples with 1262 children, located in 323 colonies (*New Nation News*, 10(4), 1977:21).

Sexual and marital developments within the Family

The shift away from an earlier, rather puritanical fundamentalism in the beliefs and practices of the Family had a number of components. Moses David became the agency not only for the voices of God and of Jesus, but also found himself the medium through which other spiritual beings and spiritual 'helpers' spoke. Notable among these was Abrahim, a former gypsy chieftain. Moses David also came to believe in aspects of astrology, particularly that astrological configurations were a considerable influence on character and personality. But most important for this discussion were Moses David's progressive elaboration of the doctrine of salvation by grace through faith and consequent relegation of the soteriological efficacy of works and conformity to the Mosaic Law, and his elaboration of the notion of God as love.

Moses David's conception of the will and nature of God derived important elements from both Old and New Testaments. He observed that Old Testament accounts showed God to have sanctioned a wider range of sexual and marital designs than that embodied in the monogamous conjugal pair. New Testament writings also contained elements which could be read as permitting deviation from the Mosaic moral code among those living a life of full discipleship. It is not my purpose here to debate the validity of these theological interpretations but only to show their role in the Family's sexual and marital innovations.

In practice, change in this domain occurred rather slowly at the beginning. Mo, identifying with the Old Testament prophets and leaders of the Israelites, took sexual companions from among his female followers in addition to his middle-aged wife (who was now known as Eve), and in 1970, when he parted from the bulk of his followers to travel in Europe — thereafter to communicate with his disciples primarily by printed letters — he took as wife and secretary a young follower named Maria. After the period of travelling, he established temporary residences in various parts of the world where he would be attended by a small group of followers, of whom some of the females — both married and single — provided sexual companionship in addition to his new wife. Some of these female companions were also seen as 'wives' of Moses David, while others were seen as having a more transient relationship.

During the movement's first few years, such sexual relationships were permitted only for Mo himself and other senior leaders of the Family. Mo's former wife, Eve, had a young companion, Stephen, and sexual relationships with married or unmarried disciples were also enjoyed by other leaders — among whom were Mo's adult children and their spouses — close to the prophet. While some lower echelon leaders suspected what was occurring, these innovations were initially surrounded with great secrecy. But, although explicit allusions to more permissiveness in sexual and marital relations did not appear until late 1972 and early 1973, Mo's writings had from the Family's earliest years displayed a high degree of explicitness concerning sexuality generally. Mo expressed the view that sex was a creation of God, to be enjoyed, and gave his married followers considerable advice on how to enjoy it better. Mo also employed a great deal of sexual allusion and metaphor in his discussion of doctrine, and in a quite intentinal way to shock his readers from their earlier assumptions. Mo clearly experienced a rich sexual phantasy life, and this he unselfconsciously displayed in the letters that he printed for his disciples, when making some point of theology clear in a familiar idiom, or when showing his disciples that he too was a man with human frailties, desires and experiences.

From late 1972 and early 1973 Mo began to make his views on sex and marriage available to all his followers, thereby facilitating the democratisation of what had hitherto been elite privileges. In his letter 'One Wife' (28 October, 1973) Mo expressed his view that marriage should not be regarded as an absolute end in itself, but only as a means, the utility of which must be judged in terms of its contribution to God's work:

> God will have no other gods before Him, not even the sanctity of the marriage god. . . God is the God of marriage, too, and the main thing is to be married to Him and His work, and when a marriage is not according to His Will, He doesn't hesitate to break it up and form other unions to further His work!

> . . . God's in the business of breaking up little selfish private worldly families to make of their yielded broken pieces a larger unit — one family.

> If you are allowed any personal private relationship with any particular individual called marriage, it can only be

76

tolerated provided it does not interfere with your relationship with the rest of God's wife — the Body, His total Bride!

We don't believe in 'to each his own', but 'to each according as he has need, of whatever God and His brethren are able to supply!'

In the letter 'Jealousy' (September 1973) Mo warned his followers against possessiveness and exclusiveness:

Selfishness is the possessiveness of private property. 'It's mine! Nobody else's! I deserve it and nobody else can have it! I'm the only one that has a right to it!' But the truth is that he belongs to others as well as to you — his time, his attention, his ideas, his thoughts and counsel.

You think he's hurting you. But if he *loves* you and is only trying to *help* somebody else, that's the furthest thing from his mind. If he loves *you* and he loves the *Lord,* he'll also love *others* and want to help *them* too. The same goes for the *fellows,* also, who are jealous of their *wives!*

In a series of doctrinal letters, Mo developed the theological basis of his views. For example, the letter 'The Law of Love' (21 March, 1974) explained:

We are the last church! We are God's last Church, the last step in God's progress toward total freedom for His Church and the last chance to prove that the ultimate Church can be trusted with total freedom in this last generation!

As in marriage and all other social relationships with each other, God's laws of love are still the same: 1. Is it good for God's work? 2. Is it good for His Body? 3. Is it good for you? . . . Does it help someone and harm no one?

Any variation from the norm of personal relationships, any substantial change in marital relationships, any projected sexual associations should have the willing consent of all parties concerned. . . .

That this letter was taken to permit sexual relationships not only outside marriage, but also between single persons who formerly had been enjoined to celibacy is evident from the rebuke Mo was later to issue. Some, apparently, had regarded 'The Law of Love' as a license of personal promiscuity and selfish pleasure, rather than in terms of whether such relationships would glorify God and assist His work ('Sex Problems', 3 March, 1975). It is not possible at this stage to determine exactly what proportion of followers have embarked on pluralistic sexual relationships, but it is evident that many married leaders maintain sexual liaisons with persons other than their spouse. Such persons may be either unmarried, or they may have some form of marital relationship to another member or leader. It is also not clear at this stage how enduring such liaisons are. My impression is that they cover a broad range from long-term to relatively transient relationships. In some cases they may result in a permanent separation between husband and wife. None the less, my observations suggest that marriages within the Family are still often stable and enduring.

'Flirty fishing'

As a movement with intensely evangelical preoccupations, committed to spreading the message of God's love throughout the world rapidly — even in countries which prohibit Christian proselytism — the Children of God were faced early in their development with a number of problems. How, in practice, could the message be spread and people influenced in societies where evangelism was forbidden? How could God's love be demonstrated to the cynical and blasé sophisticates of the Western world whose notion of love was restricted to *eros* rather than *agape?* How could a gradually aging leadership who found themselves increasingly out of touch with adolescents continue to offer a successful witness? How, in particular, would they be able to continue their work, given that the Anti-Christ would soon appear and that, after an initial *rapprochement* with the Children of God, he would seek to destroy their work, persecuting them and all those who refused to worship him? Above all, could one claim to love those to whom one witnessed but refuse to provide some concrete manifestation of it in relieving their sexual needs?

Mo's solution to these problems was the introduction of 'flirty fishing' as a mode of witness. I have elsewhere presented an account of the early, experimental stages of 'flirty fishing', and its rationale, and offered an account of the historical and situational circumstances which seem to have led to it (Wallis,

1978a). I shall here provide only a brief description of what it entails.

On his travels throughout Europe with his young wife, Mo realised that some of the men they tried to convert were more interested in Maria than in the message. Unlike the hippies and drop-outs who formed the movement's earlier constituency, the people with whom, on their travels, Mo and Maria were increasingly in contact in European capitals and resorts, were older, usually established in a career, and unlikely to be drawn by a message of sacrifice, of 'dropping out' of society. However, they were often lonely, in need of companionship, and often sexually frustrated. Mo's biblical studies soon led him to observe that in the Old Testament those favoured by God were sometimes permitted to employ the sexual attributes of their women to win the favours of powerful men (e.g., Genesis 12 and 20), or to bring about some aspect of God's plan (e.g. Judges 4; Esther 2-8; Genesis 38; Ruth 3-4). Mo also reasoned that God was prepared to go to any lengths, no matter how unconventional, if they resulted in 'good fruit' for His work. Christ had been prepared to sacrifice His life for man's salvation. Surely, then, it was not too much to ask the women of his Family to sacrifice themselves by showing their love for these lost souls in meeting their sexual needs if the result was to bring them to salvation, or to foster God's work.

From late in 1972 until 1973, Mo experimented with this idea, at first with his wife, then with other members of his household, and later with other senior leaders, The 'fisherman' would visit clubs, bars or discothèques accompanied by a number of attractive female followers. There they would dance, or engage in conversation, with men and women (but most often men) whom they met in such establishments. They would try gradually introduce them to the idea of God's love, provide friendship and companionship, and even in some cases where it was felt to be necessary, sexual relationships. From early in 1977, Mo began to encourage the whole movement to pursue this mode of witness.

It is important to stress that sex was not provided for every person approached in this way. More often, friendship and companionship were as far as things went, but in those cases where meeting the person's sexual needs was seen as the only effective means of presenting God's message, the women of the Family, married and unmarried, were prepared to provide for these needs. It is also important to note that 'flirty fishing', whether or not it leads to a sexual relationship, is not an end in itself, but is seen by the Children of God as providing an *opportunity* to make contact with people who might otherwise not listen to them, or whom they might otherwise not meet. Sexual attractiveness, sexual relationships, friendship and companionship, while provided with sincere feeling for the 'fish' concerned, are, to use the Family's metaphor, only the 'bait' hiding behind which is 'the hook' of God's word and Spirit that will bring them to salvation, or lead them to assist in God's work.

The sociological problems

That the male members of the Children of God should be prepared to undertake short-term or pluralistic sexual relationships with non-spouses is not a problem requiring explanation here. Men in most societies are believed to be more promiscuous than women, and a willingness to engage sexually with women other than their wives has historically been regarded as a characteristic male proclivity when the opportunity presented itself.

The issues that will be addressed here, then, are why members of the Children of God are prepared to 'sacrifice' their spouses either temporarily or permanently to other members or non-members and why the *female* members are prepared to enter into pluralistic, short-term sexual relationships.

Serial monogamy

It is perhaps least difficult to explain why men and women in the Family are prepared to exchange one semi-permanent stable relationship for another when all concerned are Family members. Given the high divorce and remarriage rates prevalent in advanced industrial societies, the pattern of serial monogamy has become well established as a component of popular consciousness. This is particularly so for urban America, whence came many of the Children of God.

Marriage has been recognised in such societies as a precarious institution due to the pressures upon it. An ideology of maintaining the family unit at all costs, of the preservation of a marriage as vital to respectability and an end in itself, has been displaced by a more relativistic conception which subordinates it to the ends of individual happiness of its partners and their offspring. While this view of marriage as a means rather than end has been carried over into the Children of God, the hedonic calculus has been tempered by the notion that the ultimate end to which marriage should be subordinated is not merely that of individual happiness, but that of carrying out God's work. The relativisation of marriage has itself been sanctified in the idea that *all* activities and relationships in the Family must be subordinated to the need to pursue God's mission as effectively as possible. If a particular marital relationship becomes a hindrance for the individuals concerned, limiting their ability to carry out their tasks as God's messengers and prophets, then those concerned are faced with a choice between doing God's will and preserving their marriage. Few Children of God would opt for the latter against the former. That they are in the Family at all is predicated on the assumption that they are there to do God's will. Hence, faced with such a preceived choice, a failed marriage should be abandoned, although only as a last resort since Mo does not *encourage* divorce for trivial reasons, and only with the consent of both parties.

Hence, although acceptance of the practice of serial monogamy has perhaps been slower among women than among men in industrial societies, it has become sufficiently common and accepted so that in the context of the Family, and with the added incentive of the injunction that activities should 'bear good fruit' for the parties involved and for God's work, and with the availability of alternative partners among the high proportion of single disciples, it poses no major problem of explanation. Where wives are unwilling to agree to divorce and the remarriage of their husbands to another partner, polygamous marriage is an accepted possibility, and some cases of polygamous marriage are known at various levels in the Children of God.

Sexual Pluralism

The issues of why the female members are prepared to engage in short-term pluralistic sexual relationships, and why both male and female members are prepared to 'sacrifice' their spouses to such relationships are perhaps more difficult, and therefore more interesting. One way to approach these questions is to examine why they can be seen as problems *at all,* i.e., what assumptions are implicated in construing as problems the preparedness of partners to engage in pluralistic sexual relationships and of other partners to accept such activity? We can then proceed to an analysis of the extent to which such assumptions are denied or mitigated within the Children of God.

In Western industrial societies generally, extra-marital sexual relationships are typically hedged in secrecy. They may bear a general *stigma*, particularly if they result in the break-up of a marriage, most especially if there are children in the family for whom such events might be emotionally traumatic. They are normally kept most secret from the spouse, since such relationships are viewed as a threat to the interests of the spouse in terms of ego-investments as well as real property and life-chances contingent upon the prevailing marital situation. Knowledge of an extra-marital relations is thus often a *shock* for the spouse.

While this is perhaps less the case today than in earlier periods, a marital relationship still tends to retain an element of *property in persons* analogous to real property. An extra-marital sexual relationship thus carried a connotation of the loss of theft of property rights in the spouse involved. In the case of marriage in conventional Western society, extra-marital sexual relationships and marital disintegration must be considered together, since although the former may not inevitably lead to the latter, it is normally seen as posing the threat of separation or divorce.

In cultures dominated by the 'romantic love complex', in which personal identity and a sense of individual worth and fulfilment are expected to come as much from intimate personal relations as from the performance of roles within broader social institutions, *particularly for women* who after marriage may have no significant involvement in social institutions outside the home, an extra-marital relationship or the desire of one spouse to end an existing marital relationship, carries a connotation of *personal failure*. The 'innocent party' has failed to provide what the 'guilty party' required from the relationship.

There is also the problem of *remarriageability*. Having invested probably one's most marriageable years in the relationship, the 'innocent party' faces the prospect that a break-down in the marriage will return him or her to the marriage market with fewer marketable attributes, threatening a subsequent life of relative social isolation and loneliness. This may be particularly acute for women in societies where marriageability and sexual desirability are associated with youth. Where the 'innocent party' is male, there is particularly likely to be a problem of *alternative sexual access*.

At the most mundane level, too, marital disintegration poses problems of a *economic* kind. There is the loss of the labour of one party, the problem of supporting two homes and families from one income where the male remarries, and the problem of dividing jointly-owned property.

Contingent upon all this disruption and the real and psychic costs to the 'innocent party' is likely to be a sense of *guilt* felt by the 'guilty party' at being its cause. I now propose to consider the situation in the Children of God in order to show the existence of various structural and motivational factors which minimise the impact of the economic, social and psychic costs described above.

Of major importance is the communal character of life in the Family. Members live in small groups of seven or eight persons in each 'colony', sharing the economic support and labour required. Income comes predominantly from soliciting donations for Mo Letters on the street, but also from gifts, and from 'provisioning' food and other consumables from local businessmen and Christian friends. Most colonies are located relatively near a number of other colonies which provide service facilities (office colonies; school colonies; publications colonies where translating and preparation of the Mo Letters for printing and distribution take place; club colonies; etc.). Since all colony members participate in the labour of the household, and child-care is spread between several persons, the burden of economic support and household labour is considerably less than in the nuclear family. Marital partners are thus less dependent upon each other in terms of income or labour since alternative resources are available. Living a communal life, little real property is owned by individuals. The problems of economic responsibility or of complex financial obligations and investments contingent upon the conventional family in the form of mortgages, hire-purchase, bank accounts and joint property are, thus, negligible in the Children of God.

Living communally in a group which places a high degree of emphasis on love and in which affectivity is a diffuse property of all social relationships, loneliness and social isolation are unlikely to result from the separation of spouses. There is, moreover, an understanding that the community, the Family, must meet all the legitimate needs of its members. Sexual release and companionship are viewed as legitimate needs and other members will be encouraged to meet them if marital separation takes place. Hence isolation and lack of alternative sexual access are unlikely to be problems in the Children of God.

As children are reared in a communal life-setting, their identity is early vested in the collectivity as a whole rather than exclusively in a particular adult pair. Children certainly continue to have strong emotional bonds with their parents, but they can also readily form such bonds with other adults. Children over the age of three usually spend four days a week in a school colony where they are often taught and looked after by adults other than their parents. The affectively-laden nature of all relationships spreads the burden of a child's ego-involvement and identity widely beyond the parent-child relationship. Hence marital breakdown in the Family is less likely to be a source of trauma to the children of the couple.

The costs of marital breakdown are thus very much slighter than in the conventional family, hence both *stigma* and *guilt* are less likely to result from being the cause of such costs. The high proportion of unmarried members in close proximity renders the formation of an alternative stable relationship highly likely. This is particularly the case for women since there are twice as many single men as single women in the Family. Marrying a woman with children is not more costly than marrying one without children in a completely socialised economy. Hence one conventional inhibitor to remarriage is removed. Most of the female members of the Family are still young so they are not far removed from the apex of marriageability, but even for older women this is less likely to be a problem. In a context of such pervasive diffuse affectivity, romantic love is less pressing a concern. Members who have been prepared to sacrifice career, education, possessions and much else conventionally thought of value; and who have humbled themselves so often before in the face of insult and scorn from non-members, the chastening of leaders, and the ego-deflating consequences of soliciting money from strangers, have such a high level of commitment that many would be prepared to take a partner because they believed it to be God's will rather than because that partner displayed the most desirable attributes. Members are committed to the need to share with their fellows to provide for their needs, and to sacrifice their own private and personal interests in the general good. But since the members of a conjugal pair are not *restricted* to sexual relationships solely with each other, the costs of marrying someone without all the desirable attributes are lower and can be compensated by the availability of extra-marital sexual contacts. Moreover, since married women are not isolated in the nuclear family household, but form an active part of the wider collectivity, their need to invest their identity in a particular or indeed *any* marital union is very much less than in the world at large.

While there may remain some element of a sense of personal failure, this is greatly mitigated by the fact that personal happiness as it may be discovered in marriage is not the major life-purpose to be sought. Peforming God's will is the real purpose with which adult members identify, hence not only is marriage simply less central as a life-interest, but it is seen as much more important to remove impediments to God's spirit or the conduct of His affairs than to be successful in one's marriage. This is not, however, to say that the Children of God make no effort to achieve a satisfactory marital relationship. Quite the contrary. They are encouraged to do all they can to interest, stimulate and attend to the needs of, their partners. But meshed in the context of the Family as a whole, the conjugal unit has fewer strains to bear. Less is demanded of it than in the conventional nuclear family.

Permanent separation of spouses thus appears less problematic in the sect than in the nuclear family and the account given above goes part of the way to show why the *threat* of permanent separation posed by an extra-marital sexual relationship is less severe. But there are other factors minimising the threat of such relationships. Sexuality is given very explicit recognition in the Family. It is openly discussed as a need and as a set of techniques in much of Mo's writing. Particularly in the case of leaders, spouses may be separated for periods of time because they have to perform tasks in different locations. It came to be accepted that — in the absence of a spouse — the partner might need to achieve sexual release with someone else. (From these early transient sexual relationships in the absence of one partner there have devloped more stable patterns of sexual bonding of an unusual kind to which we shall allude later.) Such transient relationships, as with more permanent relationships, are sanctioned only if *all* the parties approve. Hence, no problem of a secret affair arises. There is no sense of shock and betrayal as in the conventional world. The provision of sexual resources is seen as no more taboo for a spouse separated by Family business than the provision of laundering or cooking facilities. They are needs which equally have to be met realistically and openly. Again no sense of personal failure need attach here, any more than would be the case for a woman who could not launder or cook for an absent spouse. The meeting of these needs by other loving brothers and sisters is seen as *positively contributing* to God's work rather than as an indication of personal failure. This is enhanced by a feature of members of the Children of God deriving from their pre-membership background. Many, particularly among the early followers now in leadership positions, came from a youth culture which rejected the ethics of the isolated nuclear family and possessive life-long monogamous, sexual relationships. Although they were prepared to subordinate their inclinations towards a freer structure of conjugal role relationships and less taboo ridden style of sexual engagement while this was enjoined by God's prophet, they were also generally willing enough to return to and even move beyond these inclinations when this was legitimated by the logic of Mo's developing antinomian doctrine.†

Finally on intra-Family sexuality and marriage, the communalisation of life and the commitment to 'forsaking all' and 'sharing' bear the consequence that a sense of ownership of a spouse, of property in persons, is absent. Only God and the wider Family have property rights either in real goods or in persons. Individuals are merely stewards of that property and must administer it for God's glory and His work rather than for personal enrichment. As Mo has put it in his Letter 'One Wife': 'It's the very last vestige of forsaking all to forsake even your husband and wife to share with others.'

From all this, it can be seen readily enough why 'flirty fishing', even when it leads to sexual relations with non-members, is acceptable to the husbands of those involved. But there remains the problem of why the women are prepared to allow sexual access to chosen outsiders, many of whom may be physically unappealing. How is it that they are able to overcome the traditionally characteristic sexual commitment of women to a single partner? The elements of the explanation have already been provided but perhaps need to be brought together at this point.

The commitment to the prophetic vision — the validity of Mo's access to God and their own role as God's messengers — is the dominant feature of the lives of the Children of God. They see their primary purpose as that of witnessing to God's message revealed through their prophet, the central elements of that message being God's love for mankind, and the imminence of the Endtime. As a small band of disciples they cannot hope to reach the entire world before the rise of the Anti-Christ, therefore the urgency of the situation demands that they make an impact now, especially upon the influential in the world. Bringing a 'King' to salvation may forward God's work more rapidly than bringing a drop-out. This is not to say that the poor or humble are to be neglected, but that the influential must also be reached and this may require novel methods. Christ was prepared to sacrifice everything to win souls. How can they, with what little they have to sacrifice in comparison, do less? They feel that it is hypocrisy to talk of love but to be unwilling to display it in a concrete way; to talk of their spiritual freedom and their life of sharing with others and yet to be unwilling to share themselves sexually; and that sex is no more taboo than food or drink. Hence, just as one would feed a hungry man in demonstration of God's love, so one should be prepared to have sexual intercourse with a sexual frustrated man if that is what is necessary to 'really touch his heart'. But a particularly encouraging factor to engage in such activity is the reports of those who did it first, describing the changes it wrought in the lives of those 'hooked' by this 'bait'. The transformation achieved with those who joined the Family as a result of 'flirty fishing' convinces the formerly faint-hearted that this method of witness does indeed 'bear good fruit' for God's work. Moreover, the *very* first to do it were Mo and Maria, and if God's prophet and King is prepared to share his wife in this way only false pride can keep the prophet's followers from making a similar sacrifice. These innovations in the belief and practice of the movement have led to the emergence of novel connubial patterns in the Children of God, taking the form of *networks* of sexual relationships rather than strictly bounded reciprocal sexual ties. Such networks take the form in Figure 1.

As can be seen from Figure 1, a complex pattern of connubial relationships may prevail at any particular point in time among a cadre of Family leaders. Not only may a particular member of the network be married to another member and have a sexual relationship with a third, but in the course of 'flirty fishing' a sexual relationship may also have developed with a non-member. (That this is a possible pattern for men as well as women in the Family is signified by the $A \text{---} \bar{Z}$ bond). In some cases this may lead to a formal marriage between a member and non-member as shown in the case of $Z === \bar{C}$. One can only

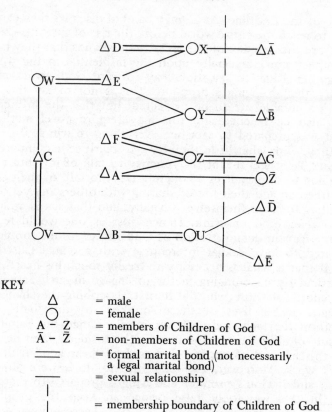

KEY

△	= male
○	= female
A – Z	= members of Children of God
Ā – Z̄	= non-members of Children of God
══	= formal marital bond (not necessarily a legal marital bond)
──	= sexual relationship
¦	= membership boundary of Children of God

Figure 1. *Connubial Networks in the Children of God*

assume that such a marriage would not be legally bigamous since formal marriage relationships within the Family are not necessarily solemnised in a legally binding form. (Even if that were not the case, while not actually wishing to flout the law, the Children of God do believe themselves bound to follow God's will in situations where it is seen to conflict with the law of the State.) Normally, by the time the 'bait' (Z) and the 'fisherman' (let us assume A to be the 'fisherman' in this case), other 'interested' parties (F), and other leaders with whom they would counsel (perhaps Y, W, E, B), were prepared for a formal marriage between Z and C̄ (the 'fish'), C̄ would have been taught much of the Family's beliefs and practices. He would have been socialised into many of its norms of behaviour, and probably have come to accept the fluidity of the boundaries on sexual bonding that prevail within it. He would certainly have undergone a conversion experience, and normally, by the stage of formal marriage his assimilation, symbolised by the marriage itself and would have been all but complete. Hence such a marriage bond signals the point at which the membership boundary would have to be redrawn to include C̄ inside it.††

Conclusion

In this chapter I have sought to show how the structure and ideology of the Children of God have facilitated innovation in the sexual and marital lives of members, and in their mode of witnessing to the world beyond. The communal style of life inhibits the development of conjugal economic dependency. The diffuse affective character of relationships inhibits conjugal emotional dependency. Commitment to a belief in sharing, meeting the needs of all members, and placing God's work above all else, inhibits personal possessiveness and exclusiveness.

While many youth communes, which developed in the 1960s, sought to implement a more permissive style of sexual relationships than those prevailing in the wider society, they characteristically failed to endure as a result of jealousy and a sense of sexual exploitation (Whitworth, 1975). Only the sincere belief of the Children of God that they are carrying out God's will as revealed through His prophet keeps this group from following a similar path. Firm in this belief, they have been able to institutionalise a disciplined form of sexual freedom without the costs or resistances that could be expected to accompany such innovations beyond their 'sacred canopy'.

* A scholarly — and not at all polemical — study of sex and marriage in nineteenth-century American utopian communities can be found in Muncy (1973).

† A number of Family members have previously been associated with other communal ventures, and some doubtless found as did one ex-communitarian respondent quoted in a study I can now unfortunately neither identify nor locate, that sexual freedom in such groups often 'meant freedom for the women to get f - - - - d over by the men'. That is, sexual freedom in prior 'permissive', youth-cultural surroundings, had often been an ideology legitimating the continued, or even the increased, sexual exploitation of women.

†† This pattern of final assimilation into the Family at the point of marriage can be seen in the case of the Duke Emanuele who married one
of the wives or consorts of Moses David. The entire pattern of gradual
socialisation and integration into the beliefs and norms of the Family
can be seen in the case of Arthur, discussed in a long series of 'Mo
Letters' (see Wallis, 1978b). This account of connubial networks draws
heavily on my conversations with the Rev. Rex Davis, whose first
hand knowledge of the Children of God throughout the world is
unrivalled.

II
CONTRIBUTIONS TO THE SOCIOLOGY OF MORAL CRUSADES

CHAPTER VI

Theories of moral indignation and moral crusades

The sociology of morality has never figured very prominently as a sub-discipline, and despite the massive transformations that have thoroughly re-fashioned the character of moral commitments and behaviour over recent decades, morality and the debates connected with it have received little sociological attention. One area that has generated theory and research to some extent has been connected with the phenomenon of *moral indignation,* and its mobilisation in the form of *moral crusades,* social movements oriented to resisting social changes in the nature of norms and values relating to moral issues, or the creation or enforcement of moral rules.

The source of moral indignation has, for example, been argued by Emile Durkheim to arise from infractions of the *conscience collective* (Durkheim, 1933:102). A challenge to, or contravention of, commonly held sentiments represents a threat to social solidarity, which is reaffirmed through punishment of the offender. The 'true function' of punishment is, therefore, the maintenance of social cohesion. It is, on this account, essential that social solidarity 'be affirmed forcibly at the very moment when it is contradicted, and the only means of affirming it is to express the unanimous aversion which the crime continues to inspire, by an authentic act which can consist only in suffering inflicted upon the agent' (Durkheim, 1933:108).

There are a number of problems in applying this theory to the explanation of moral indignation displayed by social movements in modern society. Without rehearsing the gamut of criticisms of functionalism, we may say that the premise of a *conscience collective* covering any extensive range of moral norms in industrial societies seems unjustifiable. Moral crusades emerge precisely because there is no sentiment common to all or even to a substantial majority of members of that society, concerning a particular norm or set of norms. The members of moral crusades may *feel* that the very foundation of society are threatened by some form of behaviour, but they organise in the defence of that view for the very reason that it lacks consensual acceptance. Moreover, Durkheim fails to explain why some acts call forth moral indignation in some periods and some societies, but not in others. Nor does he provide any explanation of why it is that such repressive sentiments in a pluralistic society affect some social groups and not others, nor a means of ascertaining which groups these will be.

As Howard Becker has observed,

> Rules are not made automatically. Even though a practice may be harmful in an objective sense to the group in which it occurs, the harm needs to be discovered and pointed out. People must be made to feel that something ought to be done about it. Someone must call the public's attention to these matters, supply the push necessary to get things done, and direct such energies as are aroused in the proper direction to get a rule created (Becker, 1963:162).

Hence an understanding of moral indignation and its organisation in the form of moral crusades requires as a minimum a means of differentiating and identifying those who are particularly likely to become 'moral enterpreneurs' (Becker, 1963). Any viable theory needs to account for the differential distribution of moral indignation in relation to particular sets of issues.

Ressentiment and envy

Max Scheler attempted to identify the sources of moral indignation in his elaboration of the notion of *ressentiment*. Scheler argues that *ressentiment,* an attitude of condemnation arising from the 'cumulative repression of feelings of hatred, revenge, envy and the like' (Coser, 1961:23), 'can only arise if these emotions are particularly powerful and yet must be suppressed because they are coupled with the feeling that one is unable to act them out — either because of weakness, physical or mental, or because of fear' (Scheler, 1961:48).

Scheler suggests that women are more likely to be subject to *ressentiment* than men whose attributes and status they secretly crave. The spinster excluded from both the prestige of the male role and from the satisfactions enjoyed by married women, is particularly vulnerable to *ressentiment*. The aged, threatened with displacement by the young, in power, prestige, and sexual gratification, are similarly likely to respond with *ressentiment* to the succeeding generation (Coser, 1961:26). Scheler proposes a 'sociological law' to the effect that *ressentiment* 'will spread with the *discrepancy* between the political, constitutional, or functional status of a group and its *factual* power' (Scheler, 1961:50).

Svend Ranulf, while viewing his own thesis as identical with that of Scheler (Ranulf, 1964:199), condemns his failure to provide any evidence in support of his argument. Scheler's reliance on 'the experience of everyday life' should, Ranulf believes, 'be met with the objection that such supposed experience might possibly, after all, prove to be nothing but a system of generally accepted prejudices'. Ranulf (1964:1), proposes that envy is the predominant source of moral indignation, and locates the life experience of the lower middle class as its major generating milieu (Ranulf, 1964:2, 36). Drawing on an idea of Werner Sombart's, he argues that moral indignation 'is a distinctive characteristic of the lower middle class, that is, of a social class living under conditions which force its members to an extraordinarily high degree of self-restraint and subject them to much frustration of natural desires' (Ranulf, 1964:198).

While he seeks to locate empirical support for his theory in various historical situations, including the rise of Puritanism and Nazism, Ranulf's theory also raises certain objections. Lasswell, in his preface to the work, suggests that Ranulf did not distinguish fully enough between 'the indignation of the rising middle classes and the defensive indignation of declining social formations' (Ranulf, 1964:vi). Gusfield, whose theory we shall shortly summarise, objects that the Ranulf-Scheler theory does not account for the early stages of the American temperance movement, in which the primary orientation of the reformers was towards converting and assimilating the drinker, rather than coercing him into conformity. 'If the Temperance adherent secretly craved drink, he should have responded in the same way to all violations of the norm. He didn't' (Gusfield, 1963:113-14). Moreover, there is no evidence that supporters of the Woman's Christian Temperance Union, the particular moral crusade analysed by Gusfield, *did* envy the drinker, or that they secretly craved the alcoholic liquors for the consumption of which they proclaimed distaste. Finally, Ranulf's theory does not enable us to account for the moral indignation aroused on some issues, in social groups other than the lower middle class. The desire to retain capital punishment for certain classes of sexual and homicidal offence, for example, can certainly be located in substantial sections of the working class.

Moral crusades as status defence

In a fascinating and seminal study of the Woman's Christian Temperance Union in the United States, Joseph Gusfield has proposed that issues of moral reform can be analysed as one way in which a cultural group may act to preserve, defend, or enhance its dominance. Moral reform campaigns can be seen, on this account, as a form of status politics. The public affirmation of a set of values and beliefs, and their support by institutions of the state maintains or enhance their status against competitors, and thereby symbolicially affirms the status of those who adhere to them.

Gusfield's analysis draws upon Max Weber's conception of status. Weber identifies the *status situation* as 'every typical component of the life fate of men that is determined by a specific, positive or negative, social estimation of *honor*. This honor may be connected with any quality shared by a plurality . . .' (Weber, 1970:187), and he goes on to argue that 'status honor is normally expressed by the fact that above all else a specific *style of life* can be expected from all those who wish to belong to the circle (*ibid.*). Social honour or prestige is differentially distributed between status groups. At times of social change the styles of life associated with particular groups may begin to acquire greater prestige and traditional status elites may experience a loss in social honour. At such times, status movements may emerge 'which attempt to raise or maintain the prestige of a group' (Gusfield, 1963:20). This they seek to do through symbolic rather than instrumental means. Through the symbolic affirmation of some component of their life-style through legislation or executive action, the dominance of their way of life is reaffirmed. 'The fact of political victory against the "enemy" shows where social and political dominance lie. The legislative victory, whatever its factual consequences, confers respect and approval on its supporters' (Gusfield, 1963:23).

Gusfield then analyses the American temperance movement in these terms. He argues that temperance had become a significant symbol differentiating the life-style of the old, rural, Anglo-Saxon Protestant middle classes in America from the life-style of new, urban, middle-class groups which were often Catholic and recent immigrant in composition, and in which drinking had an accepted place. Gusfield argues (1963:7-8) that 'The establishment of Prohibition laws was a battle in the struggle for status between two divergent styles of life', and that 'A function of Temperance activities was to enhance the symbolic properties of liquor and abstinence as marks of status' (Gusfield, 1963:59).

Gusfield here presents the unexceptionable claim that attempts to secure the sanction of state and other legitimating agencies for some norm may have the *consequence* of maintaining or enhancing the social honour or prestige of a particular status group against the claim to improved status made by some challenging group. This is clearly so in the case of white dominance in the Southern United States or South Africa. Zoning regulations which sought to restrict the domiciles of blacks to particular locations have the consequence (and usually the purpose) of preventing the assimilation of blacks into white status groups.

On the basis of this *functional* argument, Gusfield defends himself in anticipation, against the charge of *reductionism*. That a *function* of temperance activities was to enhance the status of the old, rural, Protestant middle classes, 'is not an assertion that this was its only function nor is it an assertion about motives. It is merely pointing out that as a consequence of such activities abstinence became symbolic of a status level' (Gusfield, 1963: 59).

This defence is sound. To identify the consequences of an action as tending to enhance status does not impugn the religious and moral motives of those involved. But the defence fails for Gusfield, since as he clearly recognises, sociologists are not merely interested in the *consequences* of action, but in their *causes*, and in the course of his analysis, Gusfield slides from functional claims to causal claims and thus falls prey to the charge of reductionism. This drift into causal claims can be documented from a number of passages:

The drive for political enforcement was *an attempt to defend* the position of social superiority which had been stabilised during the nineteenth century but was threatened during the first two decades of the twentieth (Gusfield 1963:88, my emphasis).

In the first phase . . . Temperance represents the reaction of the old Federalist aristocracy to loss of political, social, and religious dominance in American society. *It is an effort to re-establish control* over the increasingly powerful middle classes making up the American 'common man'. In the second phase Temperance represents the *efforts of urban, native Americans to consolidate their middle class respectability* through a sharpened distinction between the native, middle class life styles and those of the immigrant and the marginal laborer or farmer (Gusfield 1963:36-7, my emphasis. See also pp. 111, 102, 80, 12, for similar, if less explicit, formulations).

The language of an 'attempt to defend', 'an effort to re-establish control', and of 'efforts . . . to consolidate' is explicitly the language of *cause* and *motivation,* not of *function,* and Gusfield therefore stands committed to a causal thesis concerning the origins and meaning of this crusade.

Gusfield's analysis purports to show that the power and prestige of the old, rural, Anglo-Saxon, Protestant middle class was being challenged and that this group formed the main source of support for temperance activity. However, this does not show as he seems to suggest, that we can therefore conclude that because temperance crusading had the 'latent function' (consequence) of reaffirming the style of life of the old middle class, his *causal* thesis is also supported. There are clearly grounds for moral indignation other than resentment at lost status. Moral indignation directed towards Nazi atrocities or towards atrocities in Vietnam scarcely seems related to status loss. Moral indignation is a normal response to the violation of any deeply cherished norm or value. There is no reason to believe that an increasing disparity between the standards of morality and behaviour which one has grown up to believe were true and right and those displayed and legitimated in the surrounding society can not *of itself* provide the ground for commitment to a movement of moral reform.

Hence the hypothesis of status discontent needs to be supported by independent evidence other than the objective loss or challenged status of a group, and its involvement in a social movement, the success of which would enhance their status.

The most satisfactory evidence would be that found in the accounts of movement participants. There can be little doubt that they would be so located in the case of movements clearly based on status discontent (among other things): black civil rights, women's liberation, gay liberation. However, Gusfield either does not seek or find such accounts among temperance supporters. In the case of moral crusades I suspect that members' accounts would loudly disclaim any desire for the improvement of the status or prestige accorded them (and evidence in support of this view is presented in Chapter 9). In the absence of such confirming accounts, we can perhaps conclude three things:

1. They are dissembling and *really do* desire status improvement and know this to be the case, although they will not admit it.
2. They are motivated by unconscious desires for status improvement which they fail to recognise.
3. The hypothesis of status discontent is false.

To support (1) or (2) we should need to secure independent evidence of 'real motivation'. In the case of alternative (2) this would probably need to take the form of psychological testing or other clinical evidence. A decision in favour of (1) or (2) can hardly be made merely by reference to the social composition of the membership and the imputation of 'latent functions' to the movement's ideology which are then covertly construed as the motivational bases for adherence.

However, there is a much more fundamental issue to discuss. This is the issue of whether Gusfield has, in fact, identified a status group at all. Weber's definition does not permit us to identify *any* aggregate of people sharing some component of their life-style as a status group. Or, if it does, it should not. Rather such an attribute must not only be shared and differentially evaluated, it must also have some significance for life-chances. It is clear that not any shared life-style characteristic will do if we consider the landed peer and the bookmaker who both own a Rolls-Royce. The two are likely to see themselves as having *nothing* else in common. For a life-style characteristic to form the basis for a status group then, it is clear that something else is needed. Three possibilities suggest themselves. Either shared life-style characteristics must derive from some other common features (sex, race, religion, source of income, exercise of political power, etc.), which *are* significant determinants of life-chances. Or, since even with changes in these structural characteristics a status group may continue to maintain a high level of prestige, and of exclusiveness, the life-style characteristics must be themselves significant determinants of life-chances. That is, as in the cases of Brahmins, monks, or a politically and economically waning aristocracy, possession of the relevant life-style characteristics must involve the exercise of rights and privileges not shared by non-possessors of those characteristics. Or, as in the case of an achieved status attribute like higher education, the status characteristic must provide access to differentially distributed rewards, rights or privileges.

Gusfield argues strongly that temperance crusaders shared not only a set of life-style attributes, but also structural characteristics based in the class structure, viz. that they were rural, Anglo-Saxon, Protestant, old middle class. But his evidence for this rather throws the matter in doubt. As he indicates, the WCTU was not the only organisation involved in the temperance movement and others, such as the Washingtonians, were acknowledged to comprise people of lower social standing. But even examining Gusfield's evidence for the WCTU, it is clear that in 1885, nearly 30% of the local *leadership* was composed of wives of labouring husbands (Gusfield 1963:81). Since leadership in voluntary associations tends to be disproportionately middle class even compared to their membership, this suggests that a very substantial body of support for temperance came from the working classes. We also have no way of telling how large a proportion of the middle-class membership was, in fact, from the rural, Anglo-Saxon, Protestant, old middle class.

The high proportion of working-class leaders even at the high point of its career (in terms of social composition) suggests that the norms of the respectable middle classes had *diffused* to social classes and to status groups well beyond those whose social dominance led to the association of prestige and social honour with an abstaining life-style. By 1925, 43% of the local leadership was from a labouring background (Gusfield, 1963: 130). Gusfield provides us with no evidence that these supporters of temperance shared any characteristics with the old, native middle classes except that they valued the same style of life. This life-style was no longer uniquely associated with some set of structural characteristics determinative of life-chances. There is, moreover, no evidence in Gusfield's account that style of life carried with it any differential rights and privileges by the turn of the century. Hence, what we have here is not a *status group,* but a *cultural group.* Temperance crusaders identified with the same view of what respectable life and behaviour involved. They fought to preserve this style of life, or culture, against the increasing erosion which it faced as the dominant culture in American society. What we have in Gusfield's account is not the politics of *status defence,* but the politics of *cultural defence,** and the two are not necessarily the same.

Gusfield's theory has also been adopted by Zurcher and Kirkpatrick (1976) in their analysis of two anti-pornography crusades in the United States of America, occasioned by a pornographic book store in one case, and a 'skin-flick' movie house in the other. Their analysis is rendered more complex than Gusfield's by the fact that they are unable to identify as readily two alleged status groups in opposition. Hence they are more cautious in their claims. Nonetheless, their model is substantially similar. They argue that anti-pornography crusades emerge as a traditionally dominant status group (i.e. a group of persons with traditionally dominant beliefs and life-styles) faces challenges from rising social groups with contrasting beliefs and life-styles. Attitudes to pornography provided a summary symbol of this contrast. Those who joined the anti-pornography crusades were 'status dis-contents' (Zurcher and Kirkpatrick, 1976:307) seeking 'to defend the prestige and power of their style of life' (Zurcher and Kirkpatrick, 1976:266).

The force of Zurcher and Kirkpatrick's argument is weakened from the outset by their inability to display even to the same extent as Gusfield that supporters of the anti-pornography crusades could be identified as possessing any distinctive differentially evaluated attribute which could form the basis for a status group and hence for status protest. The supporters of anti-pornography movements are rather a heterogeneous group only distinguishable from persons who exhibited opposition to their crusade by an overall tendency to attend church more regularly, to have non-professional occupations, to have been more likely to come from small towns or cities, and to have had less higher education. But this diverse range of characteristics are not uniquely possessed by the anti-pornography supporters, nor do all anti-pornography supporters, exhibit them. Hence, the only characteristics shared by the anti-pornography crusaders were certain norms and values including opposition to pornography. They possessed certain values and commitments which were traditionally dominant in America. But discontent at the decline in the prestige of certain values and norms and an attempt to enhance or promote them, is not necessarily the same as discontent at the decline in the prestige of certain *groups* or an attempt to enhance or promote them through the enforcement of certain norms. This can only be conceived as status enhancement in the truistic sense that the supporters of a successfully legitimated belief or action tend to receive greater prestige than their opponents. Winners are more prestigeous than losers, whatever the issue. Zurcher and Kirkpatrick do not provide evidence that any distinguishable status group was involved. That is the crusaders neither share any structural characteristic determinative of life-chances, nor is there any evidence that their shared life-style carried with it any distinctive rights and privileges.

Zurcher and his associates therefore change the ground of their argument to include aspects of the theory of *status inconsistency,* hypothesising that supporters of the anti-pornography crusade would 'tend towards an over-rewarded status inconsistency pattern of higher income and lower education and far lower occupation' (Zurcher and Kirkpatrick, 1976:266; see also Wilson and Zurcher, 1976). The evidence, to say the least, does not loudly acclaim the validity of this hypothesis. In terms of their measures of objective status attributes (education, occupation, income) there is little evidence in their study that a particular pattern of status inconsistency provides the motivation for moral indignation.

Zurcher *et al.* urge us to accept a consensus that over-rewarded inconsistents 'could be expected to resist . . . changes in their social environment which might threaten their somewhat precarious over-rewarded situation'. There are two particularly striking puzzles here. First, no evidence is offered that the situation of the 'over-rewarded' is at all precarious in American society. Secondly, and more important it is extremely difficult to see how the existence of a 'skin-flick' movie house and a pornographic book store (which were the precipitating factors leading to the two crusades) could conceivably 'threaten' the alleged over-rewarded status of the anti-pornography campaigners. Nor do Zurcher *et al.* exhibit any evidence that the campaigners saw these offending agencies as any kind of threat to their over-rewarded *status*. They did indeed see them as a threat, but to the moral climate in which they lived and the way of life of which they morally approved. These are very different from a concern about their status situation, and it is a fundamental mistake to conflate them.

Zurcher *et al.* therefore again shift their ground to the claim that *perception of status threat* is more significant than status inconsistency. Wilson and Zurcher assert, for example, that active supporters of the anti-pornography campaigns were found to be 'status discontents defending against social change' (1976:523). However, examination of the original study (Zurcher and Kirkpatrick, 1976) reveals that no data on perceived status discontent were gathered. Supporters of the campaigns exhibited discontent solely over changes that had taken place in the *culture* of American society, not over their position within the *status structure* of American society. The explanation of attitudes towards pornography and their mobilisation in moral crusades must be located in social and historical changes which differentially affect commitments to traditional cultural values, not in threatened social status. Pornography crusades are a matter of *cultural defence,* not *status defence.*

The theory of symbolic crusades

The two studies discussed above share a number of problems. They assume that because crusading in connection with a moral issue may lead to status enhancement for some group of people, it is the desire to achieve enhancement of their status that motivates involvement. It is doubtful whether either study identifies a distinguishable status group whose status would thus be enhanced. Neither study provides independent evidence for a *perceived* challenge to status, nor that the group in question *experienced* status discontent. In particular, neither study offers any clear evidence that desire for status improvement *motivated* the crusading activity. The evidence they provide only substantiates a claim that people sought to foster norms and values once dominant, but now challenged.

Both studies display a *debunking* drift. Things are not what they seem. Moral crusaders may say that values and behaviour once widely viewed as virtuous and right are now being ignored, and that they still hold to those values and norms and have a desire to see others return to the paths of righteousness, but we know better. We know that the *real* reason they choose to defend these values and norms is a sense of lost status and a desire to restore the public deference formerly their due.

It is interesting that such a form of analysis impugning the motives of movement followers has only been applied to conservative groups. Zurcher and Kirkpatrick argue that such an analysis could be applied to reformist movements, but they are confused by their failure to distinguish a desire for status *for a group* from a desire to promote the status of certain *values and norms*. Anyone who seeks to foster some value or form of behaviour wishes *it* to have increased status. Opponents of capital punishment believe it better not to hang murders than to hang them, and wish to maintain or *foster the status of their view*, but it is nonsense to believe that the desire to end the use of capital punishment is motivated by a desire for their status enhancement as persons, or as a group. Students of social movements have not applied such analyses to reformist groups, I suggest, because they tend to sympathise with such groups or at least do not seek to impugn their motives. White people engaged themselves in black civil rights activity not to improve their status but because black civil rights was an obviously adequate source of motivation to an idealistic person, and similarly with opposition to the Vietnam War, campaigns for nuclear disarmament, etc. Only conservative groups do not wear their intentions on their face. Only for conservative groups do we need to ignore their own statements of motivation and look elsewhere for the *real* reasons. Hence I suggest a covert ideological bias in the theory.

This bias is also evident in the notion of *symbolic* crusades. 'Symbolic' is a term used ambiguously in these analyses. It is first, and appropriately used to imply that the avowed object of protest actually stands for a range of issues which are in reality the subject of protest. But it is also used in a covert constrast with 'instrumental' or 'effective'. The object of the crusade is merely a symbolic one, of achieving a change of a ceremonial or ritualistic rather than a real or effective kind. The evidence for this is usually drawn from the aftermath of the crusade when legislative implementation of the crusaders' views, is in fact, found not to solve the problem. People still drink after Prohibition. People are still able to consume pornography after the passage of restricting legislation. Hence, it is argued, since the crusaders have settled for a resolution which is not in fact effective, they only sought a symbolic or ritual affirmation of their values.

This view should be treated with scepticism. Again it imputes a motivation for which evidence of an appropriate kind is rarely drawn. Some crusaders believe — mistakenly — that legislative change alone will solve the problem. Others, faced with the difficulties of securing effective legislation, settle for something less rather than nothing at all. Some continue to agitate and protest even after the passage of legislation to ensure that it becomes more effective, and that it is implemented. And others are glad to see legislation passed even though they may not wish it enforced, because they believe that the existence of laws against some form of behaviour may discourage some people from pursuing it, and in particular may lead young people to recognise that this is not a form of behaviour approved in society and therefore discourage them for experimenting with it. None of these can be construed as merely symbolic in the sense of ceremonial or ritual. The protesters desire effective action, but may not always know how, or be able to secure it. Or they wish it to be instrumental or effective in ways the investigator has not considered. Again, we rarely see reformist movements referred to in *this sense* of symbolic. Civil rights, nuclear disarmament and anti-Vietnam War campaigns are seen as aiming at effective change and going about it in the best way they know how. I suggest that a little more interpretative charity is required towards groups that resist change at least of the order of that shown towards groups that promote change.

* I owe this term to Professor David Martin.

CHAPTER VII

Morality and the media: The National Viewers' and Listeners' Association

This chapter presents an analysis of a moral crusade, the National Viewers' and Listeners' Association (NVALA), and seeks to explain the emergence of this crusade in terms of a theory of cultural defence. Observations of the NVALA were carried out over a period of three years in which the author systematically perused the movement's periodical publication the *Viewer and Listener,* ephemeral documentation, mimeoed speeches, submissions to committees of inquiry, and national press reports. The autobiographical writings of the movement's leader, Mrs. Whitehouse (1967; 1972), have also been utilised, and the author attended three national coventions of the movement.

The moral crusader: a portrait of Mrs. Whitehouse

The National Viewers' and Listeners' Association is both brainchild and vehicle of Mrs. Mary Whitehouse, having little independent life of its own. A Christian of long standing, Mrs. Whitehouse's Anglican convictions were early strengthened and moulded in the direction of moral reform through contact with Moral Re-Armament. Mrs. Whitehouse lived and worked in the Midlands, an area of Britain where the impact of the cultural changes, which overtook the country in the aftermath of the Second World War, was perhaps both less severe and less rapid than in the more cosmopolitan South-East and London. Nevertheless, when she emerged from the relative isolation of seventeen years as a mother and housewife on her return to work as a schoolteacher in the early 1960s, she was, she reports (White-

105

house, 1967, 1972), suddenly faced with the fact that significant changes had taken place in the moral and cultural climate. 1963, the year in which she began actively to concern herself with these issues, was notable for, among other things, the Profumo scandal and the book, *Honest to God,* written by John Robinson, Bishop of Woolwich.

As a teacher with responsibility for the moral welfare of the children at her school, her memoir recounts that she was distressed by their divergence from Christian standards that she accepted. When the children referred to material which they had seen on television to legitimate their views, she felt that they were being won over to a 'sub-Christian concept of living' (Whitehouse, 1967:16). In the summer of 1963 she wrote to, and visited, the BBC and ITA to discuss her fears. She was well received by a senior BBC official in the absence of Sir Hugh Carleton Greene, the Director-General, and given a sympathetic hearing for her account of the 'harmful' effects of some programmes on young people (Caulfield, 1976:Ch. 2). During the summer she also approached her local MP; the Bishop of Hereford; and the Minister of Health. She believed that once apprised of the facts, the BBC would effect changes. While no transformation seemed to occur immediately, she believed that the issues as she saw them would be raised in parliamentary debate when the BBC's charter came up for renewal, and that the Corporation would then be obliged to mend its ways.

After a season of 'kitchen sink plays' on BBC television and the renewal of the BBC's charter she realised, however, that her protests had had no impact. Individual protest, she concluded was not enough (Whitehouse, 1967:22). At this point she determined to form a protest movement. Aided by the wife of an Anglican vicar, also an MRA supporter, the Clean-up TV Campaign was launched. It began with a manifesto published early in 1964. The manifesto asserted a belief 'in a Christian way of life' and objected 'to the propaganda of disbelief, doubt and dirt that the BBC projects into millions of homes through the television screen' (Whitehouse, 1967:23). Publication of the manifesto was followed by a meeting in Birmingham Town Hall in May 1964. The issue — an attack on the media — itself aroused the interest of the mass media, and the meeting was covered by press and television, which captured and found particularly newsworthy the heckling which disrupted it.

Mrs. Whitehouse shortly discovered that the active life of a moral crusader was incompatible with full-time teaching, and as the requests for talks and guidance increased, it became necessary for her to give up her teaching career. The Clean-up TV Campaign was organised to secure signatures for a petition to Parliament, embodying the manifesto, which was duly presented in June 1965 bearing 365,00 names (Whitehouse, 1967: 55).

Although it provoked discussion both in the press and in Parliament, it seemed the battle was not to be won so easily. The Director-General of the BBC construed the Clean-up TV Campaign as a minority opinion, and declined to attribute much significance to its views. The CUTV Campaign had also been criticised for the negativity of its stance by sectors of society whose support Mrs. Whitehouse sought to win (e.g. representatives of some Church-related organisations), and it was in response to this pressure that a new organisation, the Viewers' and Listeners' Association, later National VALA, was shortly formed, and the Clean-up TV Campaign allowed to disappear. NVALA was established, according to Mrs. Whitehouse, to promote a 'positive philosophy' rather than merely to protest against TV productions.

The ideology of NVALA

NVALA adopts a position of cultural fundamentalism (Gusfield, 1963) in the face of changing values. Its literature expresses the virtues of fidelity in marriage and chastity before marriage; respect for authority; patriotism; hostility to drugs and alcohol, to 'foul language', homosexuality, pornography and abortion; and belief in traditional, denominational Christianity. The values of the NVALA are held to be those also of the nation as a whole. While its membership, though growing, is numerically small, NVALA literature claims to represent the sentiments of the vast majority of British people. Hence, the norms and values to which it objects can be seen by members as belonging only to a small, but well-organised, minority who are seeking to impose their views on society at large through the mass media.

While Mrs. Whitehouse and the NVALA see themselves as defenders of the culture on which our society is founded, they view this culture as seriously threatened from without by the forces of world communism; and from within by commercial pornographers, and more particularly by political and sexual radicals for whom moral change and the transformation of sexual behaviour are a means of undermining capitalist society as a whole. These latter youthful radicals are seen by at least some members of the NVALA as a 'fifth column', or perhaps as inadvertent fellow travellers, working for the success of world communism, which is perfectly prepared, they believe, to utilise drugs and pornography to achieve its ends (*Viewer and Listener,* Autumn 1970:3; *Viewer and Listener,* Spring 1971:4). Ensconced in the BBC in positions of power, it is said, are men who, whether politically motivated or otherwise, support the views to which NVALA members are inexorably opposed. That a perspective of this kind easily slides into a conspiracy theory, is familiar from such populist movements as McCarthyism. In the case of NVALA, members have accused at least one Director-General of the BBC towards whom they felt particularly hostile, of 'encouraging and harbouring near-communists on his staff. . .' (Whitehouse, 1972:88). This view that the decline of contemporary morality is planned or encouraged by a communist conspiracy seems a common theme in a number of contemporary moral crusades (Kirkpatrick, 1971:78; it also appears in the conversations of members of the Festival of Light whom I have interviewed).

There prevails in the NVALA the view that the social, political and economic ills to which the country is perennially subject, derive from a moral crisis which requires solution before any substantial change will occur elsewhere. The movement's Treasurer has argued (at the 1974 NVALA Convention) that 'We would not have an economic and political crisis in this country if it were not for the moral crisis', and this position is one that Mrs. Whitehouse, deriving at least some of her views from the philosophy of Moral Re-armament, readily supports (Whitehouse, 1967:186-7). The mass media are held to have a determining role in creating, enhancing, or undermining the prevailing moral climate. 'Who controls the media controls the country', Mrs. Whitehouse asserted at the 1975 NVALA Convention. However, magazine pornography and sex-education can similarly have a decisive effect on the state of modern society. Mrs. Whitehouse quotes with approval in one of her works the view that sex education has been responsible for the level of contemporary violence (Whitehouse, 1972:124). Elsewhere, 'obscenity in the paperbacks and magazines, and on the motion picture screen', has been presented as 'a basic and major contributing factor to violence . . .' by Mrs. Whitehouse (*Viewer and Listener,* Summer 1970:3). But whatever the immediate causal factors, crime, promiscuity, juvenile delinquency, drug addiction and alcoholism are encouraged by a 'permissive society' (*Viewer and Listener,* Autumn 1970:1).

> The 'Permissive Society', with its much vaunted 'freedom', is now seen for what it is — a bitter and destructive thing.

> The arts are degraded, law is held in contempt and sport fouled by outbreaks of vandalism and violence. The national purse takes the strain of a health service over-burdened with increasing abortion, drug addiction, mental disturbance, alcoholism and an epidemic of venereal disease.

Television can lead to the commission of crime by portraying violence, encouraging sexual behaviour and glamorising criminal behaviour (*Viewer and Listener,* Spring 1970:4). Its impact is, indeed, believed by the NVALA to be *determinative* of the prevailing culture. One issue of its newsletter conveyed with approval the view that: 'Without a change in the character of our television programmes no change [is] possible in Britain' (*Viewer and Listener,* Autumn 1970:6).

The NVALA thus see society as engaged in a battle against forces of structural, cultural and personal disruption. The social order is precariously balanced, and hence potentially responsive to concerted action by either challengers or defenders of our culture (*Viewer and Listener,* Spring 1970:2):

> The society in which we now live can as easily rise to a fresh resurgence of spirit as it can collapse into decadence. Everything depends upon how many of us are prepared to get underneath and push, or climb the heights and pull.

The imagery of war is prominent (e.g. Whitehouse 1967:50; *Viewer and Listener,* Spring 1975:1). In this battle the mass media are important weapons, and television, entering almost every home and affecting almost every member, is peculiarly powerful. The battle metaphor is reinforced by the movement's title, members preferring the form National VALA, which, when spoken, can be heard as National 'Valour'.

Children are seen as particularly vulnerable to new styles of life, and modes of thought, belief and behaviour, displayed on television. 'Children . . . are . . . pressurised into alien patterns of behaviour . . .' (Whitehouse 1972:134. This theme is also common to other anti-pornography crusades, see e.g. Kirkpatrick, 1971:76). They must be defended. The protection of the child legitimates an urgency and stridency in the NVALA's message, less easily supported by the simple demand for the reinstatement of one's own values. The sensitive adult who has hitherto been sheltered from some of life's more primitive features must also be protected, and the privacy of all must be preserved against the instrusion of alien language, behaviour and opinions. The BBC, a symbol of all respectable British institutions, should be at the forefront of this reassertion of the traditional culture, but has, instead, been subverted from within, and become one of the worst offenders against 'good taste' and 'decency'. Mrs. Whitehouse lists first amongst the offences of the BBC that 'It derides accepted standards of conduct . . .' (Whitehouse, 1967:119).

It is not, however, only respectable institutions like the BBC which have deserted their positions of trust. As Bridget Pym has observed of the resurgence of groups like NVALA, formed to defend traditional values: 'In the past the orthodox could depend on their values being defended by social workers, teachers, etc., without having to think about the matter, but in the current world, none of these agencies is wholly reliable' (Pym, 1974:148). The churches have temporised and compromised, failing to defend traditional Christian views on questions of morality.

> Many of our traditional leaders, especially in the universities and to some degree within the Church and State have abdicated. They have been so fearful of appearing authoritarian . . . that they have forfeited their moral authority (*Viewer and Listener,* Autumn 1970:1).

NVALA members have complained that one cannot always be sure of the support of ministers of the Church in their struggle. There are those clerics, it seems, who are even prepared to accept some 'X rated' films. Mrs. Whitehouse has argued that the churches have abandoned their responsibilities in the prevailing climate of moral relativism (Whitehouse, 1972:37-40), and that their failure to provide a united front has undermined the Christian cause. She relates an occasion on which three clergymen presented different views on an issue in a television programme: 'many people felt that the cause of Christianity was not forwarded by the spectacle of so wide a disparity of views, and apparent lack of sympathy between a group of people calling themselves Christian' (Whitehouse, 1972:159).

Such indecisiveness, and differences of opinion among

purveyors of respectable culture have a demoralising effect, particularly on the young. Dr. Sturdy, who before his death held executive office in NVALA, objected to schoolchildren being allowed to 'question and doubt' rather than being taught 'sound doctrine' (*Viewer and Listener,* Winter 1973:6), and other members have inveighed against the tendency in some television programmes to invite in children 'a critical attitude towards parents . . .' (*Viewer and Listener,* Summer 1972:5). Members appear to be unhappy at the prospect of children being left without dogmatic moral guidelines, to make up their own minds, since they might make them up in what NVALA supporters would construe as the wrong way. A team of NVALA programme 'monitors' reported on a schools' broadcast in which the faults of contemporary society and the problems of modern warfare were discussed that it 'lacked any moral yardstick', and that

> The general effect of such a programme is bound to be to make the younger generation feel 'Better to be Red than dead'. It could lead the young generation to associate themselves with the Hippy cult — to opt out of society . . . (*Viewer and Listener,* Summer 1971:4).

Mrs. Whitehouse has objected to broadcasting time being given to political critics of the prevailing order, e.g. Jerry Rubin and the Yippies (*Viewer and Listener,* Spring 1971:4); Bernadette Devlin and Tariq Ali (*The Times,* 27 April, 1972); and other groups which 'might want to destroy society' (*The Times,* 21 December, 1970).

The rhetoric employed by the NVALA seeks to display the forces behind the trends of which they disapprove as a small, conspiratorial and sinister group, while presenting its own concerns as those of all right-minded men, or of the nation as a whole. Its literature refers to the 'politically motived interests' of the radical left. The enemy is driven by narrow political concerns, or 'vested interests', while the NVALA, one may infer, is guided only by conscience, patriotism and good sense. The enemy is depicted as only a minority interest, while NVALA represents the 'licence-holder' in general, and legitimates its views by reference to what '*people* deeply resent', or to the 'moral and religious values of the *mass* of the people' (Whitehouse, 1967:119, my emphasis). Discussion of membership figures of several thousand is usually buttressed by the claim that these, in fact, 'represent' several million people.

Mrs. Whitehouse has observed (Caulfield, 1976:Ch. 6, emphasis in the original)

> I talk to every kind of audience up and down the country and I've absolutely no doubt that the majority of people support what we do. At all my meetings, I find that whatever the enthusiasm shown, however, only an infinitesimal number actually join VALA. *But the support is there.* I've no doubt in my own mind that we've got widespread support throughout the whole country and among all classes.

The movement's first manifesto claimed that the forces which they opposed sought to 'flout at will the conscience of millions' (Whitehouse, 1967:148). The rhetoric sometimes raises the contradiction in their position between the claim on the one hand that the NVALA represents the silent majority and on the other, their occasional presentation of themselves as a beleaguered and vilified minority in an increasingly alien culture.

As Orrin Klapp observes, 'The goal of a crusade is to defeat an evil, not merely to solve a problem. This gives it a sense of righteousness, of nobility . . . thus the crusader may think of himself as a hero and define his opponents as villains' (Klapp, 1969:274). The issue between NVALA and its opponents is therefore drawn in sharp terms. The debate concerns 'genuine freedom' or 'total licence'; 'cultural responsibility' or 'cultural anarchy' (Whitehouse, 1972:122). NVALA members 'defend decency' while their opponents' views contain 'the essence of the worst kind of dictatorship' (Whitehouse, 1972:122). NVALA seeks to defend the *'accepted* standards' (Whitehouse 1967:24, my emphasis) or *'sound* standards' (Whitehouse, 1967:54, my emphasis), while its opponents seek to use television 'for purposes alien to the character of the nation and the true interests of the British people' (Whitehouse, 1967:171), with the result that they become 'pliant material for any kind of alien philosophy' (Whitehouse, 1967:165). There is, moreover, a rudimentary apocalyptic vision in NVALA ideology, indicated by the ominous prophecy that 'Time is running out for Britain', and hence urgent measures are necessary.

Structure

As I indicated earlier, the NVALA is very much the personal vehicle of Mrs. Whitehouse. It has nevertheless grown within recent years to a membership of some 30,000 (that is *individual* members and does not include, as far as one can tell, *block* membership by organisations). The membership subscription is only 25 pence a year, which includes the cost of an irregular publication, the *Viewer and Listener* mailed to members usually twice a year. The membership fee is kept at this low figure, despite frequent suggestion that it be raised, to facilitate ease of recruiting at public meetings and, it is said, in order that the total sum received remain below a level at which Value-Added Tax would be incurred. Further funds are obtained, however, by the practice said to be widespread among members of sending a donation with their subscription.

The membership is nominally organised on a regional basis. Some regions have a core of active members who promote public events to further the aims of the NVALA, but the active duties of members are slight. They are asked to monitor broadcasts on radio and TV and to complete cards produced by the organisation on which they can indicate whether programmes infringe the standards which they uphold. They are also urged to contact radio and TV authorities and voice their complaints when programmes are broadcast which contravene the moral code supported by the Association. Each year an Annual General Meeting is held, attended by approximately one hundred of the more active adherents, followed by a public meeting which has in recent years attracted 300-400 people.

Members have little voice in the running of the movement. Its executive committee is re-elected each year almost automatically and replacements suggested by the committee are usually elected without any dissenting voice. Since any suggestion, organisational or ideological, which is made by a member in the face of disapproval by the executive committee, seems dangerously close to a challenge to Mrs. Whitehouse, it is usually not pursued against such opposition.

Tactics

NVALA employs a variety of tactics to serve its ends. Its most prominent and probably most effective tactic because of Mrs. Whitehouse's 'newsworthiness' is that of public statements to the press by the leader. Mrs. Whitehouse's protests regarding programme content are good copy. The movement has also mobilised its following to secure signatures on petitions to

Parliament. The second petition organised in association with the Festival of Light obtained some 1,350,000 signatures.

On at least two occasions Mrs. Whitehouse has sought to mobilise the Director of Public Prosecutions to bring actions against the BBC. Warning letters have been sent from NVALA's solicitor to the BBC. Mrs. Whitehouse made representations to HM Customs and Excise in order to secure the exclusion from Britain of the film 'Deep Throat' (Caulfield, 1976). More recently she sought to bring a private prosecution of a film 'Blow Out', but her action was unsuccessful. Members have brought similar actions, and where these failed, appeals for financial support have been circulated to the membership at large. Less spectacularly, Mrs. Whitehouse and NVALA members regularly write and telephone broadcasting authorities with complaints concerning programmes to which they object.

Members have sometimes also formed themselves into local pressure-groups for public morality, aiming to bring pressure on local cinema managers not to exhibit films they find objectionable, and on local councils, seeking to prevent such films receiving a certificate to be shown.

On one occasion the NVALA sought to pressure advertisers to withdraw advertising from the vicinity of programmes of which they disapproved, or by publishing the names of such companies, to censure their inaction. Members have also sought to discover whether MPs for their constituencies are prepared to support an Indecent Displays Bill; to oppose 'permissive' legislation; or to press for revision of the BBC's charter. A telegram was despatched by the movement to President Nixon, urging him to 'stand firm' in the face of advocacy of repeal of the United States Obscenity laws by the Presidential Commission on Pornography and Obscenity (*Viewer and Listener,* Autumn 1970:2) Mrs. Whitehouse has also engaged in the other activities typical of the leader of a pressure-group: writing letters to the press; submitting evidence to government inquiries such as the Annan Inquiry into broadcasting; or circularising policy-makers and legislators with the NVALA's views, or commentary, on some current issue (*Viewer and Listener,* Spring 1973:7). The NVALA sometimes co-operates with other pressure-groups, as in a demonstration in association with the Festival of Light and the Salvation Army, outside the offices of the Greater London Council in 1975, when the question of the abolition of film censorship in the London area was being debated.

114

Cultural fundamentalism and social change

Data on the class composition of NVALA have not yet become available. While there is every reason to believe that the membership is largely middle class, there are also grounds for believing that support for the position adopted by the NVALA comes not only from a retreating *petit bourgeoisie,* as the Ranulf-Scheler theory might suggest, but also from a substantial section of the respectable working class. Witness a letter in the movement's periodical, the *Viewer and Listener* (Spring 1975:5)

> . . . it is an insult to the working class that anyone should suggest that the desire for standards of decency is a feature of middle-class morality. The middle-class do not have and never *did* have a monopoly of 'virtue'. . . For quite large sections of the working class, moral codes have been very strict indeed.

It is, indeed, a truism of contemporary sociology that the working class tend to be poorly represented among the membership of voluntary associations of almost every kind. Hence, this suggests that we need to look beyond Ranulf's theory for an explanation of the moral indignation displayed by NVALA. There is, moreover, contrary to Scheler's theory, no evidence that NVALA's protest against sexual permissiveness, on television and elsewhere, masks a covert prurience.

It remains the case, however, that NVALA is protesting against the erosion of norms and values to which its membership is committed as part of a broader way of life, and these norms and values have historically been linked to certain social groups. They adhere to and proclaim traditionally respectable norms and values which were dominant in British society in the late Victorian era, and which remained symbolic indicators of 'respectability' at least up to the Second World War. Frank Parkin (1968:21), in his analysis of the Campaign for Nuclear Disarmament, speaks of

> certain institutional orders which occupy a key place in the social structure, and the values surrounding which exercise a dominant influence throughout society. Even within a highly diverse and complex normative system it still makes sense to conceive of, . . . a set of dominant values, or core values, which are in a way central to the society, which give the society its defining characteristics. . .

The norms and values which NVALA members support are those embodied in the 'Protestant ethic': thrift; abstemiousness; diligence; commitment to Christianity; and belief in the virtues of hard work, restraint and the deferment of gratification. Such norms have usually been identified with the enterpreneurial and commercial middle classes.

It cannot be stressed sufficiently that this is *not* to say that *NVALA members* therefore *occupy* such class positions. Rather, once a particular set of norms and values becomes established as did those of the entrepreneurial bourgeoisie, during the eighteenth and nineteenth centuries, as the dominant norms of a society and therefore as the bases for the attribution of 'respectability', they tend to become 'lodged' in certain areas of the social structure where they are resistant to social change. As a result of social and economic change and the emergence of new dominant values, commitment to the traditional norms and values may therefore by subject to a process of *differential erosion*.

Traditional Protestant ethic morality has been eroded by a variety of social forces. A major factor is that the power and income position of the independent entrepreneurial middle class has itself been undermined by social change. The changing scale of industry and commerce and the increasing rationalisation of industrial and commercial enterprise have led to widespread replacement of individual entrepreneurial capitalism, and hence a bourgeois and *petit-bourgeois* capitalist class (the main bearers of Protestant ethic values) by a class of corporate bureaucrats.

The traditional middle class has also suffered dilution through the expansion of the middle strata during the present century. Bain *et al.* (1972:92) conclude that the most striking characteristic of the occupational structure during the period 1911-66 is the 'rapid growth of the white collar labour force', both absolutely and as a proportion of workers in the labour force as a whole. A new bureaucratic, salaried and often effectively tenured, middle class has emerged with the increasing technologisation of production, and the expansion of state intervention and responsibilities. This relatively secure middle class has been less constrained to maintain the appearance of support for formerly 'respectable' standards, as, indeed have workers in general, in an era of generally high employment.

It is also at least arguable that there has been some erosion of the relative income superiority of the traditional middle class as a result of the redistribution of wealth by progressive income tax and welfare provision. Bacon *et al.* (1972:80) argue that the effect of progressive income tax has been to distribute after-tax incomes more equally than before-tax incomes, a trend that may have become more marked since 1949. But pre-tax incomes have also become more evenly distributed in recent years, they suggest.

The political position of the entrepreneurial middle class has been undermined to some extent by the return of Labour governments, and the growing political power of organised labour. The institutions of the traditional middle class have also correspondingly undergone some decline. Currie and Gilbert (1972:409), for example, document overwhelmingly that 'Adherence to organised religion has in general decreased since 1901'. The Church of England as an important repository of middle-class values, has suffered particular depredations. Its nominal membership, as a proportion of the population in England, declined from 9.5% in 1901 to 5.4% in 1966 (Currie and Gilbert, 1972:444). But here it largely mirrors the plight of the other major Protestant denominations. Secularisation has severely undermined the viability and prestige of a major legitimating institution for traditional middle-class values and behaviour, and has thereby removed the transcendental constraints on various hitherto tabooed forms of behaviour and their public display. The disappearance of domestic service also marks the loss of a major institutional mechanism whereby the manners and morals of the middle classes were assimilated by substantial sectors of the working class (I am grateful to Dr. Bryan Wilson for this point).

In a high technology, mass production economy, there has, moreover, developed an increasing concern with generating consumption as well as production. Marketing strategy has eagerly drawn upon and exploited as a source of customer appeal, bases of human motivation hitherto shrouded in secrecy and surrounded by religious constraints. At the same time, social control over behaviour has become more difficult to maintain. Increased urbanisation reduces the possibility of surveillance over behaviour in another part of the urban ecology by employers, neighbours, or clients, and therefore limits the degree of informal control which can be exercised to ensure the maintenance of 'respectable' standards (Wilson, 1970a).

The specialisation and rationalisation of production have

117

decreased the degree of instrinsic job satisfaction to be found in work for much of the labour force. Their involvement in work is instrumental, and seen as a necessary evil which provides resources for the enjoyment of non-work. As work has become devalued, and lost its rationale as an end in itself, so the values associated with, and increasingly restricted to the world of work, have declined in prominence and been replaced by values associated with leisure.

These basic shifts in the economy and social structure then provide the grounds on which the values of the traditional middle class have come to be challenged. In a comsumption-oriented age, earlier stress on the virtues of restraint, deferred gratification, asceticism, hard work, self-control, discipline and respect for authority, is seen as an ideology more suitable for an age of scarcity and entrepreneurial enterprise aimed at accumulation (Kirkpatrick, 1971). With the acquisition of a level of widespread affluence, some sectors of society begin to reject accumulation for its own sake; and others are less willing to sacrifice 'spontaneity', 'personal integrity' and the desire for full 'experience' for the sake of further increments in their material standard of living. Hence greater affluence has led not only to the emergence of new social groups, but to the spread of values and behaviour which fundamentally deny the legitimacy of the life style and culture of the entrepreneurial middle class (Davies, 1975:1). Their norms have come to be identified with a narrowing domain, finding their repository in the world of work. As leisure has increased, hitherto 'subterranean values' of play (Young, 1971) have come to occupy an increasingly prominent place within the culture, acquiring a wider legitimacy and respectability in consequence. Short-run hedonism has come to replace this-worldly asceticism as the dominant value system of a mass-consumption society.

These factors also suggest where erosion of the values of an entrepreneurial middle class is likely to have been greatest and least, and therefore should enable us to locate those social categories which are likely to have been resistant to it. Parkin observes that 'to claim that a society has distinguishable complexes of dominant values is not at the same time to claim that all strata are necessarily committed to them in the same degree' (Parkin, 1968:28). The remaining sectors of the entrepreneurial *petit-bourgeoisie*, lacking economic security, remain jeopardised by failure to adhere to traditionally respectable norms and values. The elderly are more likely than the young to have been socialised into respectable culture, and to identify with an earlier cohort of heroes. Those living in small towns and rural areas are likely to have suffered less of the impact of these social and cultural changes than city-dwellers. Christians are more likely than non-Christians to have had the traditional virtues buttressed by their faith and reinforced by the social circles in which they move. People with middle-class upbringings are more likely to have been socialised into traditional norms and values than those brought up in working-class homes, the working classes having had less commitment to the dominant culture in the first place. Those who have not been exposed to the questioning and criticism of conventional beliefs experienced in some areas of contemporary higher education are more likely to remain committed to the morality that prevailed in their youth, than those who have been thus exposed. Frank Parkin (1968:178), for example, concludes from his findings concerning adherents to CND that 'exposure to certain forms of advanced education has the effect of undermining . . . total acceptance [of dominant values] among middle-class members. To this extent it could be said that the minority of the non-manual stratum which has undergone formal intellectual training beyond the sixth form constitutes a permanent source of potential opposition to certain commonly accepted socio-political values . . .' Finally women, who are more likely to be isolated from economic and social change in the home, to be more susceptible to surveillance by neighbours, and to have received severer childhood socialisation on matters of morality, are also therefore more likely to display a stronger commitment to traditional standards of respectability, than men.

Observation, albeit of a very limited kind, of the membership of NVALA, suggests that the social categories identified above as less susceptible to the erosion of respectable culture, do in fact provide the major sources of NVALA's active support.

The NVALA, then, are defending a disappearig culture, but why is *television* the focus of their concern (BBC television especially), and sexual norms and values the particular target of their crusade? One reason is that earlier targets of protest at the infraction of respectable norms, such as drinking, no longer adequately differentiate the respectable from the reprobate in a period when moderate consumption of alcohol has become acceptable in all social strata.

In a modern industrial society, occupational and social differentiation give rise to a wider range of sub-cultures embodying more or less distinctive life-styles, consumption and behaviour patterns. While these continually threaten to impinge upon each other and hence provide the grounds for conflict, there is nevertheless a degree of segregation and insulation of competing sub-cultures. This is accomplished temporally (some sub-cultures only operate late at night for example); and geographically (particular locations in the urban area may be more or less explicitly reserved for particular sub-cultural activities); as well as by the proliferation and differentiation of institutions. The net result of this has been, however, that in the public domain no man can expect his norms and values to old exclusive sway. The institutions which provide supports and vehicles for his beliefs are only more or less differentiated, and more or less precariously segregated, from those of other cultural groups. Before the onset of radio and television, however, one domain remained sacrosanct as an institutional basis for a particular style of life: the home. Within the confines of their home, parents could expect to enact their beliefs and transmit them to their offspring largely unchallenged. Radio, as a mass commodity challenged that autonomy in a way which newspapers could not. They at least had to be *brought into* the home and could be excluded if their values did not conform to those prevailing in the parental domicile. Radio, once it was accepted as a domestic necessity altered this situation. It was always there, and the potential for conflict between the values it purveyed and those fostered by the parents always existed.

Under the aegis of Lord Reith, radio in Britain stolidly preserved the attitudes, modes of speech, Christian beliefs and social values of an upper middle class which set the pattern for respectable thought and behaviour in this country. Asa Briggs calls attention to the public image of the BBC under Reith's management. 'In several respects this was to be an image drawn from upper class or upper middle class life' (Briggs, 1961:292). Radio announcers were even required to wear evening dress for several years from 1925.

Reith displayed a considerable preoccupation with broadcasting as a moral force (Briggs, 1961:138). He was concerned with 'building character' through the BBC (Briggs, 1961:253). He held to a paternalistic view of the responsibilities of broadcasting *vis-à-vis* the listening audience. Even news broadcasts, he believed, should include what the BBC thought listeners *ought to* hear (Briggs, 1961:267). He had strong if somewhat amorphous Christian feelings (Briggs, 1961:272), and ensured that radio broadcasting exhibited a concern with maintaining religious faith (Briggs, 1965:227). He is reported to have been quite unwilling 'to give freedom of the air to those who wished to attack or question the religion of large number of people' (Briggs, 1961:272). NVALA members look back to the days of Lord Reith with the fondest nostalgia. As Asa Briggs records, 'By the end of 1923 in most people's eyes he *was* the BBC. To many people . . . he has remained the BBC over since . . .' (Briggs, 1961:135).

Television, however, changed everything. As it quickly demonstrated, its power to attract and hold an audience was greater even than that of radio. It rapidly also came to be seen as a domestic necessity. Its visual impact conveyed the messages it transmitted with even greater force than radio, and under the direction of a new breed of broadcasting professionals in postwar Britain, whose own values were less likely to have been shaped by the traditional middle-class institutions of public school, the Church of England, and the army elite corps, the beliefs and attitudes it conveyed shifted away from those of the respectable middle class which had earlier dominated broadcasting.

The BBC had to legitimate its activities and its cost, and a readily available measure of cost-effectiveness lay in audience figures. Securing a large audience became an important concern, particularly with the emergence of a competitive situation after the establishment of commercial television. As the commercial media, cinema and independent television, sought to maintain an audience by defining their purpose in terms principally of entertainment and the accepted standards of the market, the BBC, in order to retain its own audience, was also forced to adapt away from education and moral uplift, towards entertainment.

As Table 1 shows, while by 1948 only 4.3% of the adult population had television sets in their homes, by the early 1960s, few homes were without one (Halsey, 1972:552).

The point at which NVALA emerged, then, was that at which the distribution of television sets in Britain reached saturation level. The adherent to 'respectable' values found the legitimacy of his life-style and beliefs challenged in his own home. Mrs. Whitehouse records that her co-founder of the Clean-Up TV

121

campaign, Mrs. Buckland, had been approached by mothers, concerned that 'the training they were trying to give their children was being undermined by television' (Whitehouse, 1967:21). A message sent to the Queen from their first public meeting, expressed their desire 'to banish from our homes and theatres those who seek to demoralise and corrupt our young people' (Whitehouse, 1967:38). The respectable parent came to find his offspring quoting the authority of television against him.

Table 1 *Growth of Television Reception 1947-64 UK (% ages)*

Year	Proportion of adult population with TV sets in home
1947	0.2
1948	4.3
1955	39.8
1960	81.8
1964	90.8

If this argument is accepted, the NVALA can be seen as a protest against the challenge television presented, within the homes of its members to a set of values no longer accorded universal respect in British society.

The bearers of an increasingly challenged culture turned to coercive reform (Gusfield, 1963) exhibiting their moral indignation through a protest movement, when they found themselves deserted by the groups and institutions which had traditionally supported their values and been identified with them. The legislature, the courts, the press, even the Church, they felt had abandoned them and compromised with modernism. The BBC, a major symbol of respectability and hitherto a bastion of all respectable virtues was also succumbing. The NVALA directed its moral indignation in particular therefore at the institution which it felt had the greatest obligation to support respectable morality since its message was conveyed with the greatest immediacy to a larger proportion of the population than that of any other institution; and whose desertion from traditional standards was also therefore the most visible.

NVALA has attacked television for its failure to maintain a wide range of values and norms: patriotism, motherhood, abstemiousness, non-violence, respect for Christianity and respect for authority. While the role of each of these allegedly neglected values must be understood, it is evident that it is the sexual 'permissiveness' and the explicitness of sexual behaviour displayed on television which generate the severest criticism from this source. Why should this be? Earlier studies of anti-pornography crusades have not ventured further than suggesting that sexually exciting material or pornography provides a 'summary symbol for threats and challenges to the life-style of anti-pornography crusaders' (Zurcher *et al.*, 1973:70). But why was this symbol so highly salient?

In a most thoughtful and detailed analysis of the relationship between late Victorian sexual respectability and the prevailing social and economic system, Peter Cominos describes the way in which sexual respectability — continence before marriage, late marriage and restraint thereafter — was seen as intimately related to the desire to maintain and improve both economic circumstances and social position (Cominos, 1963:223):

> Continence was good. Attained by sublimation through industry, it resulted in the accumulation of wealth. Incontinence was bad. The outcome of idleness and yielding to temptation, it resulted in poverty and early marriages.

Sexuality was seen as an animal passion to be suppressed by reason. Its sole purpose, according to the strictest expression of the respectable norm, was for 'the propagation of the species in the holy state of matrimony' (Cominos, 1963:21). Sexual indulgence for 'mere pleasure' was strongly disapproved. All 'sexual excitment' should be controlled, and so permeated by guilt was the entire domain of sexual emotion, Cominos argues, that guilt spilled over to emotions generally, rendering them suspect. 'Reason and feeling were diametrically opposed . . .' (Cominos, 1963:25).

Sexual repression was thus intimately linked with the maintenance and enhancement of respectable status through sublimation in labour and accumulation. The shift in norms and values which accompanied the social and economic changes outlined earlier, was most pronounced in the area of sexual behaviour and attitudes. The widespread availability of effective contraceptive technology broke the vital link which buttressed a repressive Victorian morality by ending the almost inevitable correlation, between sexual indulgence and social and economic ruin, for the precariously balanced middle classes.

Sexual permissiveness thus represented one of the most fundamental challenges of new norms and values to traditional respectability, attacking a central, and a highly emotionally-charged, component.

The declining commitment displayed in the mass media, the courts, and the legislature to the respectable norm in the post-Second World War period, through acceptance of homosexuality, abortion, pre- and extra-marital sexual relations, and the wide public exposure of sexually exciting material, all indicated graphically the shift in dominant values away from those of the respectable middle classes. Sexual behaviour as it was displayed in a particularly influential mass medium which entered virtually every home, was therefore a particularly salient target for protest.

The other more peripheral norms against the public infraction of which the NVALA protested, similarly formed a part of the culture of the respectable middle classes. Patriotism, respect for motherhood, marriage as an institution, respect for authority and denominational Christianity, formed a syndrome of norms along with sobriety, thrift and punctuality which had a strong elective affinity for a class of entrepreneurs and their functionaries whose status was founded upon accumulation in a period of industrial development, nationalism and familism, and whose standards of morality and behaviour had become widely diffused as this class rose to a position of social dominance. Violence, to the portrayal of which on television (even in newsreels) NVALA also objects, can be seen as falling within this same syndrome. Violence represents an abnegation of the norms of restraint and self-control valued by the respectable middle class. It may represent the victory of spontaneity over planning; the desire for immediate gratification over deferred gratification; the triumph of ego-expressivity over conformity to bureaucratic rules; or of the search for excitement over subordination to routine and predictability; in short the victory of what Jock Young (1971) has called 'subterranean values' over 'formal work values'.

Developments in the NVALA

The NVALA has grown and undergone various developments during the course of its history, and the climate within which it exists has also changed. The moral ethos of British society has become slowly more permissive and thus increasingly divergent from the culture of the traditional entrepreneurial middle class. As 'respectable' culture has been increasingly challenged by these changes and its values have lost sway, so the appeal of cultural protest through the NVALA has increased, and with it the membership of the movement. But while the prevailing moral ethos has further isolated the NVALA, the mass media have become more accommodating toward it, and succeeding Directors-General of the BBC have sought to 'cool-out' the NVALA by adopting a less intransigent posture towards it than did Sir Hugh Carleton Greene. Mrs. Whitehouse is attended to by the media, and has become a public figure, even a media 'personality'. She is invited to universities to debate, appears on television regularly and her articles are solicited by popular magazines and prestigeous newspapers.

Perhaps in response to this increased respect accorded her, and certainly in order to facilitate her presentation of NVALA's views in such settings, Mrs. Whitehouse has resisted pressure by members to present a more fundamentalistic and more explicitly repressive content in her public pronouncements. Her speeches tend to express less hostility towards television today than in the earlier years of the movement, and Mrs. Whitehouse now admits that the Clean-Up TV Campaign was too sweeping in its denunciations of the BBC (Caulfield, 1976: Ch. 8).

At recent Conventions, representatives from the BBC and the IBA (Independent Broadcasting Authority), have attended and addressed the meeting. Their presence, particularly that of the BBC officials, represents a victory of recognition for Mrs. Whitehouse. For her followers present at the Convention, the availability of these television officials provides an unparallelled opportunity to arraign and criticise, forcing Mrs. Whitehouse to defend the representatives of the 'enemy' from her own followers. Mrs. Whitehouse has built up 'relationships and friendships with television people. When I began compaigning there was a great gap between me and the television people' (quoted in *Daily Mail,* 20 May, 1970). However, while the reduction of the gap between herself and television personnel can be deployed as part of the rhetoric of her success, it carries with it certain dangers.

In an increasingly alien cultural and moral environment, Mrs. Whitehouse's compromising approach carries the danger of alienating her more fundamentalistic followers. Currently her enormous prestige in the NVALA prevents any open conflict, but as the pressure on respectable norms increase, Mrs. Whitehouse may find the members are correlatively more inclined to challenge her position.

The trend towards greater sexual tolerance in the wider society also creates the problem of sustaining the credibility of NVALA's stance both internally and externally. Their response to this is to claim on the one hand that the shift in prevailing values and behaviour only *apparently* receives widespread acceptance. There is, they suggest, a vast 'silent majority' whose views they represent, and whom they strive to mobilise to more active opposition to the trend. On the other hand, in the face of evidence that contentious programmes such as 'That Was The Week That Was' and the early series of 'Till Death Us Do Part' had massive followings,* NVALA claims less to represent an appalled silent majority, and more to represent a group of people concerned to maintain higher standards, whose views are legitimated by transcendental imperatives, or by their role as interpreters and defenders of the cultural heritage which they claim is being eroded.

The failure of NVALA to secure a return of society to traditional values has led them to face threats to their culture on a widening front. One response to this has been for NVALA, on Mrs. Whitehouse's initiative, to expand the scope of its activities. She has observed that while her current involvements may seem a far cry from cleaning up TV, they are the necessary outcome of the increasing trend away from respectable values:

> . . . what is happening now is but the inevitable sequel to the denigration, the ridicule and the destruction of moral values which, in the sixties, so effectively prepared the ground for anarchy (Whitehouse, 1972:133-4).

Mrs. Whitehouse has become involved in recent years with other national movements for moral reform in Australia, New Zealand, the United States, Canada and in Europe. The changes in values experienced in Britain over recent decades are being experienced sooner or later, in every developed nation. The battle has become an international one, and NVALA and movements in other societies are combining to fight it more effectively in concert.

In Britain itself, Mrs. Whitehouse and her followers have increasingly directed their attention to the cinema and sex-education; and during the late 1960s and early 1970s they invested much energy in the wider field of pornography generally. As the dominant culture shifted further away from traditionally respectable morality, the NVALA has both broadened the focus of its crusade and shifted the nature of its demands from the *enforcement* of existing legislation, which they now recognise to be inadequate, to the *creation* of new, more effective legislation. After the appearance of the *Little Red School Book,* and the trial of those associated with the 'School Kids' issue of *Oz,* NVALA joined forces with the Festival of Light to launch a Petition for Public Decency 'calling upon the Government so to revise the Obscenity Laws that they become an effective and workable instrument for the maintenance of public decency' (Whitehouse, 1972:138). The Association has agitated in favour of the Indecent Displays Bill which a Conservative Government attempted to pass, but which was shelved after its electoral defeat. NVALA has sought to gain assurances from all major parties that the Bill would be proceeded with, but received these only from the Conservative Party.

Under adverse circumstances, maintenance of the faith of the movement's following becomes more problematic. While successful prosecutions of films, or their withdrawal, can be heralded as a victory, the loss of a legal action can still be seen as a 'moral victory' (*Viewer and Listener,* Summer 1974:1). The views of favourable television critics or public personalities can be reprinted in Mrs. Whitehouse's books or the movement's periodical, to indicate the success and influence of the movement and its message (*Viewer and Listener,* Summer 1974:3). Or again, the rhetorical constituency from which NVALA claims its mandate can be invoked:

> Mary Whitehouse pointed out that, as a result of experiences in obtaining signatures for the Petition for Public Decency, 'our impression is that we do in fact represent not a minority, but the "silent majority".' Eighty-five per cent of those approached, she said, did in fact support the Petition... (*Viewer and Listener,* Spring 1974:3).

Now, moreover, Mrs. Whitehouse can stress that National VALA has become part of an international movement, setting the reverses of the local scene in the context of a planetary battle against the forces of 'licence' and 'anarchy'.

In order to sustain such a position, however, it is vital that the Association be able to display a concrete increase in the support which its views receive. Hence, recruitment has come to be viewed as a prime imperative for NVALA, and members are encouraged to recruit as widely as possible. In 1970, a 'membership drive' was announced (*Viewer and Listener,* Summer 1970:2):

> To be effective, National VALA must be based on the steady support of ordinary people and their willingness to be active and vocal. . . . Nationwide extension of the work of National VALA, together with rising costs. will involve increased financial provision. . . . . The increase of income necessarily must come through increase in membership. . . . In order to increase membership every member needs to enlist at least one new member in the current year. *(Viewer and Listener,* Autumn 1970:4).

Conclusion

A moral reform movement, the National Viewers' and Listeners' Association has been described and features of its ideology, structure, tactics, and development have been analysed. The NVALA can be construed as a movement of cultural fundamentalism which seeks to reassert traditional values in the face of massive cultural change. Economic and social changes have eroded the supports for formerly dominant values borne by a class of individualistic enterpreneurs. This erosion has been more pronounced for some social categories than others. Due to their socialisation; their continuing dependency upon 'respectability' as part of the necessary conditions for maintaining a livelihood; their greater isolation or insulation; some social groups have proven resistant to new norms and values and their members are therefore mobilisable in the defence of the earlier standards of morality to which they still adhere.

Sexual permissiveness has been the most prominent feature of moral change and hence provides a ready focus for moral and cultural protest. Its visual presentation in the form of 'pornography' at first sight seems an unpromising object of reformist intervention. The consumption of visually erotic material can be construed as a victimless transaction (Duster, 1970), since the consumer is presumably in normal circumstances a willing party. The rhetoric of NVALA transforms the presentation of erotically stimulating material into a circumstance in which there is a victim, by protesting against the public visibility of pornography; designating the young as vulnerable and liable to corruption by it; and presenting themselves as the defenders of children, the unwitting shop-user, passer-by, or television viewer, rather than merely as representing their own interests and values.

The BBC as a former bastion of the respectable culture of the entrepreneurial middle class, became a particular target for such protest as it came increasingly to reflect the norms and values of contemporary consumption-oriented society and of newly prominent social groups; and was therefore seen to have deserted its traditional constituency. However, NVALA has been able to achieve little in reversing the prevailing cultural trend. It has rather found itself increasingly challenged, and in response has sought to counter-attack on a wider front. It has become involved in protest against 'pornography' in films, magazines, and in sex education, as well as on television, and now seeks new legislation rather than the enforcement of existing legislation.

The gradually increasing social tolerance displayed towards permissive sexuality has resulted in an increase in the membership of NVALA. At the same time, however, the movement and its founder have become increasingly accepted, resulting in some moderation of its public pronouncements on the evils of television. These circumstances may give rise to greater tensions within the movement, between a leadership forced to present its message in hostile, liberal, surroundings, and the more culturally fundamentalistic of its members urging for an unambiguous declaration of a belief in censorship as the solution to the contemporary 'moral crisis'.

* Fletcher (1970:89) found that on a week sampled in December 1968, between 40-50% of all TV sets in Britain, varying from region to region, were switched on to 'Till Death Us Do Part'.

CHAPTER VIII

'Goal displacement' and 'routinisation of charisma' in the Nationwide Festival of Light

Introduction

A characteristic mode of analysing social movements proposes that they arise on the basis of strains or relative deprivations experienced by a social constituency. Hence social movements are seen as providing explanations and remedies in the form of an ideology and goals which attract those experiencing the appropriate strain or deprivation (see Smelser, 1962; Aberle, 1966; Glock and Stark, 1965). Movement goals and ideology are construed as objective 'facts' against which changes in presentation and practice can be measured. In the initial stages of movement mobilisation the charisma of the leader is seen as a major factor, followed by institutionalisation and a shift to rational-legal forms of authority and administration.

This chapter explores the validity of this view in the context of a case-study of a British moral crusade, the Nationwide Festival of Light (NFOL). It aims to suggest that movement goals may be elaborated *in the process* of recruiting support rather than providing an unambiguous stimulus object which mobilises those appropriately frustrated, strained, or deprived; that the following of a social movement engages in selective perception and interpretation of a movement and its goals; and that the notion of a goal or goals for a social movement is a rhetorical device to which appeal can be made by different organisational leaders with different strategic aims, rather than a fixed point of analysis against which changes in state of the movement can be compared. The chapter also proposes that charismatic and rational-legal orientations may be *immanent tensions* within a social movement, rather than *sequential phases.*

Emergence of NFOL

The Nationwide Festival of Light developed from the inspiraton of a young evangelical Christian, Peter Hill, who returned on leave from several years of work distributing Christian literature in India. On public hoardings, in bookstalls, and in neighbourhood newsagents he found advertisements and magazines 'selling sex in a way that he thought four or five years ago would surely have been carefully hidden out of sight' (Capon, 1972:6). As he travelled around the country talking about his work in India, the state of Britain increasingly preoccupied him. Late in 1970, during a period of prayer and meditation 'he had a vision of tens of thousands of people many of them young, marching for Christ in London and "taking a stand for righteousness" . . . He felt that God might be calling him to take some part in a demonstration such as he had seen in the vision . . .' (Capon, 1972:8). His conviction that this was God's purpose was confirmed by a March of Witness organised by the Bishop of Blackburn, particularly when one of the leaders of a Prayer and Bible week conference he was attending at the time suggested that such a March of Witness should be held in London, with a rally at Trafalgar Square and Hyde Park. Thus the basic structure of the event was crystallised, a March of Witness; a rally in London; and a demonstration for 'righteousness'. But what Hill had largely formulated was a set of *means* with only the vaguest and most amorphous of goals (a 'stand for righteousness'). In the course of securing influential support for the demonstration, Hill's purpose was to be respecified by others in particular directions which followed their own interests and orientations. At the same time, the public presentation of the developing movement's goals would remain amorphous in order to incorporate under the same rubric groups and persons oriented to very different ends.

Hill began securing initial support in the same way that mass mobilisation would later follow. Both personal contacts and an 'organisational field' (Curtis and Zurcher, 1973) were utilised. Hill and his wife already had contact with a number of evangelicals. As a result of discussions with them he was also passed on to people prominent in protest against changes in public morality. The Reverend Eddy Stride, as well as being prominent

131

within the evangelical wing of the Church of England, had engaged in previous small-scale demonstrations against pornography and obscenity in films and the theatre. Stride provided an important component of the specification of the movement's aims by conceptualising it as a form of political protest. 'What Peter had no conception about . . . was the political thing . . . When he came to me, I said to him . . . this must be political. Peter had a vision, he saw people marching. He saw Jesus as the answer, but he didn't see anything political' (interview with Rev. E. Stride, February 1975). Stride put Hill in touch with Mary Whitehouse whose National Viewers' and Listeners' Association was already engaged in protest and lobbying activities in connection with sexual explicitness in the media. Mary Whitehouse provided other contacts later to play a major part in the movement. And it was one of these, Malcolm Muggeridge, who thought of the name Festival of Light for the movement.

There were, therefore, by this early stage in the mobilisation of support for the realisation of Hill's vision, two types of personnel with analytically distinct orientations. One orientation was that of evangelical Christians who saw the proposed activities as primarily a means of witness and evangelical revival. The other was that of the moral crusaders like Eddy Stride and Mary Whitehouse who saw the proposed activities as primarily a means of securing a renewed moral conscience in government and the mass media, together with changes in the law or its implementation.

> I think that Peter Hill and some others did see people marching for Christ as a Witness, and I think that was all fine. There were others of us who said: To march isn't sufficient. It's got to be a means to an end, not an end in itself (interview with Steve Stevens, March 1975).

In practice many of the early leaders, as well as the later followers, combined in varying proportions the two orientations. But the activity originally envisioned by Hill had now come to possess a dual purpose:

> Ever since Peter Hill's first contact with Eddy Stride and in all subsequent discussions with other people, the project had been thought of as having a twin purpose — to protest against 'sex-ploitation' in the media and the arts . . . and to proclaim the Christian Gospel as the positive answer to

132

it. It was natural that some of those present at the initial planning meeting were particularly concerned to make a civic and political protest against moral pollution, whilst others emphasised the potential for presenting the claims of Christ in an evangelistic context (Capon, 1972:13).

The demonstration was therefore planned to secure support as widely as possible by holding two separate rallies, one in Trafalgar Square oriented to the civic and political aims and another the same day in Hyde Park oriented to the evangelistic aim, both being linked by the March of Witness. The mobilisation of support also pursued this dual course. On the one hand through local NVALA followers, on the other through evangelical groups. Hill was, for example, able to interest the son of the late Tom Rees a well-known evangelist who had planned a massive campaign for the autumn of 1970 entitled Time for Truth (Capon 1972:15-16). He was given the mailing list of supporters for the Time for Truth campaign. The 'Statement of Intent' drawn up by the rapidly formed Executive Committee in 1971 also incorporated the now entrenched dual focus. This document displayed a sense among the Committee members that their culture was under attack: 'There is clear evidence that a determined assault is being made on family life, moral standards and decency in public entertainment and the mass media' (Statement of Intent). Existing institutional resources were failing effectively to resist this attack. 'There seems to be a reluctance in the government departments, the media and even in some church circles to affirm any absolute moral standard' (*ibid.*). And the Statement also clearly indicates that what was at issue was a cultural matter, the assimilation of new moral standards and forms of behaviour to the realm of acceptable public norms, rather than the existence of such activities *per se:* 'While filth has been portrayed in the past, it was done surreptitiously. Now it is being shown openly as being "normal".' The notion of 'moral pollution' which had appeared in nineteenth-century Evangelical thought (Trudgill 1976) was revived to describe the general area of changes in publicly presented depictions and writings which were seen as eroding and replacing traditional moral standards and attachments. The objects of NFOL were therefore listed as follows:

(a)   to alert and inform Christians and others like-minded to the dangers of moral pollution;
(b)   to translate into action the concern that hundreds of

thousands feel about the moral pollution in our nation today;

(c)   to register the support of people of goodwill for Christian moral standards in such a way that the national leadership is influenced;

(d)   to witness to the Good News about Jesus Christ.

While (a) and (b) are directed to alert a constituency to the dangers and mobilize them for action, (c) expresses an instrumental goal in producing effective changes in the policy of national leaders, and (d) expresses the evangelical commitment of a large section of NFOL's following.

The mobilisation of a following for the Festival took various forms. Hill began to build up a network of 'regional co-ordinators' throughout the country, whose role it was to secure local support, provide information, organise local events, and to seek to maintain the effort after the nationall rally. Hill obtained people for this task through his own contacts, and those of the Executive Committee, ramifying the movement's central dualism into its local organisation.

The widely differing perceptions of the movement at grass-roots level can be readily observed from the following quotations taken from interviews with local co-ordinators and followers.

The main object of it all was the evangelical side.

In the beginning the aim wasn't youth evangelism, but it just seemed to turn out that way.

In this area we were more concerned with moral pollution. . . I personally think the Festival should have carried on as it was doing, attacking the moral aspect all the time. . .'

The biggest aspect of the FOL was not so much its negative side but . . . (its role as) a positive movement for love, purity, that which is good in life . . .

While many followers and local organisations happily combined both aspects of the movement's rhetoric, in their activities they tended to emphasise one aspect more than another. Generally, this was the evangelistic orientation.

Apart from personal contact, followers were mobilised by more impersonal means which also followed the prevailing dualistic tendency. Volunteers distributed leaflets at the annual evangelical Keswick Convention. Leaflets were inserted in the organ of the Evangelical Alliance, *Crusade* magazine, in *Decision* the periodicial of the Billy Graham Evangelistic Association; and the rally was also promoted in the newsletter of the National Viewers' and Listeners' Association (*Viewer and Listener,* Summer 1971).

Early in September 1971 an inaugural rally for the Festival was held in London. There the dual focus was symbolised among the platform speakers by Malcom Muggeridge who had in pre-rally press interviews prophesied cultural doom and social collapse as a result of the 'present Gadarene slide into decadence and godlessness' (*The Times,* 12 July 1971), and Lonnie Frisbee representing the American Jesus People. Disruptive tactics by sectors of the underground — Gay Lib, Women's Lib, etc. — ensured, as had several years earlier been the case for NVALA, that the meeting received wide press coverage.

In the subsequent week beacons were lit at local rallies throughout the country, drawing symbolically upon the historic parallel of the warning beacons lit at the appearance of the Spanish Armada.

Support for these rallies, as for the major London rally later in the month, was mobilised by regional co-ordinators who typically drew upon existing organisational resources. Local ministers and leaders in the more evangelical denominations were approached for support (Baptists, Pentecostals, Plymouth Brethren); inter-denominational organisations, Christian women's and youth associations were circularised and mobilised.

On 25 September 1971 the national rally was held in London. In Trafalgar Square a crowd of perhaps as many as 30,000 was addressed by civic leaders and prominent personalities. Mary Whitehouse, Malcolm Muggeridge, MPs and peers had been secured to speak and addressed themselves primarily to the civic and political issues, castigating the established institutions for failure to provide moral leadership. Moral pollution presented a threat to mental health, family life, the dignity of man. The Churches, Government, and mass media were enjoined to mend their ways and take a firmer stand on sexual display, encouragement to permissive moral standards and violence.

About two-thirds of those present in the Square were under twenty-five years of age, and while the platform speakers inveighed against the civic and political problem, a large proportion of the audience seemed engaged in an expressive demonstration of solidarity, singing, chanting Hallelujah and shouting 'J-E-S-U-S, Jesus!' (Capon 1972:76). The rally then marched to Hyde Park where an unambiguously revivalist Gospel meeting had been arranged. The platform speakers, notable among them the American evangelist Arthur Blessitt, were all evangelicals. The music was provided by popular Christian singers like Cliff Richard and Jesus music groups. The performers and speakers were all young. The talk was of Jesus, Christ, the Holy Spirit, repentance and conversion, rather than of 'moral pollution'.

Goal displacement and routinisation?

The 25 September rally was the culmination of Peter Hill's vision. God's message revealed through an individual particularly sensitive to His call and to the state of the nation had been charismatically realised in a mass demonstration of enthusiasm, solidarity and protest. This, on the face of things, should have been the end of the matter. But as theories of movement transformation would predict, the Nationwide Festival of Light did not cease operation at that point.

The classic statement of the theory of goal displacement is to be found in Sheldon Messinger's (1955) study of the Townsend Movement. Originally organised to promote a specific programme of improvements in welfare benefits and pensions for the aged, the movement found its goals progressively undermined by State and federal initiatives in improving conditions for the elderly, and by the adoption of the less idiosyncratic parts of its programme by other organisations. The leadership responded to the movement's declining impetus by progressively introducing entirely new goals, particularly the provision of consumer commodities aimed at the elderly, and the promotion of recreational activities for the elderly at its local facilities. Here the movement is seen as having undergone a process of 'goal succession' where one set of specific goals is replaced by some other set of specific goals. A further process is that of 'goal diffusion'. After a movement achieves one set of goals, new ones are introduced which are still largely in line with its original 'charter' but involve a broader range of targets. The National Polio Foundation was set up to secure financial support for research into a cure or prophylaxis for poliomielytis. After the succes of the Salk vaccine, the Foundation, which had developed an elaborate bureaucracy and machinery for charity promotion and collection, found itself with nothing to do. Rather than disband, the leadership changed the organisation's name to the National Foundation and reoriented it as a less specific agency for the mobilisation of charity. A similar process has been described for the YMCA (Zald, 1970). The third type of change in goals is that of 'goal-extension', where the short-term programme of a movement is gradually extended temporally and expanded programmatically in response to the success of earlier goals. The Festival of Light would seem to fit into this category, since following the London rally, a further and broader programme of activities was introduced. The development of the NFOL would therefore seem to follow one of the classic patterns of goal displacement, and Wallis (1972) presents an analysis of NFOL following this model. The explanation of these processes is usually held to lie in the development within the movement of a leadership cadre or body of officials with vested interests in the maintenance of the organisation or movement structure, who seek to adapt the organisation to ensure its survival, and the maintenance of their interests. The movement is seen as recapitulating in modified form Michels's (1958) 'Iron Law of Oligrachy'.

On this account, movements and their organisations are seen as possessing clearly visible 'charter' goals which are adapted or supplanted as the movement develops a structure operated in a rationalistic way. Charisma is routinised and rational stragegy replaces utopian aspiration. An analysis of the NFOL suggests that this theory may only be viable if the movement, and particularly the operation of its leadership are viewed at a distance. A closer inspection may reveal that while there is a broad acceptance of the denotation of the movement's official statement of its goals, the connotation of that statement may convey very different things to different people. The differences in interpretation which may arise, form the basis for ongoing negotiation and debate about the direction and purpose of the movement, and in some cases, for overt conflict, factionalism, or schism. Viewed in this light it is less evident that there exists any 'real' movement goal at the outset, which is subsequently transformed. Rather changes in movement policy and practice reflect the shifting balance in the power, influence, or activism, of factions or looser groupings differing in the connotative interpretation of the movement's aims and means.

In the Festival of Light, the evidence does not indicate any clear factions informally organising to produce particular shifts in the direction of the movement. There are, however, signs that some leaders of the NFOL, particularly those whose interpretation of its purpose was more civic-political, had a more rationalistic conception of its structure and duration, in contrast to the charismatic conception of a unique event of witnessing. Eddy Stride, who had earlier engaged in anti-pornography demonstrations and in Church work related to trade unions, had in the July preceeding the rally, raised the issue of what should happen thereafter (Capon, 1972:32). Although it was agreed that a 'follow-up' committee should be formed nothing seems to have been done to implement the idea.

It was not until after seeing the success of the London rally and because of requests from churches and Christians 'throughout the country' (Capon, 1972:127; Dobbie, 1972:125) that the Executive Committee felt that God had called them to continue for another year. Some limited formalisation of the movement organisation occurred when Peter Hill and a man who had been very active in assisting him, Steve Stevens, were appointed honorary secretaries. Copies of the proclamation read in Trafalgar Square were distributed, and smaller rallies were held in the north of England, and in Scotland later in 1971. With the decision to continue for another year the tension between evangelical and civic-political orientations, charisma and rationality, became more pressing. The evangelistic interpretation largely prevailed during 1972 with the bulk of NFOL's efforts going into a London Festival for Jesus. This five-day Festival was an explicitly revivalist enterprise. Young Christians were to be encouraged to witness to their faith by morning 'teach-in' sessions on Jesus' place in contemporary life, and 'training in gospel outreach' An introductory leaflet described it as follows:

> *Objective and method* of the Festival for Jesus is that it shall be in the open air, where thousands can be invited to come freely to listen to music, song, testimony and message. Special meetings will be held where Christians and new converts can be instructed. . . .

> Thousands are converging on London with smiles, T-shirts, 'God loves you'! banners, hallelujahs, sleeping bags, stickers, laughter, bibles, guitars, and prayer.

One afternoon in the Festival for Jesus was devoted to a symbolic dramatisation of the threat to Britain and the need for a 'miracle of deliverance' by a demonstration in a parade of boats up the Thames, referred to as 'Dunkirk Miracle '72'. But the orientation of the event was evangelistic and revivalistic in character, although perhaps inevitably, in a secular society involvement in the activities was largely restricted to the already converted, and succeeded in heightening commitment and reaffirming solidarity, rather than leading to extensive proselytisation in any systematic way. This aspect of the movement continued to draw upon the imagery of the Jesus People in seeking to awaken a more vigorous enthusiasm in young Christians.

But while all the Executive Committee and a substantial proportion of the following were probably committed to revival as the ultimate solution to the nation's problems, this was not the priority all saw as important for NFOL to pursue.

> There was no tension over pornography. We were all agreed about pornography. But there was tension, certainly, about the emphasis we were going to put in our actual activities, and I said a number of times in the committee: If this is simply an evangelistic agency, I have no part of it, because we have the Movement for World Evangelisation, we have the Billy Graham Association, we have the Eric Hutchings set-up, we have the Don Summers set-up. We have tons of people doing the evangelism thing, and I'm not going to be party to having another one doing it. . . . As far as I'm concerned, while it evangelises, it's here to make this *social* witness, and if it isn't, I'm not part of it . . .

> To be quite honest, I was personally not happy with the Jesus Festivals the following year. I felt this would take us off what I believed the Festival of Light had to do. . . I felt we were getting off the nitty gritty of tackling the brutalising of the culture . . . (interview with Rev. E. Stride, February 1975).

During 1972 the civic-political reformist orientation took a subordinate part, but was displayed in 'Operation Newsagent' which sought to mobilise supporters to visit local newsagents and encourage them to examine the more titillating and sexually explicit literature which they were selling, and to cease purveying it. In collaboration with Mary Whitehouse's National Viewers' and Listeners' Association, supporters were also urged to collect signatures for a 'Petition for Public Decency' which demanded firmer anti-pornography legislation and tighter control over radio and television and sex education.

Again in 1973, the emphasis was primarily evangelistic. While still urging supporters to protest personally and by letter to MPs, local councils, the Home Office, etc., about pornographic magazines, or obscene or violent films, NFOL effort was largely directed during 1973 into providing support for a rally organised by the Billy Graham Evangelistic Association, called 'Spree 73'.

But throughout 1972 and 1973, there seemed to be a lack of impetus and direction in the movement. Apart from the 1972 'Festival for Jesus' and 'Spree 73' and exhortation to supporters to make individual protests, little attempt was made to mobilise or organise the following of the movement. One provincial Regional Co-ordinator complained that during 1973 the co-ordinators found little coming out from headquarters. 'They let it all flop. By the time they turned again to moral matters, the following had been lost' (interview, 1976). Circulars were sent out occasionally and these made oblique reference to the apparent loss of interest. A 'Broadsheet' in June 1973 urged supporters to 'break your silence and let us know what you have been doing in your area!' It also referred to the fact that 'there have been very few donations the past few months'. While the evangelistic orientation had prevailed, it was not clear to those who fostered it what could be done next with a movement of this kind. As one leader put it to me, 'We couldn't go on having Festivals for ever'. The evangelists sought to mobilise enthusiasm, to display the fervour of their faith, to secure converts, and to heighten the intensity of their own religious commitment. But since this programme was fundamentally charismatic in character and organisation, being led as the Holy Spirit directed, it became incongruous that such charismatic enthusiasm should be programmed annually, scheduled and organised; that indeed, it should become routinised. Continual repetition of the Festival/Jesus rally, style of activity threatened to undermine the charismatic legitimation which gave it force and purpose. Enthusiasm of the evangelical variety is not readily amenable to institutionalisation and regular periodical display. It tends, as in the denominationalisation of conversionist sects (Wilson, 1959a), to become accommodated to the more routinised forms of worship of the established denominations — whose lack of evangelical fervour NFOL was in fact protesting — to lose its enthusiasm, and hence to become less convincingly sincere because it has to be generated to order.

The evangelical enthusiasts therefore seemed to lose interest or at least to wane from their earlier height of commitment to NFOL as a vehicle for national revival. Peter Hill became more fully committed to work with the charismatic House Fellowships, and the local organisers of evangelical inclination were being attracted to less ambiguously revivalistic enterprises such as the 'Jesus musical' *Come Together* which could convey the conversionist message with greater impact and immediacy for the young. The youthful following of NFOL, attracted by the Jesus People imagery and enthusiasm found protest meetings, lobbying and pressurising local newsagents lacking in appeal. The evangelical enthusiasts lacked patience with the slow, long-term instrumentalism necessary for the pursuit of social-moralistic goals through pressure on legal institutions and agencies. The tactics associated with this orientation did not receive very great support at rank and file level. Followers were not so eager to go round newsagents bringing pressure to bear to cease display of erotic material, or to gather signatures for a petition for greater legal control, as they were to engage in collective witness to their Christian faith. Such activities provided no occasions for collective expression of commitment, the reaffirmation and reawakening of solidarity, or the emotional context for the saving of souls. At both leadership and grass-roots levels, therefore, interest and activism waned.

In this context, the field seems to have been more open for the civic-politically oriented leaders to influence the direction of the movement's development. Early in 1974, Raymond Johnston, a former University lecturer was appointed Director of NFOL, his salary for a period of three years having been covenanted by a group of supporters. Steve Stevens became General Secretary, and subsequently an Assistant Secretary was appointed.

Mr. Johnston's style of leadership was altogether different from that of Peter Hill. While committed to the view that religious revival was vital for Britain's moral and social future he did not view the Festival of Light as appropriate to that role. An organisation was needed to concentrate specifically on combating the erosion of moral standards through patient and arduous collation of evidence, and the presentation of that evidence and the NFOL point of view in long-term lobbying activity directed at influentials like Church leaders, MPs, ministers and media officials, rather than through the periodic mobilisation of mass demonstrations. Through memoranda and submissions to committees on broadcasting, films and legal reform, as well as through debate in the press and personal contacts, Johnston sought to represent the views of Christians committed to an absolute stand on matters of morals. The only demonstration held between 'Spree 73', and the rally again in Trafalgar Square in September 1976, on NFOL's fifth anniversary, was a small-scale demonstration of about 100 people outside the offices of the Greater London Council during a debate on the abolition of control over films displayed in the London area.

While concentrating its efforts on moral reform rather than evangelism, the NFOL expanded its brief by broadening the range of moral issues concerned. Initially the movement had concentrated on the display of 'pornographic' magazines in newsagents. Under the influence of Mary Whitehouse, it had become associated with the NVALA-initiated 'Petition for Public Decency'. One of its leaders, Peter Thompson, had long been concerned with obscenity and violence in films, and ensured a vigorous level of publicity in this area. Later, the NFOL issued pronouncements on the resignation of two Government Ministers for their revealed liaisons with call-girls, and on homosexuality, abortion, euthanasia and religious education.

Out of the vague and amorphous imagery of Peter Hill's vision had developed a movement which recruited persons who could conceptualise this vision in terms of evangelistic revival based on inspirational demonstrations which would both witness to the world and heighten personal commitment. It had also recruited persons who while often of evangelical persuasion were anxious to pursue a strategy of long-term legal reform and enforcement in connection with matters of morality. The movement could have disappeared after the 1971 London rally, but while it continued and managed to retain both charismatic and rational-legal orientations among its leadership cadres, it was almost inevitable that institutionalisation of the movement would draw it towards emphasis on moral lobbying. Those who supported this approach had been much more prepared from the outset for a lengthy battle against 'moral pollution' and for the slow, painstaking process of accumulating evidence, engaging in negotiation with bureaucratic agencies, and pressure-group politics. The evangelists more clearly had a picture of the Festival as a 'one-off' event of witness and reaffirmation and when drawn into prolonged activity continued to view it in terms of spontaneous revivalism. As the revival rallies began to become ritualistic and repetitive, they proceeded to invest their energies in more experiental forms of witness, vacating the NFOL programme for the rational-legal strategies of the moral reformers. Charisma and rationality were co-existent tensions in the NFOL rather than sequential phases. Charisma was not routinised into rational-legal organisation. In the face of the possibility of routinisation, the charismatically-inclined tended, *particularly* at national leadership level, to abandon or lower their commitment to NFOL, permitting the rational legal orientation greater scope for developing its own strategy and formalising that strategy through the appointment of a small staff of professional officials.

Similarly, the goals of the movement were also not displaced from 'utopian' to 'accommodation' or 'organisational-maintenance' aims. Rather the 'goals' of the movement were an amorphous rhetorical device interpreted and deployed by leaders in different ways. While the evangelistic orientation exercised the greatest influence under Peter Hill's leadership, this interpretation took an evangelical-revivalist form. As the evangelists were faced by the dilemma of routinisation and lowered their activism, so the civic-political orientation vested the movement's goals with a connotation more suitable to their own aims and strategies.

Conclusions

This chapter has suggested that analyses of social movements conducted at a distance from the 'action' may lead to the glossing of internal processes and differentiations which are always present, as distinctively different stages. Charisma and rationality may be co-existent tensions rather than sequential phases in movement leadership and, indeed, rather than charisma becoming routinised and giving way to rational-legal administration, the case of NFOL suggests that rational-legal administration may come to predominate as the charismatic leadership vacates the direction of the movement in the face of threatened routinisation.

The notion of 'movement goals' which come to be 'displaced' has been a prominent model in the analysis of social movements. Analysis of the NFOL suggests that the notion of movement goals is a rhetorical device, providing a sense of unity and continuity to the differing aims of groups and persons who seek their realisation through the agency of the social movement. The rhetoric deployed in statements of movement goals provides a resource which can be mobilised by participants in the pursuit of their own purposes, and is interpreted differentially by participants.

Thus the sequence typically suggested in analyses of social movements, whereby strains or deprivations are experienced, explanations and remedies formulated, and a following mobilised by unambiguous movement ideology and goals, glosses vital processes. Statements of 'movement goals' and strategy are first formulated *in interaction* with initial recruits. The aims and purposes proposed for the NFOL initially were of the vaguest and most amorphous kind, and were respecified in interaction with persons who sought to utilise them in a fashion very different from the original intentions of the movement's founder. Even then, they were differentially and selectively perceived by later recruits, in line with their own aims and interests.

CHAPTER IX

They rallied to the call (with Richard Bland)

In this chapter we report the methods and findings of a survey of participants in a rally held by the Nationwide Festival of Light in London, five years after its inaugural rally.

The Rally

Observation of the movement prior to the 1976 rally had led then to the view that NFOL had emerged with a dual orientation but that since its early years it had moved increasingly towards a focus on civic-political goals directed towards the implementation of stronger formal social controls, based around a moralistic message, rather than evangelistic goals. NFOL's public pronouncements were increasingly explicit in their focus on opposition not only to pornography, but also to abortion and legal permissiveness in respect of homosexuality. This impression was strengthened by the nature of the publicity for, and the content of, the anniversary rally held five years after NFOL's first rally — on 25 September 1976.

The broadsheets circulated to followers and sympathisers quoted Solzhenitsyn's polemics in drawing a picture of Britain stressing the 'dwindling of our freedoms and a deep moral decline', and the consequent potential 'for collapse and take-over by the well-armed, ever-expanding imperialism of Soviet Russia'. The pre-eminent message of the rally was to be a reiteration of the Ten Commandments, and 'the standard of the Word of God which is the final arbiter. The Festival of Light, a non-political body, stands for those clear values given in Scripture which it is the Church's task to announce as God's will for men in society'.

God has provided His law and the two basic community structures of civil society — the family and the State — to restrain sinfulness of all kinds, including propaganda for perversion, and to guide men into ways of happiness and fulfilment in society (all quotations, unless otherwise indicated, are from NFOL's *Summer Broadsheet,* 1976).

A leaflet handed to participants in the rally specified as the first item in a 'Declaration' to be made by the rally:

Moral law and man-made law must be rooted in God's Law, the heart of which we recognise in the Ten Commandments. Law protects, law sets standards. Law shapes behaviour. Good laws protect men and their neighbours from violence, corruption and exploitation. Unjust laws drive people apart.
We declare our dependence upon God in Government and Law.

This theme was elaborated in speeches from the platform during the rally:

The first speaker was Mr. Ian Percival, QC, MP for Southport, who reminded the meeting that we need rules to prevent us being blown off course and harming others as well as ourselves. This needed to be said because many people were deliberately rejecting all moral guidelines, including the Ten Commandments (NFOL, *Autumn Broadsheet,* 1976).

A Swedish pastor referred to his own country where 'every part of the Ten Commandments has been attacked by a law which has legalised what the Word of God calls sin and transgression' (*ibid.*). Other speakers deplored the desertion of a firm traditional moral stand by national leaders:

The real trouble is that so many of our leaders in national life have either grown timid in the face of the corrupting influence of pornography, violence and greed, or do not even recognise that a problem exists (speech of Sir Bernard Braine, MP, as reported in *ibid.*).

The amount of rhetorical attention given to conversion and saving souls was negligible in comparison with the attention given to morality, secular law and God's law.

A major question of interest to us, therefore, was the extent to which involvement in the rally reflected the civic-political

146

and moral protest direction which the movement had taken. Our hypothesis was that we would find two distinct orientations among participants deriving from an earlier dualistic pattern of recruitment and continued dualistic pattern of mobilisation. However, we had expected that due to the shift away from evangelistic goals, this orientation would be less evident among participants than a civil-political orientation. In this latter expectation we were quite mistaken.

Method

A questionnaire was designed (included as Appendix A) which aimed to generate information of a sociographic kind on rally-participating supporters of NFOL, and to investigate (a) whether supporters were primarily engaged in an expressive activity or an instrumental one; and (b) whether participation could be explained in terms of a desire to defend the *threatened status* of those mobilised. If they were not expressively oriented what were the instrumental ends they sought, and if they were not motivated by a concern with status defence, by what were they motivated?

Two thousand and thirty questionnaires were prepared in the form of two single-sided foolscap sheets stapled together with a covering letter from the Director of NFOL and attached to a stamped, addressed return envelope.

Distribution was, of course, a major problem of method. No conventional random sampling procedure was practical in the circumstances of the rally. Nor, by the same token, could complex quota sampling be employed in the absence of prior demographic and other relevant information. The investigators were thus faced with the problems of how to distribute the questionnaire, and of how to minimise sampling bias. Distribution during the course of the rally was ruled out by the organisers and by the likely density of people in the Square particularly in proximity to the platform. On practical grounds, then, a strategy was devised to distribute the questionnaires as participants entered the Square for the rally, and as they departed thereafter. Seven distributors were positioned at entry points to the Square. They took up their positions at 12.30 p.m., each with three marked bundles containing respectively 40, 60 and 90 protocols each. They were instructed to distribute the first bundle between 12.30 and 1.00 p.m.; the second between 1.00 p.m. and 1.30 p.m.; and the third between

1.30 and 2.00 p.m. This stragegy was predicated on the assumption that the flow into the Square would increase with proximity to the rally's starting time at 2.00 p.m. Distributors were instructed to adopt a self-correcting distribution policy, distributing initially during each time-zone on the basis of an arbitrary number of entrants, then increasing or decreasing that number if the half-hour's protocols were going too fast or too slowly. They were warned against picking any particular kinds of people, but were required to ask the individual selected 'Are you going to the rally?' to eliminate casual travellers across the Square, tourists, etc. At the conclusion of the rally, distributors again took up position with a further 100 protocols each which they handed out a people left. The departure rate was so rapid that no particular policy of distribution could be effectively and consistently followed. All questionnaires were distributed.

Attendance at the rally has been variably estimated. The Director of NFOL suggested an attendance of 20,000, the *Sunday Times* only 8000. Our own estimate falls between the two at approximately 12,000 persons. 2030 questionnaires were distributed, or to approximately one in every six participants. About 20-25 refusals were met with. Most people seemed happy to take the questionnaire just as they took the various other NFOL and other leaflets and programmes proffered to them.

Respondents were instructed to complete the questionnaire at their leisure and to return it in the stamped, addressed envelope supplied. January 2 was arbitrarily chosen as the cut-off point for receipt of returns since their number by that stage (1106) did not merit further delay in the analysis. This gave a return rate of 54·5% of questionnaires distributed. A further six questionnaires were returned thereafter but not included in the analysis. 96% of the returns were received during the first five weeks after the rally. A further nine weeks were required to produce the final 4% of returns.

The completed questionnaires were coded and the data transferred to punched card. The resultant data set was screened for errors and inconsistencies introduced by coding and punching, using the DATA CLEAN program (Bland, 1976).

1. Main characteristics of respondents

We here briefly summarise the main characteristics of the respondents. Our first question was directed to discovering the prior active participation in NFOL of the participants in this rally. Prior active participation was defined in terms of five national events which NFOL had organised or to which it had lent its support:

(i) The inaugural rally in Trafalgar Square and Hyde Park held in 1971.

(ii) A Festival for Jesus, and a symbolic parade up the Thames, with associated meetings in 1972, known as the 'Dunkirk Miracle'.

(iii) The collection of signatures for a Petition for Public Decency in association with the National Viewers' and Listeners' Association in 1972.

(iv) Operation Newsagent, a campaign in association with NVALA to persuade newsagents not to stock magazines regarded as pornographic, also conducted in 1972.

(v) Spree 73, an evangelistic campaign organised by the Billy Graham Evangelistic Association in 1973.

Table 1 shows the proportion of respondents who had engaged in each of these events.

Table 1 *Prior participation in NFOL Activities*

	Activity	%
(i)	1971 Rally	25·7
(ii)	1972 Festival and Dunkirk Miracle	10·0
(iii)	Petition 1972	14·9
(iv)	Operation Newsagent 1972	3·9
(v)	Spree 1973	15.9

We concluded from this table that prior active participation had been greatest in events which were presented as primarily evangelistic in purpose, and provided occasions of a collective kind for affirming and reinvigorating Christian commitments. Activities of a civic-political kind directed to some moral rather than evangelistic end were less well supported. This is particularly evident in the case of Operation Newsagent which required personal and individual confrontation with shop managers and owners in an effort to persuade them, or to monitor their sales. The high rate of participation in collecting signatures for the Petition for Public Decency can be accounted for, we believe, by the fact that such collection could often be conducted among a sympathetic audience through Church-related organisations. We also computed the proportions of respondents who had engaged in one or more of the above events, and found that 56·0% had not participated in *any* of these activities. Hence 44·0% had been involved with at least one prior activity, but only 21·9% had been active in two or more.

Our second question was directed to discovering the referral route by which participants had been mobilised to take some part in the 1976 rally. This question proved to be inadequately sensitive to the complexities of the circumstances in which individuals were mobilised to attend the rally. Overall, however, it is quite evident that participants were mobilised primarily on the basis of pre-existing associational affiliations.

Respondents were evenly divided between the sexes with, surprisingly, a slight over-representation of men. Of the 1102 responses 53.6% were male, 46.4% were female. Their marital status is shown in Table 2.

Table 2 *Marital status of rally respondents*

Status	%
Single	59·4
Married	35·7
Widowed	2·5
Divorced/separated	2·5
Total	100·1

n = 1102 (4 responses uncodable)

30·8% were found to have one or more children. The age distribution of respondents is shown in Figure 1. We were surprised to find a relatively low proportion of middle-aged and elderly persons in our sample. The modal age-group was between 16-20 years and 74·3% of respondents were found to be under 40 years of age. It may be surmised that younger supporters of NFOL would be more likely to attend a rally in London which would involve standing in Trafalgar Square for 2-3 hours, than its older supporters. Hence, on this ground it is probable that the data collected is disproportionately biased towards the views of NFOL's more youthful supporters.

The denominational affiliation of respondents was requested.

Figure 1 *Age distribution of respondents in five-year bands*

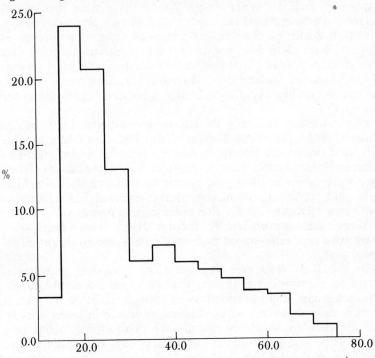

Respondents not infrequently listed more than one attachment and the 1193 responses were found to be distributed as follows:

Table 3 *Denominational attachments of rally respondents*

	Denomination	n	%
(i)	Church of England	502	42·1
(ii)	Baptist	260	21·8
(iii)	Pentecostal churches and House Fellowships	108	9·1
(iv)	Interdenominational (including 'None' or Missing)	75	6·2
(v)	Evangelical/Free Evangelical	67	5·6
(vi)	Methodist	62	5·2
(vii)	Catholic	40	3·4
(viii)	Brethren	37	3·1

151

No other single denomination secured more than 1% of the responses, and the remaining 3·5% of these were distributed among Congregationalists (*n*=8); United Reform (*n*=9); Salvation Army (*n*=9); and a number of other denominations scoring fewer than five responses each: Church of Christ (2); Church of Scotland (3); London City Mission (2); Presbyterian (3); Church of Ireland (1); Mormon (1); Unity (1); Philanthropic Assembly (1); Seventh-Day Adventist (1); Community Church (1).

Participants in the rally then were drawn primarily from the Church of England and Baptist Churches. Respondents who indicated no attachment or simply wrote in 'Christian', or 'All', indicated elsewhere a high level of church attendance. Hence they were taken as having no *particular* denominational affiliation, and as seeing themselves self-consciously as Christians *tout court* rather than denominational members. It was therefore felt appropriate to include these respondents with those who *explicitly* stated membership in some *inter*denominational body.

Of the 1097 responses to a question on church attendance, *only one* respondent indicated that he never attended church. An amazingly high proportion of 96·4% claimed to attend church at least once a week, and many wrote in comments to indicate that, in fact, they attended church far more often than that. The occupational circumstances of respondents are indicated in Table 4:

Table 4 *Occupational circumstances of respondents*

	%
Full-time employed	54·8
Student (including school)	25·8
Housewife	11·6
Retired	4·4
Unemployed	2·8
Other/Uncodable	0·6
	100·0

n = 1106

Given the age distribution of respondents it is not altogether surprising that over one-quarter should be students. As can be seen from Table 5, the classification of the occupations of the employed (plus father's occupation of students, husband's occupation of housewives, and last occupation of retired) shows the respondents to be overwhelmingly located in the non-manual sectors of society. 78·8% of those who responded to the occupational questions were associated with non-manual occupations.

Table 5 *Respondents' distribution by Registrar-General's Social Classes*

Class	%
RG I	21·5
RG II	40·7
RG III Non-manual	16·6
RG III Manual	10·5
RG IV	5·3
RG V	1·1
Services	1·0
Unemployed	3·3
	100·0

n = 1056 (60 uncodable)

By this criterion then, participants in the rally were overwhelmingly middle class. A further indication of the types of occupation found can be gained from noting that 37·5% of the quoted occupations fell into Occupational Order 25 — Professional and Technical Workers and Artists. These included 21 Doctors; 59 Nurses; 140 School, College and University Teachers; 18 Accountants; 73 Clergymen; and 17 Social Workers.

The 283 students in the sample were largely composed of school children (46·3%) and university students (25·1%), with others attending teacher training colleges, polytechnics, etc. 27·9% were still engaged in full-time education. Of those who had completed their full-time education, only 36·3% had done so before the age of 17. Hence, bearing out what is shown by the distribution by Registrar-General's Social Class, the respondents were clearly above average in the length of their education.

To gain some indication of whether respondents came from Christian homes, they were asked to indicate whether or not their parents were 'regular church attenders'. As can be seen from Table 6, a high proportion (64%) had at least one parent

153

who was a regular church attender, and almost half had parents both of whom regularly attended church.

Table 6 *Regular Church attendance of respondents' parents*

Parent	%
Neither parent	36·0
Mother alone	14·0
Father alone	2·0
Both	48·0
	100·00

n = 1030 (76 uncodable)

Status defence, expressive politics, and assimilative and coercive reform explanations of moral crusades

Further areas investigated were the motivations of respondents for participation in the rally; their response to the possibility that no concrete changes might result from it; and the priority that they placed upon *evangelism* rather than more effective *legislation* for reversing the 'moral decline of Britain'.

Status defence

Participants were asked to rank five statements purporting to be reasons for attending the rally in the order in which they most nearly reflected the respondent's own feelings. The statements were designed to signify five types of motivation.

(i) *Evangelistic* was designed to typify motivation primarily directed towards evangelising others, and spreading the 'Good News' of Christ.

(ii) *Moral Protest* was designed to typify motivation primarily directed towards protesting against changing moral standards.

(iii) *Legalistic* was designed to typify motivation primarily directed towards securing legal repression of what participants viewed as immorality.

(iv) *Status Protest* was designed to typify motivation primarily directed towards protesting against the loss of status experienced as a result of moral change.

154

(v) *Solidaristic* was designed to typify motivation primarily directed towards showing, and experiencing, the solidarity of Christians and an assertion of their right to a respected opinion.

Table 7 *Reasons for attending the rally given first ranking*

Reasons		Ranking	% who gave 1st ranking
(i)	Evangelistic:	To witness publicly to my Christian faith in the hope of bringing others to Christ	41·3
(ii)	Moral Protest:	To protest against the continuing moral decline of Britain	20·2
(iii)	Legalistic:	To secure more effective legislation against immorality	3·5
(iv)	Status Defence:	To protest against the loss of respect and esteem shown to people who live a respectable life	1·7
(v)	Solidaristic:	To join with others in showing that there are still many Christians in Britain and that they have a voice	40·7

(As '1st equal' was a possible ranking, the percentages sum to more than 100).

Joseph Gusfield (1963), and Zurcher and Kirkpatrick (1976) have argued that the motivation to engage in a moral crusade derives from the status situation of the crusaders. We presented earlier a critique of the 'status defence' theory which we believe to suffer many conceptual difficulties. In our view the language of 'status defence' is entirely misleading for many, perhaps most, moral crusades, in which a concern with *status* — the defence of a differentially evaluated position of social honour — is evident only in the mind of the researcher rather than the participant.

Our findings evidently belie any simple 'status defence' theory of motivation in moral crusades. The first preferences of respondents show a *marked* disinclination to select the status defence reason as a description of their motivation for participation. It might, of course, be said that the respondents were, in fact, dissembling; that status defence is a reason which would not receive general approbation; and that it was therefore avoided in the selection of first rankings. But even considering rankings as second, third, or fourth most important reasons, 'status defence' emerges as *clearly the least* important for our sample as a whole. If it played any significant part in motivating active support for the rally, one might have expected some reason considered morally more legitimate to be selected for first ranking, and for 'status defence' to figure prominently in second or third place. In actuality, it is ranked as of least significance and indeed nearly 40% of our respondents gave it a zero ranking which we provided to indicate that any statement offered 'has no relationship to your own feelings'. Proponents of the theory of status defence must, if they are to convince us of its validity, provide some alternative means of locating a form of motivation which makes no appearance in the movement's literature, and which is ranked as the very last consideration by participants.

We sought to determine whether the small number of respondents who gave a first ranking to the 'Status Protest' reason for attending the rally could be differentiated in biographical terms from other participants. No association was found between first ranking on 'Status Protest' and Registrar-General's Social Class or age. An effect on Age at End of Education did, however, seem to be present: the 15 respondents who gave first ranking (and for whom we have education data) had, on average, two years less education than the mean, and the 405 who dismissed it as irrelevant (by responding 'O') had almost one year more. The retired, too, had a greater preference for this category than did the sample as a whole. These findings are not inconsistent with the theory of status protest presented by Zurcher and Kirkpatrick (1976). However, the small number of respondents involved is a clear indication of the irrelevance of status considerations for the overwhelming majority of our sample.

The distribution of first rankings of reasons for attending suggest that the principal motivations for participation were evangelistic in orientation, concerned with the conversion of non-believers rather than their coercion into conformity with standards of respectable behaviour. The assertion of a Christian presence in the public debate concerning morality, or the collective reaffirmation of Christian commitments appears to have been a source of an almost equally large proportion of choices. The position of 'Moral Protest' as third in significance suggests that participants' motivations for participation displayed a substantial divergence from the leaders' principal

156

concerns as exhibited in the publicity material and the speeches from the platform. This is further supported by the *very* low proportion who defined their reason for attending in 'legalistic' terms.

Symbolic crusades as expressive politics

Frank Parkin (1968) has proposed that social movements which emerge to fight for ends of a *symbolic* or diffuse value kind, rather than for specific concrete increments in material benefits or political power, can be viewed as a form of *expressive* activity in which the end lies in the activity itself, rather than in the successful attainment of some *instrumental* goal. This distinction is not altogether as clear as it may at first appear, since there is no obvious reason why 'benefits and satisfactions which the activity itself affords' (Parkin, 1968:34) should not be found in a movement pursuing specific, concrete, material goals; nor why 'activity . . . directly geared to the attainment of concrete and specific goals' (*ibid.*) should not have a non-material end in view. There is often a tendency among materialist and positivist sociologists to define the instrumental (and the 'rational') in rather narrow terms under which only economic and power goals are likely to fall.

In examining this issue in the context of the Campaign for Nuclear Disarmament, Parkin asked his respondents if they agreed or disagreed with the statement: 'Protests and demonstrations which fail to achieve their aims are a waste of effort.' The results were as follows:

Table 8 *Parkin's findings concerning instrumental vs expressive politics* (Parkin, 1968:36)

	%
Agree/Strongly agree	10
Disagree/Strongly disagree	86
Don't Know/No response	4
	100

($n = 358$)

Parkin concludes from this (and a further question concerned with the Labour Party putting 'principles before power') that CND supporters largely displayed an expressive commitment.

We sought to explore this issue in the context of supporters

157

of the NFOL rally. We asked our respondents: 'Would you feel that your participation in today's rally will have been wasted if no concrete changes in our society come about as a result of it?'

The initial impression from our data is that they are in tune with those of Parkin and his conception of the pursuit of goals concerned with 'symbolic' issues as expressive rather than instrumental in character. Only 9·8% of our respondents adopted an obviously, directly, instrumental view, and indicated that they felt participation *would* have been wasted if no concrete changes came about.

However, unlike Parkin, we gave those respondents who answered 'NO' to this question an opportunity to indicate *what* they felt would have been gained. Their answers throw considerable doubt on the idea that the bulk of the participants were expressively rather than instrumentally oriented. We coded the answers to this open-ended question in seven categories (plus an 'other' category). The proportions indicating each of these categories is listed in Table 9.

Table 9 *Reasons why participation in the rally would not have been wasted*

	Rally not wasted because:	Percentage mentioning
1.	A moral stand had been made	37·1
2.	Personal encouragement had been received	13·3
3.	Others would be encouraged to take a stand	11·7
4.	An evangelistic witness had been made to non-Christians	21·8
5.	Fellowship or solidarity had been experienced or demonstrated	13·2
6.	God's will had been obeyed	3·8
7.	There would be a subtle or delayed effect on public opinion	14·8
8.	Other	8·2

(All responses were coded and the percentages therefore sum to more than 100.)

The only relatively clear *expressive* categories are (6), that participation was in accord with God's will whatever the result; (5) that the participants had experienced or demonstrated their solidarity, unity or fellowship; and (2) that the rally had been a source of personal encouragement to those present at the rally. These categories, however, received a fairly low rate of mention.

Category 6 (obedience to God) is captured in the following comments:

> I obeyed the will of God in going to the rally. God's blessing follows obedience (Respondent 1004).

> Because I believe that God is more concerned that the rally should take place than that it should have particular man-made results (Respondent 0173).

Category 5 is shown in the responses below:

> Fellowship with other Christians (Respondent 0002).

> A unity of Christians in the fight against the moral decline of our country (Respondent 0192).

> For those that were there a feeling of unity and hope for the future (Respondent 1206).

> The fellowship, reunion and joy of being with other Christians, plus impact on society in general, plus the opportunity to praise God made it well worth while (Respondent 0141).

Category 2 (personal encouragement received) is shown in the following comments:

> It will have served as an aid to greatly strengthen the faith of many of those present (Respondent 0170).

> Strength from meeting with other Christians. Happiness in obeying Christ's injunction to witness (Respondent 0114).

> The rally encourages Christians who may not come from large fellowships to realise they are not alone in following Jesus, and upholding his standards (Respondent 0107).

A particularly common theme was that captured in category (1) (moral stand made) in which respondents took the view that at least the Christian voice will have been heard on the moral issues concerned, that NFOL's position will have been made clear, and that the rally will thereby have created awareness among politicians and other notables and caught public attention for the views the rally upheld, thereby helping to stem the tide of 'permissiveness'. In part this response expressed the view that *without* such a stand the views of secularists and supporters of 'permissiveness' would succeed by default. At least such a stand would make *this* less likely. Some examples of such comments are given below:

> At least Christians will have made their opinion known which is better than failing to say anything (Respondent 0038).

> Leading members of society will know there is a large body of people willing to make a stand for morality (Respondent 0047).

> That at least a voice has been raised at long last in protest against the decline in morality and hopefully the floodgates to further activities have been opened (Respondent 1027).

The poor mass media coverage of the rally suggests that those who believed it would succeed in attracting the attention of public and politicians were largely mistaken, but whatever the *result*, this was clearly an *instrumental* orientation.

Equally instrumental was the second largest category of 'evangelistic witness' (Category 4), in which we coded all responses which took the view that the rally was worth while, whatever the concrete changes in society, because it will have led to *conversions*.

> It is worth while in my eyes if only, say, just one single person was brought to the Lord as a result of it (Respondent 0051).

> A stand will have been made for Jesus Christ our Saviour; and the challenge of Christianity may reach an unsaved person thus planting a seed which the Holy Spirit may use to bring that person to a saving knowledge of Jesus (Respondent 1048).

> . . . even if only a few become believers it will be worth it (Respondent 0197).

Individuals may have heard the good news of God's love and forgiveness for the first time (Respondent 0160).

Bringing others to salvation may not seem instrumental to the secular-minded, but it is clearly an end beyond the expressive benefits of mere participation in the event.

A substantial proportion took the view that although the rally might result in no immediate concrete changes, it would have an effect in a more subtle way, influencing attitudes *in the long term* (Category 7).

'Concrete changes' in our society will not come about through a 'rally', but I believe that such manifestations of opinion and concern can play a cumulative part in altering (if only slightly) public opinion and that of private individuals (Respondent 0013).

Some seed has been sown which must have results somewhere sometime (Respondent 0016).

It may have a gradual, snowballing, long-term influence on people (Respondent 1030).

Changes will come about as a result of a series or many events and developments, not of one rally (Respondent 1026).

The media are beginning to take note of voices raised against evil in society. Continued frequent 'Speaking out' and demonstrations will effect changes in time (Respondent 0133).

Finally, a substantial proportion indicated that the rally would have an effect by encouraging others, particularly Christians and Church leaders not in attendance, to speak out against 'declining moral standards', as well as leading to a recommitment among Christians and renewal in the Church (Category 3).

Christians will have stood up to be counted, and this may lead to more Christians taking a firm stand for their beliefs (Respondent 0089).

Christians have been encouraged by thousands of other Christians taking a stand (Respondent 0040).

161

Our results indicate that the view that crusades or demonstrations concerned with symbolic issues are largely expressive rather than instrumental in orientation, receives little support from our data on the NFOL rally. While participants may have been aware that little of an immediate, concrete kind would change as a result of their activity, they often also believed that instrumental gains of a broader and longer-term kind might be achieved. It must also be remembered that many respondents gave *multiple* responses. Thus the proportions giving apparently *expressive* responses need to be interpreted remembering that the expressive comment was only part of a multiple response, other components of which were *instrumental* in character. Thus, if we look at those endorsing *only* one or more of the three 'expressive' categories, we find that only 28% of the sample do so.

Assimilative and coercive reform

Joseph Gusfield (1963) in his study of the Women's Christian Temperance Union in America suggests that a distinction can be drawn in terms of modes of moral reform. A secure status group widely recognised as embodying the normatively approved standards of behaviour and moral conduct will tend to regard those who depart from such standards with pity rather than anger. Their moral reform activity will be *assimilative* in character, aimed to reform the lives of the reprobate through kindness and conversion, to raise them to the recognised standard of respectable life. However, when the reformers find their values and norms increasingly challenged, to the point where established social elites and institutions begin to defect from them, they are, Gusfield suggests, likely to shift their efforts at reform in a more *coercive* direction, seeking to impose through the force of law and the power of official agencies of social control, norms and values no longer regarded as the self-evident standards of respectable conduct.

In the literature and activities of the NFOL there has been some ambiguity concerning which mode of reform the movement should pursue, as we showed in the previous chapter. This ambiguity, however, appears to have disappeared in the more recent direction of activities, and in the pronouncements of leaders. The September 1976 rally seemed quite unequivocally concerned to focus on the rule of law which should be derived from a traditional conception of biblical moral standards. It appears, that is, to have stressed a *coercive* rather than an assimilative approach to moral reform. Moreover, NFOL literature and public pronouncements had clearly expressed a feeling that traditional moral standards were increasingly being abandoned by dominant social groups and social institutions, such as Parliament, the mass media, the courts and the Churches. Hence it could be expected to pursue a policy of 'coercive reform' and for this orientation to inform the view of priorities for action held by rally participants. A question in our protocol was designed to explore the views of respondents on the issue of which mode of reform they saw to have the greater importance:

> Many Christians feel that in order to reverse the moral decline of Britain pressure for more effective legislation on moral issues and more active evangelism are both needed. If you had to put a priority on one rather than the other for immediate action, which would you place first?
>
> More active evangelism . . . .
> More effective legislation . . . .

The response pattern to this question is shown in Table 10.

Table 10 *Priority on assimilative or coercive reform*

Priority	%
Evangelism	84·3
Legislation	13·9
Both equal*	1·8

$n = 1072$ (34 uncodable)

* Although 'both equal' was not a response we had made available, some respondents indicated this as their view, and all such responses were coded in this category.

It is clear from Table 10 that an overwhelming proportion of respondents saw evangelism, or *assimilative* reform as having the greater priority. This is an extremely important finding, since it shows the danger of taking for granted that the beliefs and values of supporters for a social movement are merely a direct copy of those disseminated in its literature and official pronouncements. This finding is entirely consistent with the small proportion of respondents who gave first ranking to 'Legalistic' concerns as their reason for attending the rally, and the relatively small proportion who gave first ranking to 'moral protest' (see Table 7).

Differing orientations to the rally

Ideally we should have liked to secure an appropriate sample of non-supporters of NFOL against whom our respondents could be compared. However, having little prior knowledge of the relevant characteristics of the rally participants this was not possible. Nor is it altogether self-evident what would have constituted an appropriate comparative group. Thus, in generating correlational data our strategy was informed by the hypothesis that the differing orientations to the rally as expressed in their rankings of reasons for attending, and to the mode of reform requiring priority, differentiated two types of involvement in NFOL which could be related to biographical characteristics of the individuals concerned.

In order to explore further the character of participants' orientations to the rally, and to discover any underlying structure of attitudes towards it, and by implication to the movement as a whole, we subjected the responses to the question on reasons for attending the rally to multi-dimensional unfolding.

The basic idea for the technique is due to C.H. Coombs (1964) and the technique has subsequently been treated as a member of the general family of non-metric Multi-dimensional Scaling techniques (see, for example, Shepard *et al.,* 1972). We preface our findings with a simplified account of the procedure.

The model which underlies the technique is that the respondent in a ranking task has a 'mental map' of the stimuli as *points in a space,* with a personal 'ideal' point located in the same space. The number of dimensions of the space is not pre-defined. If we have a (fairly large) number of respondents who (a) share the same mental map, and (b) have individual ideal points which are dispersed in the space, then the unfolding algorithm can deduce the common mental map from the differing rankings produced by the respondents. In so doing, it performs the apparently miraculous task of raising ordinal data (rankings) to an interval level of measurement — i.e. it will produce the mental map with a *metric.*

Of course, respondents do not usually share exactly the same mental map of a set of stimuli. The more respondents differ in the underlying map, the greater the 'difficulty' the algorithm will encounter in producing a common solution. This difficulty is measured by what is called 'stress'. If respondents *do* share exactly the same map, then a solution can be found with zero stress, and, equally, the greater the differences in respondents' maps, the higher the stress associated with the solution. Further, if an attempt is made to find a solution using fewer dimensions than are actually present in the respondents' maps, then the resultant solution will have high stress.

It follows that we can investigate the possibility of a common map, and its dimensionality, by looking for solutions in various numbers of dimensions and inspecting the stress for each solution. If we find that a solution can be found which has acceptably low stress, is statistically reliable (as measured by, e.g. split-half inspection), is interpretable and has a parsimoniously small number of dimensions, then we have a 'successful' use of the technique.

The question on reasons for attending the rally yielded 1098 usable responses, 8 respondents having failed to answer the question. These 1098 responses, on analysis, were found to be made up of 128 distinct response patterns. Preliminary runs showed that 28 of the patterns gave high stress in combination with the remainder, and these were discarded. The final set analysed, then, consisted of 100 response patterns, being the responses of 1023 respondents — 92·5% of the sample. Solutions were attempted in 3, 2 and 1 dimensions, giving stresses (by Stress Formula 2 — see Young, 1972:83) of 0·0055, 0·0062 and 0·1665 respectively. The two-dimensional solution thus gives a highly satisfactory stress and appears to be the inflection point of the stress by dimension graph, and is, accordingly, the one used in subsequent analysis. Table 11 gives the configuration of the stimulus points in this two-dimensional solution.

Table 11 *Configuration of stimulus points*

	Dimension 1	Dimension 2
Evangelism	-0·0906	0·7348
Moral Protest	-0·2700	-0·5944
Moral Legislation	-0·9960	-0·5069
Status Defence	1·4471	-0·3679
Christian Solidarity	-0.0905	0·7343

Of these two dimensions, Dimension 2 is of greater theoretical interest for the present study. It clearly reflects the distinction

Figure 2 *Respondents and stimulus points in two-dimensional
        space*
Dimension 1:   Self's orientation to Others versus Others'
orientated to Self, is plotted horizontally
Dimension 2: Evangelism/Solidarism versus Moral Protest
Letters denote stimuli:
        A — Evangelism
        B — Moral Protest
        C — Moral Legislation
        D — Status Defence
        E — Christian Solidarity

Note that A and E are superimposed and have therefore been
indicated by an arrow. The centres of the circles denote the
positions of respondents in the space. The *area* of a circle is
proportional to the numbers of persons located at the
centre of the circle. Circles have been amalgamated where the
centre of the smaller lay within the circumference of the
larger.

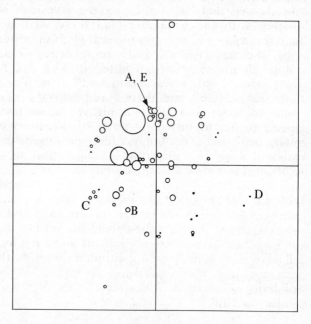

Dimension 2:
Evangelism/
Solidarism
versus
Moral Protest

Dimension 1: Self's Orientation to Others versus Others'
Orientation to Self

166

between the *Evangelistic-Solidaristic* and *Moral Protest* orientations of the NFOL. Dimension 1, on the other hand, is rather more difficult to interpret. If it is permissible to assume that 'protest against the loss of respect and esteem shown to people who live a respectable life' can be equated with protest against the loss of respect and esteem shown to people *like the respondent,* then we can take the fourth item as being concern with *Others' orientation to Self.* Dimension 1 opposes, then, this item to *Self's orientation to Others* in the form of a desire to legislate or protest against Others' behaviour when this is morally unacceptable.

The MINIRSA programme gives, as part of its output, the location of the inferred ideal points for each response pattern. One can thus create a score, on each of the two dimensions, for the 1023 respondents whose answers were unfolded. Figure 2 show the results of this operation.

Even if the extreme points at the top and bottom of the figure are ignored, it is clear that Dimension 2 (Evangelistic-Solidaristic/Moral Protest) produces a greater scatter than Dimension 1 (Self/Others), indicating that there is greater variation in the respondent's orientations on Dimension 2. The central tendency of the points on Dimension 1 is well to the left (with a mean of -0·285), and is thus shifted well away from the point corresponding to Status Defence. This point, as we should expect from the very low rankings given to this reason, is shown to be the most remote from the respondents' own orientations.

The distribution on Dimension 2 is also as one would predict from a consideration of the rankings given to Evangelism and Solidarity. It shows that in general respondents' ideal points are closer to these two points than to Moral Protest or Legislation, with a mean of 0·289. The results of this scaling exercise are entirely consistent with the view that respondents perceived the five reasons as presenting a choice between an Evangelistic-Christian Solidarity orientation on one hand and a Moral-Legal orientation on the other. Further, the results show both that the respondents' own orientations, as measured by index scores, fall at various points on a continuum between these two, and that, in general, they tended to favour the Evangelistic-Christian Solidarity orientation. A scatter-diagram of the distribution of our respondents on this dimension is presented in Figure 2.

We found, then, that the internal results of the scaling procedure were in accord with our preliminary ideas about the dual focus of NFOL, and that they confirm the finding, discussed earlier, that the majority of our respondents do *not* share the *primary* orientation towards coercive moral reform which characterised the rally's organisers and speakers.

Index scores did not, however, show any strong patterning in association with biographical variables. We looked at a variety of these and found that position on this Evangelistic-Christian Solidarity/Moral-Legal dimension was not associated with sex, religious affiliation, previous participation in NFOL activities, Social Class, Occupational Position, or parental churchgoing. Weak effects were noted on age at end of education and absolute age: there was a slightly lower tendency to fall at the Evangelistic-Christian Solidarity end of the scale among those whose age at end of education was 21 or more, and among those aged 21 to 40. These effects were independent of one another. As one would expect, index scores were associated with attitude variables such as the Reasons Why the Rally would Not be Wasted if no concrete changes resulted, and the answers concerning the priorities for future action.

We also employed the responses to the question on priorities for action to reverse moral decline as an alternative indicator. As shown in Table 10 the response pattern to this question is highly skewed. Only 14% of the sample selected legislation rather than evangelism (or both equally) as the priority.

In terms of previous participation in NFOL activities, respondents who gave their priority to more effective legislation were not over-represented in any activity except 'Operation Newsagent', the only one requiring personal confrontation with an unsympathetic audience. However, the relationship between the two was not strong. This finding is consistent with the relationship also found between ranking highly the 'Legalistic' reason for attending and participation in Operation Newsagent and the Petition for Public Decency. But in each case the 'Legalists' were only likely to have had a *marginally* higher propensity to have been active on these occasions.

Those who favoured more effective legislation were found to have a more clearly instrumental view of the rally than those who favoured conversion as a priority. 20% of the former, compared to only 8% of the latter felt their participation would have been wasted if no concrete changes in society came about.

Respondents favouring legalistic priorities were not found to differ from those favouring evangelistic priorities in sex distribution, Registrar-General's Social Class, or age at the end of full-time education. They were found to be marginally older (average age of 35·0 years as compared to 31·5 years), which is also consistent with our finding that the ages of those who participated in the civic-political activities: 'Operation News-agent' and the 'Petition for Public Decency' averaged 8 to 10 years older respectively than those who did not participate in these activities. The only evidence of a *denominational* distinction in terms of priorities for action was in the pre-ferences of Catholics, of whom 24% placed their priority on legislation compared to 14% of the respondents as a whole.

Conclusion

The Nationwide Festival of Light emerged as the product of amorphous sentiments concerning the moral and spiritual state of Britain. In the process of developing a body of support, these sentiments were respecified in terms of a dual focus on civic-political reform and evangelistic witness. During its early years, both foci were operationalised in the activities of NFOL, and through networks of individuals and organisations with both types of concern, support was mobilised for the aims of NFOL. During the first three years, the concern with evangelistic witness had the dominant place in the planning of NFOL activities. Impressionistic observation, however, suggests that in a relatively secular society, mass rallies and revivals more often provide occasions for Christians to *reaffirm* their faith, and through what is often an emotional collective enterprise, to *revitalise* and heighten their own commitments, than to bring others to coversion in any great number.

During recent years, for reasons discussed in Chapter 8, there has been a substantial shift towards the active pursuit of NFOL's civic-political aims among its leadership to the almost complete exclusion of evangelistic aims. NFOL, however, con-tinues to mobilise support through the dualistic network which it had acquired, and to publicise its efforts and activities particularly to an audience located in Evangelical churches and organisations. Hence, despite the highly *moralistic* and *legalistic* character of the rally planned for 25 September 1976, it was to be expected that participants in the rally would variously be found to define their motivation for attending in terms of some combination of (1) a *moralistic* purpose con-cerned with a restoration of traditional moral norms and values as the dominant ones in British society through social action

and control; (2) an *evangelistic* purpose concerned with converting others to their own beliefs and mode of life; (3) a
solidaristic purpose in which the role of the rally in providing
encouragement and heightened commitment to oneself and
to other believers was recognised as of importance.

A significant body of sociological theory and research also
proposed that moral crusades were an exercise in *status politics,*
and suggested that participants in such crusades would be found
to have a concern with *status defence.* A survey of participants
in the 1976 NFOL rally showed that, among our respondents,
status was quite insignificant as a motivation for their participation. In the mapping of respondents' orientations through the
statistical technique of 'unfolding', status defence was the most
distant stimulus point from the primary axis of participant
involvement.

Surprisingly, however, whole the orientations of participants
did display a substantial clustering around a dimension concerned with Evangelism-Solidarism and Moral Protest, the distribution of respondents was overwhelmingly towards the
Evangelism-Solidarism end of this dimension rather than, as
one would expect from the content of, and publicity for,
the rally, towards the Moral Protest end. This finding emphasises
the dangers of drawing conclusions concerning the motivations
of participants from the public pronouncements of movement
leaders.

The discovery of this major orientating dimension in the
minds of participants is of itself no great surprise. Not only has
this been a major theme in the life of NFOL, but a continuing
ambiguity in the history of Evangelicalism. Social action and
defence of traditional standards of morality have, historically,
been counterposed in Evangelical history with its major thrust
towards individual action in the form of conversion. Indeed,
the dichotomies between faith and works, witness and purity
and a concern with their resolution into some viable synthesis
have been major aspects of the history of Christianity as a
whole.

In general, the findings of our survey show the participants
in NFOL's 1976 rally to have been predominantly youthful
Christians drawn primarily from middle-class sectors of society,
and highly active in their religious attachments as indicated
by church attendance. These participants were found to be
engaged in the defence of a challenged set of cultural mores
largely by means of assimilative reform rather than coercive

reform. A major subsidiary theme in their participation was that this event provided an opportunity to reaffirm and reinvigorate their own Christian commitment. No particularly impressive variations were found in terms of biographical data between those who displayed a greater commitment to one or another of these orientations.

It must be emphasised yet again, that our conclusions can only relate to participants *in the rally*. It is possible that the nature of the event, involving a lengthy period on a Saturday afternoon amid a large crowd in London, may only have drawn a particular *segment* of support for NFOL as a whole. Our data do not show any very substantial variation with age. However, the possibility should be mentioned that since Evangelism and Solidarism are major motivating factors and persons considering attending the rally may have seen it as providing greater opportunity for the realisation of these goals (despite the organisers' presentation of the rally as focusing on moral reform), it is possible that supporters of NFOL more committed to moral and legal reform may not have viewed the event as appropriate to the aims that they wished to pursue. That is, it is possible that supporters of moral and legal aims may view individual or local action as of greatest importance than a mass rally in London. We have no grounds for believing this to be true, but equally we have no data on non-attending supporters of NFOL which would disconfirm it. To hold this view, however, would be to claim that the promotion of the rally by NFOL's leaders was either misinterpreted or ignored by those for whom its message had the greatest appeal. This is a most unlikely contingency.

III
PROBLEMS OF THEORY AND METHOD

CHAPTER X

A *theory of propensity to schism*

Schism, the breaking away of one group of erstwhile supporters of a social or religious movement, is a prominent aspect of the dynamics of many such movements. Indeed a substantial number of existing religious groups were formed as the result of schism. Despite the frequency of its occurrence, however, little progress has been made in securing any considerable insight into the general nature of the phenomenon.

In this chapter I propose to examine some of the scattered insights that are available. I shall argue that explanations of schism have typically rested on accounts of the *motivations* of those concerned or the social divisions underlying schism. A recent contribution by Joseph Nyomarkay, however, suggests the possibility of a fruitful shift in orientation from *motivation* or social correlates, to the *structural conditions* facilitating or inhibiting schism. I extend Nyomarkay's seminal ideas into a theory of differential propensity to schism and through the analysis of a number of cases, seek to show the utility of this approach.

Motivations for schism and social correlates

The primary concern of researchers in social and religious movements has been with explaining *why particular* schisms occurred. Their solution to this problem has typically taken the form of identifying the motivations of those involved, or, less directly, the lines of *social differentiation* along which they occurred.

H. Richard Niebuhr, for example, in his survey of Christian denominationalism, argues at one point that, 'the divisions of the Church have been occasioned more frequently by the direct and indirect operation of economic factors than by the influence of any other major interest of man' (Niebuhr, 1957: 26). Elsewhere in this volume he identifies as the immediate sources of schismatic motivation such varied forms of social differentiation as those between immigrants and native inhabitants, nationalism, ethnicity, political and cultural differentiation, as well as those directly between economic groups. Social differentiation is seen as giving rise to divergences of interest which render unified action and common commitment problematic. Hence, Zald and Ash (1966) identify 'heterogeneity of social base' as one of the two major preconditions for factionalism and schism in social movements.

Emilio Willems, in his account of pentecostal sects in Chile and Brazil, identifies nationalistic feeling against alien control as one of the major sources of schismatic developments (Willems, 1967). Doherty, in his account of the Hicksite schism among the Quakers of Philadelphia in 1827 (Doherty, 1967), identifies a developing differentiation among the Friends particularly between the wealthy urban entrepreneurs and the more rural anti-urbanite supporters of Hicks who tended to reject the accelerating urbanisation and technologisation to which the leading Friends were willing to accommodate in their commercial and industrial endeavours.

The theme of social differentiation and division leading to movement or Church division, can also be found in Christopher Dawson's (1942) résumé of the causes of schism, the discussion by Yinger (1970), and in the work of Greenslade (1953) on the early Church. Among the five causes of schism which he lists, Greenslade also includes as a factor of considerable significance, *national feeling*.

Greenslade, however, points to an alternative (perhaps complementary rather than competing) approach to that which locates in social differentiation the grounds of schism, looking particularly to the motivations of the leaders of schismatic factions. He argues that ambition or personal antipathy have often had an important part as stimulating factors: 'The personal factor is always important, but rarely, if ever, the sole cause of schism. Occasionally . . . it was the main cause' (Greenslade, 1953:55).

In a number of works touching on this topic, schisms are held to result from personality conflicts between senior personnel.

175

Alexander argues concerning left-wing radical movements in the USA for example (1953:306), that 'these schisms reveal that personalities have played too great a role in the radical organisations. This is clearly revealed by the case of Daniel De Leon, whose personality was the chief cause of the 1899 split in the Socialist Labour Party'.

Personality conflicts are often held to accompany ambition and power seeking. For example, Bryan Wilson in his discussion of schisms in Christian Science argues that 'Schism in Christian Science has almost invariably been among the teachers of the movement, and has almost always been centred on the struggle for power' (Wilson, 1961:340). Similarly in the case of Christ-adelphianism, he argues that 'Clashes of personality, perhaps specifically concerned with ambition to lead, appear to have been at the basis of most schism in Christadelphianism . . .' (Wilson, 1961:341). Calley (1965:51) employing a similar theory in his discussion of West Indian Pentecostal sects in England, argues that the motivation is not normally mere naked ambition, however:

> Although some leaders of breakaway movements may cold-bloodedly invent a doctrinal dispute after having decided to start a Church of their own, I doubt whether this is very often the case. The situation is rather that personal amibition and general dissatisfaction go hand-in-hand with a searching of the scripture for an explanation for the dissatisfaction. The saint tries to discover in biblical terms why he feels restless and dissatisfied.

Often in his search he will come across some ritual or aspect of Church government not adequately incorporated in the Church to which he belongs and therein locate the source of his dissatisfaction. Greenslade (1953), within the same general approach, points to *rivalry between sees* or ecclesiastical jurisdictions as an important source of schisms in the early Church.

Some accounts of schism have followed a less reductionistic approach, taking disputes over matters of organisation, ideology, or practice at face value, rather than seeking to relate them to what are believed to be underlying ulterior motives or social divisions. Greenslade (1953), for example, lists *liturgical disputes,* and *puritanism or rigorism* (the pursuit of religious virtuosity and an ideal of the Church as a 'congregation of saints" as important sources of schism in the early Church.

The only attempt to formulate a general model of schism

176

deriving from a search for common motivational factors is that of John Wilson (1971). While deriving his analytic framework from some components of Smelser's 'value-added' model of collective behaviour, the main force of his theory rests on the claim that 'norm-value strain is at the core of all cases of schism' (Wilson, 1971:5). By this he implies the existence of a situation 'where accepted norms are not fully appropriate to the system's values' (*ibid.*). Or, as he elaborates this, 'A schismatic group is a movement which has its origins in a dispute over norms and allegations that the main group has departed from those implicated in the values of the original movement' (*ibid.*). While this may sometimes be so, the case of the Brazilian and Chilean pentecostal sects discussed by Willems which split on explicitly nationalistic grounds seem a clear refutation. Moreover, there is a more general problem here. Departure from the patterns of the 'true' Church and the early Church as diagnosed through biblical exegesis has traditionally provided the readiest *rhetoric of legitimation* for challenges to the leadership of religious groups within the Christian tradition, and the preaching of 'false doctrine' and unscriptural ritual practice have been biblically ordained as grounds for separation, for example:

> Now we command you, brethren, in the name of our Lord Jesus Christ, that ye withdraw yourselves from every brother that walketh disorderly, and not after the tradition he received of us (II Thessalonians iii, 6).

Accounts of a number of schisms seem to suggest the *grounds* or occasions for schism are rather diverse. A wide range of social divisions have been implicated: economic, national, rural-urban, status, cultural, etc. Likewise, many schisms are seen as having resulted from personality conflicts and/or ambitions for the attainment of power or position. I would not wish to challenge the validity of any of these explanations of particular schisms. There seems, however, to be no reason to believe that we shall ever isolate any common underlying theme in these accounts of motivation or social differentiation beyond the belief that one party could no longer remain united with another, and that schismatic groups tend to be socially more homogeneous than the parent bodies from which they become divorced.

While such accounts provide insights into the circumstances of particular schisms it is clear that some motivational grounds are simply not adequate as complete explanations of schism. Nationalistic feeling may inform all participants in a schism said to be thus motivated, but personal ambition among competing leaders clearly cannot. Moreover, in general, motivation theories fail to explain a number of important features of schism. It is for example a reasonably well-founded empirical generalisation that schisms disproportionately tend to occur early in the lives of social and religious movements. They also have a disproportionate tendency to occur on the death of charismatic leaders; and more often in decentralised movements. Motivational theories typically provide no insight into these phenomena, nor do they give any guide to where we should look for the sources of schism beyond the proposal that we examine the motivations of the actors (sound enough advice but limited), and the social divisions among them. While we will always find motivations we have no clues to what these will be in particular cases, and it does not seem to be true that we will uniformly find social divisions (see, for example, Wilson, 1961:340). Nor, indeed, does the fact of social divisions provide any *explanation* of schism unless these divisions are construed as providing motivational grounds for breaking away or for remaining loyal to a schismatic leader.

Structural conditions for schism

A number of studies have provided insights into the sources of opportunity for, or the conditions facilitating and inhibiting schism. Emilio Willems, for example, discussing the continual emergence of new sects by schism among Brazilian and Chilean pentecostalists, points to the importance of 'powers bestowed by the Spirit' in many of these sects. The institution of prophethood, in which an individual filled by the Holy Spirit stands up and 'corrects the pastor who deviates from the doctrine' (Willems, 1967:257), provides a ready means of legitimating challenges to authority, and if these are resisted, for legitimating the formation of a breakaway group.

Bryan Wilson's study of three religious sects contains a number of insights into the structural conditions for the occurrence of schism. For example, Wilson suggests that among established sects, 'schism comes only from the divisions among the influential elite within each movement; no other person is sufficiently influential to cause division . . .' (Wilson, 1961:339). As he points out, in Christian Science, schism 'has almost invariably been among the teachers of the movement . . .' (Wilson, 1961:

340). Similarly, 'among the Christadelphians . . . the important divisions have all been led by men who were counted among the movement's elite, the few "prominent" brethren. . . The absence of hierarchisation and of any institutionalisation of charisma has probably assisted the process by stimulating a struggle for leadership possible only in the absence of defined roles and well defined spheres of competence' (Wilson, 1961: 340-41). He further suggests that 'it appears also to be generally true that schism is much more likely among the first generation of a sect, than among later generations' (Wilson, 1961:341-2).

John Wilson argues that organisational centralisation is an important 'structual determinant of schism. It is suggested that schism is more likely, not so much where a movement is highly decentralised, but where a movement falls at either extreme end of this continuum' (Wilson, 1971:10-11). Unusually in an area where there has been little systematic testing of the propositions offered, there has been a partial attempt to test this idea. William Gamson, on the basis of a survey of American social movements found a substantial relationship between centralisation of power and schism, 'only 25 per cent of th group with centralisation of power experienced factional splits (schisms), while this was the lost of almost two-thirds of the decentralised groups' (Gamson, 1975:104).

These are only a selection from among the many hypotheses presented in the literature concerning schism. I have selected them particularly because they have a common focus on issues of power, authority and legitimation. This focus seems, as a result of the seminal thinking of Joseph Nyomarkay, likely to be fruitful.

Nyomarkay's theory

Nyomarkay's theory, elaborated in the context of an analysis of factionalism in the Nazi Party rests on a distinction between two types of social movement. He contrasts the *charismatic* movement such as the Nazi Party with the *ideological* movement more characteristic of communism and socialism. He argues that within the former, authority and legitimation derived from Hitler's charisma, while the Marxist movements it derives from the ideology:

Hitler was the primary source of group cohesion, the focus of loyalty, and the personification of the utopian ideal —

179

he was, in short, a charismatic leader. In contrast with Marxist parties, where ideology provides the highest source of authority the Nazi party was based on charismatic legitimacy (Nyomarkay, 1967:4).

On this basis he seeks to explain why factional conflicts in Marxist parties have so often led to schism, while within the Nazi party factions never seriously affected the history of the movement.

> Charismatic legitimacy made Hitler the sole source of authority and the only point of cohesion in the otherwise heterogeneous movement. Hitler's charisma elevated him above factional conflicts and allowed him to assume the position of broker, arbiter and judge. Factions justified their existence by claiming to be Hitler's representatives, which meant that they organised not to challenge Hitler's authority but to gain his support against rival factions (Nyomarkay, 1967:145).

Only when a faction challenged his own legitimacy did Hitler decisively intervene. 'Once Hitler disowned a faction, he deprived it of its legitimacy. . . . At such moments factional leaders in opposition to Hitler found themselves isolated; their support evaporated, and Hitler emerged with his authority unimpaired and with the unity of the movement preserved' (Nyomarkay, 1967:146). By contrast, Nyomarkay argues, legitimacy within communist and socialist movements derives more usually from the ideology. Factions therefore seek 'to justify their positions by ideological orthodoxy', and unlike the charismatic leader, source of a nebulous and self-defined *Weltanschauung,* the leader of an ideological movement must equally justify his position and programme by reference to that ideology. There is no source of authority or arbitration above the dispute by recourse to which it could be resolved. Hence, factional conflicts tend to issue in splits in which each factional leader claims to be interpreting the ideology in its true light.

Nyomarkay's theory is important because it begins systematically to raise the issue of schism in a new way; to reorient the problem from the question of why schisms occur, to that of accounting for the differential propensity to schism of different movements, and (although he does not treat of it), of why they occur in some movements at one stage of development, but not at other stages.

Nyomarkay's conceptualisation is not, however, as it stands adequate to tackle these problems. As he indicates in his conclusion to the book (Nyomarkay, 1967:147), Stalin, *although not a charismatic leader* created a position of autocracy analogous to that of Hitler, and 'by the 1930s factionalism in the CPSU (Communist Party of the Soviet Union) approached the character of Nazi factional conflicts'. Hence, it seems that the matter is not simply one of an analytical distinction between charisma and ideology. The particularly seminal point in his discussion, therefore, is the identification of the sources of legitimation as the key to the explanation of different patterns of schism.

The theory of propensity to schism

We therefore need to move beyond Nyomarkay's formulation to provide a more adequate general theory of schism. Such a theory should predict the circumstances more likely to facilitate schism, and should account for the generally known prevailing patterns of schism in social and religious movements. In essence, this theory states that schism involves the breaking away from a group or social movement of an individual who is able to secure the support of some part of that movement's following. In order to win that support, the schismatic leader must be able to secure a legitimate claim to their allegiance. Thus schismatic propensity is directly related to the perceived availability of sources of legitimation within a movement. Legitimacy may be singly or severally available in the person and pronouncements of the leader; a set of sacred writings or oral tradition; diverse positions of power within the organisational structure of the movement; personal revelations directly received by members; or in the largely impersonal mandate of the headquarters organisation. By *availability* here is meant the degree to which access to the means of legitimation can be secured by all, or some subsection of, the members of a movement, independent of the mediation of (other) power-holders. ('Other', because schisms not infrequently involve conflicts *between* elite power-holders). Schism involves the mobilisation of (1) *alternative* means of legitimation to those employed by movement powerholders. For example, Zald and Ash discussing an unpublished study by Norman Miller state:

Miller has argued that the difference between Catholic

sects which remained in the Church and those which left depended on the acceptance of the ultimate authority of the Word as revealed in the Bible, and interpreted by the Fathers of the Church, versus the word of contemporary Church authorities: The Montanists of second century Phrygia and the Feeneyites of twentieth century Boston both rested their authority on the former and left the Church, whereas St. Francis bowed to the latter (Zald & Ash, 1966).

Or, it involves the mobilisation of (2) *the same* means of legitimation in those cases where access to them is widely dispersed through the movement. For example, charismatic gifts, such as prophethood, are often dispersed widely throughout the following of Pentecostal movements.

Before pursuing the details of this account further, however, we need to deal with what might appear to be a major stumbling-block. That is, that conventional religious organisations and political parties, while they may often contain many factions, appear to have less of a tendency to generate schisms from them than more 'extremist' bodies. Zald and Ash (1966) draw a distinction between *inclusive* and *exclusive* movement organisations, arguing that: 'The inclusive organisation retains its factions while the exclusive organisation spews them forth.' The inclusive organisation is identified in terms of its 'looser criteria of affiliation and of doctrinal orthodoxy'. Nyomarkay conceives the difference in terms of *totalitarian* and *non-totalitarian* movements, arguing that: 'In a non-totalitarian group the principle of legitimacy is pluralistic — i.e. based on segmental participation — and factions can exist without destroying the group. In a totalitarian movement the principle of legitimacy is monistic — i.e. based on an almost total identification — and factions can exist only if they do not attack the principle of legitimacy' (Nyomarkay, 1967:150). Unfortunately it is not clear that inclusiveness/non-totalitarianism, exclusiveness/totalitarianism can be exactly equated. The totalitarian movement may have stringent criteria of doctrinal orthodoxy but rather loose criteria of affiliation: the Catholic Church in the Middle Ages, for example.

I propose that a more useful distinction can be drawn in terms of the conception that the movement has of the nature of the doctrine or of the programme that it purveys. Those movements and groups which construe their path to truth, salvation or utopia as *uniquely legitimate** will tend to define the boundaries of doctrine rather sharply to distinguish themselves from those beliefs and programmes which they reject.

Pluralistically legitimate movements and groups, by contrast, are those that do not completely reject the validity of alternative paths to truth, salvation, or utopia. Although they may view their own as greatly superior, they are prepared to co-operate to some extent with others, to work within a set of game rules which require collaboration. They acknowledge the right of other Churches or parties to their own opinion. In politics, they will accept the role of Loyal Opposition. In religion, they will tend to be ecumenical in character. They therefore insist less rigorously on doctrinal orthodoxy and demand less commitment from members. Pluralistically legitimate movements are thus able to tolerate the existence of factional groups more readily than uniquely legitimate movements. A movement which claims that there is only one path to salvation, truth or utopia can scarcely permit alternative proposed paths within its own ranks,† which is not, of course, to say that they will never experience schism. Given this clarified usage we can happily employ Nyomarkay's terms and refer to uniquely legitimate groups as 'totalitarian', and pluralistically legitimate groups as 'non-totalitarian'.

However, there are clearly important differences between groups and movements which claim unique legitimacy. Those that achieve power within a society have available to them resources for the inhibition of challenges to their legitimacy, or the suppression of such challenges, unavailable to relatively powerless groups. The purge can be implemented by powerful totalitarian movements supported by the apparatus of state repression. Schism is therefore unlikely in such cases; the Reformation being perhaps the major countervailing case.

In what follows, then we shall be dealing with groups and movements which both claim unique legitimacy, that is, which are totalitarian, but which have not achieved substantial power in their societies. The discussion will be restricted largely to religious collectivities which fall within those limitations, i.e. to groups of a sectarian character (Wallis, 1975b), on which there is a substantial body of empirical material.

To reiterate the major theoretical claim, successful schism depends upon the ability of a factional leader to secure legitimation for separation. The propensity to schism of a movement will tend, therefore, to vary directly with the availability of means of legitimation. Nyomarkay distinguishes between monistic and pluralistic movements in this respect and sub-divides monistic movements into the charismatic and the ideological, arguing that schism will be more characteristic of the latter. However, we would argue that movements in which there is one and only one source of legitimation concentrated in one and only one individual or focus is a limiting case. In this extreme case, legitimation is available only to, or through the charismatic leader. In the case of marxist movements, while they may be construed as monistically legitimate in the sense of having only one focus of legitimacy in the ideology, *access* to it as a means of legitimation is widely dispersed. The belief-system specifies no uniquely privileged interpreter of the doctrine and hence the claim to be offering the correct interpretation is widely available to well-versed initiates. *It is a source of confusion to regard both movements as equally monistic.*

This point can perhaps be clarified by the following classification. We can construe the *means of legitimation* in a movement as being singular or plural. We can also construe *access* to the means of legitimation as available to one, a few, or many. This produces the following cross-classification.

Table 1 *Means of legitimation, availability and schismatic propensity*

| | Means of Legimation | |
	Singular	Plural
One	1.	4.
Few (i.e. an elite)	2.	5.
Many	3.	6.

Availability

This table shows that a more sophisticated formulation than that of Nyomarkay is necessary. Cell 1, which he takes as paradigmatic, fits the Nazi Party well but the marxist movements, with which he contrasts it, fit better into Cell 2 (that is, if we accept his claim that the ideology provided the only means of legitimation). Cell 3 can perhaps be seen as accommodating the situation among groups within the spiritualist tradition where contact with transcendental powers and beings is widely

believed to be available to all members and mediumistic possession thus provides a ready means of challenging established
authority. So contagious is the charisma of mediumship that is
has rarely been possible to inhibit the disintegration of a following organised at a level of greater complexity than the
characteristic professional-client relationship (for the case of
Thomas Lake Harris see Schneider and Lawton, 1942; for a
successful attempt to inhibit the diffusion of charisma in the
case of a flying saucer group, see Wallis, 1974; 1975a). Cell 4
can perhaps be seen to accommodate the situation of the
CPSU under Stalin, who could legitimate his position by means
of his claimed unique role as interpreter of the ideology but
also by his role as chief of the party bureaucracy or even as
head of state. As an example of Cell 5 we might take Theosophy. During Madame Blavatsky's lifetime, authority and
legitimation within Theosophy were split between the charismatic claims of Madame Blavatsky based on her revelations
from the Mahatmas, and the rational-legal authority wielded
by Colonel Olcott as General Secretary. Shortly before her
death a schism seemed imminent as a result of tensions between
Olcott and Blavatsky.

Since contact with the *Mahatmas* was in principle available
to an elite of committed disciples who followed the path of
Chelaship, on Madame Blavatsky's death the charisma conveyed by the claim to be in intimate communication with the
Mahatmas was readily available to William Q. Judge, already
de facto leader of the Theosophists in America, to legitimate
his schism from the international body.

As an example of Cell 6 we might take bodies within the
Pentecostal movement. Within Pentecostalism the principal
basis of legitimation is by means of the charismata of possession
by the Holy Spirit. Since the experience of being filled with the
Spirit is theoretically available to all born-again believers, this
means of legitimating challenges to authority is widely available.
Many Pentecostal groups have succeeded in institutionalising
alternative bases of authority, however, or of constraining the
freedom of access to charismatic legitimation. It is often the
case for example that interpretation of glossalalic utterances
must be carried out by an elder or the pastor. Moreover, the
congregation leader is typically viewed as *primus inter pares*
'His authority is accepted because . . . he started the congregation, but more important, because the New Testament describes
Churches as having leaders' (Calley, 1965:50). He may also be

endowed with biblically legitimated oversight, the gift of discerning spirits, which permits him to 'still' the tongues of those who challenge order, decorum, or authority (I am grateful to Dr Bryan Wilson for this point).

The major conclusion that can be drawn from this classification is that the propensity to schism increases directly with the availability of means of legitimating authority. The more bases of legitimation there are, or the more widely available they are, the greater the likelihood of schism. This claim is clearly compatible with the view that propensity to schism varies inversely with centralisation. Centralisation implies the arrogation of power and authority to a small number of persons or institutional foci. The greater the arrogation, the lower the availability of such means of legitimation and the lower the likelihood of successful schismatic attempts.

As Weber has described, and Bryan Wilson (1975) has lately re-emphasised, the greatest force for a break with an existing institutional order is that wielded by a *charismatic* leader. Charisma — the recognised claim to supernatural legitimation — thus provides the principal form of authority legitimating schism. But charisma is not the sole form of authority to which appeal may be made. On some occasions traditional authority may provide a legitimation for schism from a group or movement experiencing innovation, and rational-legal authority may provide such legitimation in a body which has become highly institutionalised. None the less, charisma, because of its very fluidity, precisely that is, because it is not tied to visible and acknowledged institutional structures and positions, is likely to be the major form of authority invoked in justification of a breach with them. This will not always, however, be charisma in its most positive and powerful form, in which an individual successfully claims for himself supernatural status as, for example, a Messiah; nor in which the individual is viewed as directly articulating the word of God in demanding a radical break with the established order, as in the case of the ethical prophet. In groups and movements where some limited form of direct access to the transcendent is regarded as available to others beyond the leader, charisma becomes diffused and, in the process as Bryan Wilson (1975) has pointed out, it becomes *attenuated*. Divisions in Pentecostal groups may therefore be frequent but they are rarely far-reaching. Groups divide and coalesce readily and schism rarely leads to broad changes in beliefs or practice.

How well does the theory account for the impressionistically well-founded observations that (1) schism tends to be characteristic of the early stages of a movement's life cycle; and that (2) schism occurs disproportionately often on the death of a charismatic leader? It seems evident enough that, assuming the accuracy of these observations, they relate to periods when the authority structure of a movement is, or becomes, unstable. During the early stages of a movement's development authority is poorly institutionalised. It remains a fluid property scarcely trammelled by routine. This is, surely, partly what is implied in the notion of charismatic authority. It has neither crystallised around certain organisational positions, nor have its limits been fully tested and defined. Members bring into the movement previously garnered assumptions concerning legitimacy which may not fully have been reduced or transformed to those promoted by the new movement's leadership. Their commitment to the particular structure of legitimation within the movement remains problematic. This is in fact a continuing problem in many movements, but on an *individual* level. For example, new recruits to a religious group like the Children of God often have had a Christian upbringing and when presented with the revelations of the leader of this group, may argue 'But the Bible says . . .', attempting to deploy the authority of the Bible against the charisma of the leader. Such recruits either learn to interpret the Bible according to the new source of authority, or never become integrated into the group, tending to leave fairly soon. But they enter as individuals, without status in the movement, and therefore entirely lack any structural basis for generating schism. In the early stages of a movement's life, many such recruits are likely, presenting therefore a collective threat to the incipient authority structure.

While authority remains uninstitutionalised, untested, and to some degree undefined, the leader may himself be unsure what the limits and definitions should be. Thus the leader may not decisively combat claims to legitimation presented by others. For example, Mrs. Keech founder of the famous flying saucer group studied by Festinger, Riecken and Schachter (1956) received revelations by means of automatic writing from a Space Master called Sananda. When a group of followers had developed around her, one, Bertha Blatsky, implicitly challenged Mrs. Keech's authority by producing revelational utterances at first from Sananda and then from the Creator himself. Mrs. Keech could have denied the validity of these revelations forcing Bertha to leave the group alone, or testing Bertha's ability to draw some of the following with her in a schismatic secession. Mrs. Keech did not take such a step. Her response seemed to show that she was not merely cynically manipulating power. She seemed indeed genuinely convinced by her revelations and simply unsure about what they implied in terms of the limits and definition of her authority. Doubtless many leaders are either more self-confident, or more sophisticated, but while *they* may not hesitate as did Mrs. Keech, their following, drawn from a milieu in which revelational indeterminancy is accepted, may not automatically accept the founder/leader's rejection of alternative revelations. For example, Ron Hubbard quickly tried to suppress challenges to his priority in the Dianetics movement, but having originally legitimated his ideas and his priority as an *inventor* or *scientist,* his followers were not all prepared to accept that this gave him unique authority, and that others could not be inventors or scientists too, developing Hubbard's ideas and practices in a manner of which he did not approve (Wallis, 1976).

While authority tends to be unstable in new movements, it tends to be *de-stabilised* by the death of a charismatic leader. The consequences of such de-stabilisation can be mitigated by extensive preparation for the transfer of authority at death so that legitimacy is smoothly passed from one depository to another without becoming available to competing claims. A case in point is that of Christian Science. Mrs. Mary Baker Eddy had established a substantial bureaucratic apparatus some time prior to her death and the membership had thus long been accustomed to direction by the Board of Directors of the Mother Church in Boston. Despite these careful preparations, however, there was a period of instability on her death as the Board sought to expand its authority to take Mrs. Eddy's place.

The only effective schism to occur after Mrs. Eddy's death was that led by Mrs. Annie Bill who rested her claim on the *Manual* of the Mother Church which clearly specified that the Pastor Emeritus — the title taken by Mrs. Eddy — must approve constitutional changes, senior appointments, etc. On Mrs. Eddy's death, Mrs. Bill claimed the position of Pastor Emeritus and established the Christian Science Parent Church to which she invited all other Christian Science Churches to affiliate (Braden, 1958; Swihart, 1931). Mrs. Bill's schismatic Church secured no large number of defections from the Mother Church. Augusta Stetson, who prior to her excommunication on Mrs.

Eddy's command, had been the most prominent teacher and practitioner in Christian Science, continued to remain loyal to the person of Mrs. Eddy. On the latter's demise, Mrs. Stetson gathered a following based on her opposition to the policy of the Board of Directors who had announced that they did not anticipate Mrs. Eddy's resurrection, and who continued to promote the 'material' form of the Church. Mrs. Stetson believed that on Mrs. Eddy's death, Christian Science should become purely spiritual in conception, and in accordance with this view, made no attempt to found a competing form of organisation. Both Mrs. Bill and Mrs. Stetson based their claims to legitimacy on an appeal to the unique status of the charismatic leader, or her role within the movement, in opposition to the transfer of authority to a bureaucratic apparatus. Neither had any substantial lasting impact. Authority and legitimacy within Christian Science had been so effectively centralised by Mrs. Eddy, that after her death dissenters had available to them little in the way of resources to which effective legitimating appeal could be made to secure the support of any substantial number of followers.

As an aside, it may be said, that by far the most serious *potential* schism following Mrs. Eddy's death, lay in the dispute between the two autonomous bureaucratic agencies which she had established. The Board of Directors was resisted by the Trustees of the publishing house which produced Christian Science literature, when the former sought to extend its authority over the operations of the latter. Both possessed the legitimation of having been vested with authority by Mrs. Eddy, and both had access to the following of the movement as a whole. A court action ensued, the judgement of which declared the Trustees to be subordinate to the Board of Directors, thereby negating their claim to independent legitimacy, and affirming the authority of the Board.

But if the death of a charismatic leader can create instabilities of legitimacy in movements where the new bases of authority have been so carefully prepared, they are clearly very much more likely to occur in movements where no alternative leadership structure has been unambiguously designated, or more problematically still, where a number of heir-designates can claim to have been indicated. The death of a charismatic leader traumatically removed the principal recognised locus of authority, leaving a more or less adequately institutionalised alternative, the legitimacy of which is problematic at least during the initial transition period. The de-stabilisation of authority renders it potentially available particularly to those who can claim some peculiar or privileged relationship with the former leader.

An interesting illustration of this type of situation of de-stabilisation is provided by the death of the Mormon leader, Joseph Smith in 1844. After substantial earlier struggles, Smith had concentrated charismatic authority in his own person, and developed an administrative apparatus headed by Brigham Young. Smith's sudden death left the Mormons without clear leadership. His immediate family proposed that Joseph's eldest son should succeed when he came of age and supported his claim by reference to statements of the founder purported to show this as his intention. James Strang, Church elder and recent convert, presented himself as successor bearing a forged letter from Joseph with whom he had been friendly, which ostensibly appointed him. Sydney Rigdon, for long Joseph Smith's closest associate and second in command, also claimed the succession, reporting revelations of his selection. When Brigham Young as *de facto* head of the organisational structure in his office as president of the Council of Twelve Apostles, won the support of the following, each of these factions was able to carry a body of support with them. Rigdon and Strang each founded short-lived schismatic Churches, while the prophet's family gathered together in the Re-organised Church of the Latter Day Saints, many of those who refused to follow Brigham Young to the West (Anderson, 1942; O'Dea, 1957).

Conclusions

This chapter has sought to show the utility of a new approach to schism, focusing on the differential propensity of different movements and the same movements at different times to undergo fission. It has been argued that the source of this propensity lies in the availability of means of legitimating a challenge to the prevailing leadership and claiming the loyalty of some body of the movement's supporters. Such legitimation may be available to a broad range of followers as in the case of groups within the Spiritualist tradition or only to an informal elite as in Christadelphianism or the early Brethren movement. It may derive from such sources of legitimation as:

1. A democratic or individualistic ideology designating no privileged interpreters of the truth, for example, pentecostalist groups, spiritualist groups, the Quakers, Marxist parties.

2. Informal personal influence and acknowledged leadership at a local level in the absence of clearly institutionalised central authority, for example, Christadelphianism, the early Brethren.
3. Institutionalised local authority which can be deployed against a centralised authority, for example, teacher-and practitioner-based movements such as Christian Science, Dianetics.
4. Competing recognised central authorities, for example, the charisma of Jeffreys as founder of Elim in opposition to the bureaucratic administration (cf. Wilson, 1961); the incipient schismatic situation of Blavatsky and Olcott in Theosophy; conflicting bureaucratic agencies as in the incipient schismatic dispute between the Board and the Trustees on Mrs. Eddy's death.

The theory proposed here then, not only provides an explanation for different rates of schism, but a means of interpreting many salient features of particular instances. While for the purposes of exposition I have drawn a distinction between theories of motivation and theories of structural conditions for schism, this distinction must now be blurred a little. Explanations for different *rates* of some phenomenon often makes reference to explanatory entities which seem to lie outside the understanding of actors and constrain their actions *regardless* of their motivations and intentions. The theory proposed above should *not* be thus construed. Rather than structural conditions *constraining* actors independently of their motivation, I suggest that in the case of schism these factors explicitly or implicitly enter into the motivation of actors to pursue a schismatic course of action.

That is, I propose that one factor under consideration when a line of conduct likely to lead a schism is undertaken, is the probability of successfully carrying some of the following or membership into separation. That probability will be seen to depend upon the degree to which a schismatic leader can successfully justify and legitimate his course of action, which will in turn depend upon whether he sees some means of legitimation as available. The degree to which some means of legitimation is seen as available is likely to correlate quite highly with the availability of such means. This is not, however, to say that a factional leader will always calculate the probabilities accurately, or correctly construe the degree to which a particular legitimatory means is available, only that such questions are likely to occur to him, and the answers will form parameters in his decision-making.

* Nyomarkay's use of 'legitimacy is not altogether clear but seems to refer to *internal* legitimacy by which he appears to mean the focus of group cohesion and loyalty — 'monistic legitimacy' thus implies one focus; 'pluralistic legitimacy' implies more than one focus.

† This is not incompatible with Nyomarkay's view of the Nazi Party. Although Hitler's *Weltanschauung* was diffuse and nebulous and he tolerated factionalism until he reached an authoritative decision on the matter in question, on incorporating that decision into his programme this became the uniquely legitimate conception to which all were required to adhere.

CHAPTER XI

The moral career of a research project

Research on human subjects perennially poses moral and political dilemmas, the diversity and acuteness of which are only rarely matched in the natural sciences. In sociology, a growing awareness of these dilemmas has developed in recent decades. The work of Vidich and Bensman (1958) on the Springdale community, and more recently that of Laud Humphreys (1970) on homosexual contacts in public facilities, posed in different ways the issue of responsibility to one's subjects. The ill-fated project Camelot raised widespread concern over the dangers of research sponsorship (Horowitz, 1967). Studies by Festinger *et al.* (1956), Humphreys (1970) and the Milgram (1974) study of obedience, all provoked controversy concerning the allowable limits of deception in social research.

Such problems are, indeed, endemic within sociology. The activity itself almost always requires incursion into areas of life which some of those involved are likely to construe as belonging to a private domain. The publication of the results of research almost always contains a potential threat to the public rhetoric or the private self-image of those who have been studied. If components of that rhetoric or self-image are matters of public dispute or debate, the work of the sociologist will inevitably be mobilised or criticised in justification or support of one or another contending party. A great deal of sociology is, therefore, in a sense, *subversive.* It inevitably provides an account of features of the social world which will conflict with the beliefs, interests, or public assertions of some individuals or groups in a pluralistic society.

The more strongly committed the actors are to the norms,

193

values, or beliefs at issue, the more threatening the attentions of social researchers are likely to prove. Those who believe they possess the truth complete and undefiled, do not need a sociologist to tell them what is going on. Indeed, his very pursuit of further or different knowledge after he has already been informed of the 'truth' of the matter by the individuals or groups concerned, displays the fact that he does not accept the ' self-evident', and perhaps even that motivated by malice; he is determined to tell some entirely different story. Few groups are committed to an authoritative conception of reality covering all aspects of their lives. Such totalistic self-conceptions are an extreme case. However, some groups approach very close to this claim to possess complete knowledge. Sectarian collectivities are particularly likely to believe that they possess all-embracing knowledge. Hence, an account of my research into one sectarian collectivity, Scientology, may illustrate the practical and moral (or, broadly, political) problems which some kinds of sociological enterprise can generate. I shall outline the history of my research relationship with Scientology and then make a few general observations deriving from this interaction.

Early in 1971, having exhausted a long list of possible thesis topics, I began work on a range of new religious movements in advanced industrial societies. It seemed to me that while traditional sectarianism had received considerable scholarly attention as a result of Bryan Wilson's research and his stimulation of an active group of graduate students, the new religious movements, many of which were only marginally Christian or altogether non-Christian, had been neglected. I proposed to begin remedying this situation by analysing a number of such movements on a comparative basis. I began collecting literature issued by, and concerning, such movements, and attending public meetings held by these groups, in order to formulate more precisely the way in which my research should proceed. One of the movements which I included, was Scientology.

Scientology is a movement based upon a religious philosophy which now claims a substantial following in all the English-speaking countries, and to a lesser degree, elsewhere. It originated as a lay psychotherapeutic movement, Dianetics which made its first public appearance in 1950. Dianetics claimed that psychosomatic illness, psychological and social disability, were the result of traumatic experiences in early, even intra-uterine life. By 1952, the movement, which had achieved craze proposititions in the USA, had foundered, and L. Ron Hubbard, its

194

inventor, had developed a more inclusive metaphysical system, which he later incorporated as a Church. Scientology holds that we are all spiritual beings, Thetans, but have lost touch with our spiritual nature and capacities. Through training, and a practice known as 'auditing', we can regain awareness of our true spiritual nature, and recover the competence to employ our forgotten supernatural powers. (On the origins, development, membership, ideology, and practices of Scientology, see Wallis, 1973a; 1974; 1975b; 1975d; 1976).

Scientology seemed particularly interesting for a number of reasons. To begin with, I must admit to having been attracted by its very 'exoticness'. As I looked over the scant material then available, I found that Scientology proposed a system of beliefs and practices which at that time seemed altogether bizarre to me. How *could* people come to believe such things, and undertake the practices they entailed? The common reaction to this puzzle, which I was later to pose to many people in the course of describing my work, was that Scientology's followers must be 'cranks', 'inadequates', or simply 'deluded'. I found these hypotheses sociologically uncompelling. The accounts which I read gave me little reason to believe that apart from holding some unusual views on the nature of man and how to cope with his problems, the bulk of the following was anything but 'normal'. I wanted, therefore, to find out more about how they came into this movement, and came to hold the beliefs to which they displayed such apparently sincere commitment in its publications.

Scientology was especially interesting for another reason. Throughout the English-speaking world, it had been a matter of controversy. Why *had* this one movement, out of the luxuriant crop of new religions, become the centre of so much debate, and even open conflict with State and private agencies, hostile individuals and the mass media? (It was, of course, followed in this respect within a few years by other new religious movements, for example the Unification Church and the Children of God.)

There was a further reason for my interest in Scientology. Reflecting upon my motivations, and aware that sociologists rarely interest themselves deeply in phenomena to which they are personally or politically indifferent, I conclude that Scientology partly interested me because as a species of social democrat, I was fascinated and repelled by the apparent authoritarianism and even occasional totalitarianism of this movement. I wanted to understand how it came to exercise such extensive control over, and to mobilise such enduring commitment from, so many of its followers.

The Scientologists often accuse me of having a preconceived idea of Scientology from the outset, which blinded me to those aspects of the movement which I saw as of minimal importance, but which they took great pains to convince me were central to their endeavours. This may, of course, be true. No one can guarantee his objectivity. Every researcher is susceptible to bias. There is perhaps even a *necessary* element of truth in their criticism. I did, indeed, formulate quite early a view about Scientology. The material which I read led me to believe that this was a dogmatic movement, intolerant of alternative conceptions of the world, and particularly intolerant of alternative interpretations of the nature and meaning of Scientology to that which it provided for general consumption through its own public relations machinery. Whether this theoretical preconception coloured my understanding of the data which I later examined, or was corroborated by it, it's always open to debate. That, it seems to me, is as it should be. However, this early working hypothesis was instrumental in moulding my methodological strategy.

It seemed clear to me that approaching the leaders and officials of such a public-relations-conscious social movement directly, for assistance with my research, was simply to invite public relations. Moreover, should they not approve of the undertaking, there was the possibility that I would even invite overt hostility. The Scientologists had been 'investigated' before. The Federal Food and Drug Administration in America; government enquiries in Australia and New Zealand that I knew of at that time; another whose report was expected imminently in Britain; and newspapers and magazines throughout the world, had investigated this movement. After reading some of this material later I came to understand better why the Scientologists reacted to public commentary and criticism, and to 'investigation' with such aggression, and even came to sympathise with them to some extent. At that time, however, I merely knew that they *did* react with virulence, and I wished to avoid it in my own case.

Hence, my research initially went little beyond reading the available material and visiting a London Scientology centre for the 'personality test' which the movement provided as a 'loss-leader', to draw further interest. At this stage, I still proposed to incorporate Scientology into a broad survey of new religious movements and their social dynamics. At an opportune moment, however, I came across a recently published book by a former member of the movement (Vosper, 1971). Having read it, I wrote to him and later met him to discuss the work on which I was engaged. The ex-Scientologist put me into contact with a number of acquaintances, most of whom, initially, had (whether permanently or temporarily) ended their connection with Scientology. Many of them agreed to be interviewed by me, and even to put me in contact with others who had knowledge of Scientology. A chain sample was developing, and I was beginning to feel that Scientology was both interesting enough, and the source of sufficient information, to make the sole object of my doctoral research.

Those I interviewed also sometimes made available to me dusty collections of papers and literature. Occasionally in this material were further names and addresses to which I wrote inquiring whether the individual concerned would be willing to see me. Or a name would reappear through many old documents, and I would badger my informants for information about how I might contact the people in question. One informant made available a mailing-list of a Scientology organisation, some years out of date, on which she had indicated those whom she believed no longer to be active Scientologists, and who might therefore be willing to discuss their experiences with me. I prepared and despatched a questionnaire to a sample of the names, although not restricting myself to those indicated by my informant.

I did not ask myself until some time later whether I had any right to employ this list. The donor was aware of my intentions and I fully intended to maintain the confidentiality of the respondents, yet it might be said that this list was an internal document of the movement and should not have been employed for this purpose without the permission of its officials. During the course of my research, I was to read many documents not meant for public consumption, and I believe the status of this mailing list differed little from other such material. I did not come by any of it dishonestly, hence I felt entitled to use it.

The questionnaire was not successful as a means of generating a random or even a representative sample of Scientologists. It was so far out of date that many of those sampled were no longer at the same address. A number of those to whom questionnaires were sent had only got onto the list as a result of buying a single book on Scientology, and had had no further contact. Nevertheless, some completed questionnaires were returned and some of my respondents subsequently indicated that they were willing to be interviewed. A grant was made available by the Social Science Research Council, which enabled me to travel around Britain conducting interviews, and later to visit the United States to conduct more, and to examine documentary sources. The interviews took various forms. Whenever possible I tape-recorded my conversation with respondents. I began with a fairly well-formalised list of questions, but gradually developed a looser, more flexible and open-ended style, talking round various themes of interest to me, and allowing the respondent to converse at length on matters which he regarded as important. These interviews were conducted in locations as diverse as a London taxi-cab, and a Japanese restaurant in Oakland, California. Some respondents were unwilling to be tape-recorded, and in these cases I sought to recall the content of the conversation as soon afterwards as I conveniently could.

Scientology provides a wide range of courses on its theories and methods, some acquaintance with which would, I believed, prove indispensable to my research. I proposed to secure some insight into this aspect of the movement, by engaging in participant observation. Having left my name and address when I had taken the 'personality test', and having purchased books by mail from the organisation, my name had appeared on their current mailing list. In consequence, I received several dozen circulars and letters, many of which encouraged me to visit the headquarters at Saint Hill Manor, East Grinstead, in order to take the introductory Communications Course.

One letter, dated 1 July 1971, for example, ends as follows:

Should you ever be near East Grinstead, come up and see us and have a look round. You will be welcome.

A further letter in July 1971 concluded:

I hope you will take the first basic course in Scientology as soon as you can. This is the Communications Course which costs only £5 and the results are invaluable. It takes only three weeks to do.

The literature which accompanied such letters indicated no constraints upon who would be acceptable to take the course. I therefore concluded that it was open to the public at large, and that I could in good conscience participate in it without revealing any more than that I was an interested outsider.

Early in 1972, I visited East Grinstead and registered for the Communications Course and arranged lodgings at a Scientology boarding house. This seemed an ideal opportunity to engage in participant observation on the movement. When I registered for the course and paid my fee I was shown a list of conditions, to which I was asked to agree. Due to the character of my role and the circumstances in which this took place, I was unable to make any note of the nature of these conditions. I recall, however, that I had early decided that while I did not feel covert participant observation to be unethical in this context, I was, nevertheless, not prepared to lie about my interest in Scientology. I was only prepared to represent it less than fully. Hence, I believe that the conditions were not such that my assent to them would have been a lie. Much later in the history of my relationship with this movement, its officials claimed that among other things, I had agreed to 'use knowledge gained from the course for Scientology purposes only'. A copy of a list containing conditions for course entry was sent to me. I now have no way of telling whether or not this was a duplicate of the list to which my assent was requested. My feeling is that this list, and the one to which I gave my assent, were *not* the same, but clearly this *could* be rationalisation.

Would it have been unethical behaviour to agree to such a list of conditions and then to break them? I do not believe there is a general answer to the question of whether or not certain kinds of behaviour are ethically impermissible in all situations. The ethics of social research involve a complex weighing of values in relation to particular situations. In *this* particular situation I feel that agreeing to constraints one did not intend to keep would have been morally reprehensible and the information which I required should have been secured some other way. It is important to note, however, that the facts of the case are not altogether clear on this occasion. My own view is that I did not agree to any conditions which I could not keep.

Having registered for the course, I spent two days at Saint Hill Manor working on the materials, stapled in folders, which I would have to assimilate in order to complete it. I early felt uncomfortable in my role. Prior to this piece of fieldwork, I had engaged in participant observation at services and meetings of various groups, but there, I had been one of a (usually small) crowd. My presence signified nothing beyond an interest in what was taking place. On those occasions too, I had felt uncomfortable when I was approached on a personal basis, when a group leader or speaker would stop for a few words of welcome to a new face among the regulars. Disguised or covert participant observation is easy when no participation beyond mere presence is required. When the interaction moves to a more personal basis and participation of a more active kind is necessitated, role-playing dilemmas present themselves.

How should one exhibit oneself? As an interested newcomer seeking some transcendental commodity which this group or individual may be able to provide, or as a disinterested observer viewing this group or individual as one case of a general class, and personally indifferent to, perhaps even sceptical of, the transcendental knowledge which is being offered? Good participant observation required a particular personality or discipline, which I did not possess. Outside a 'mass' context, I felt uncomfortable in my role. It felt like spying, and a little dishonest. In general, I tried to shift the situation to an 'open' interaction context as quickly as possible. I conveyed as early as I conveniently could that I was a sociologist, that I worked in a University, and that while I was interested in what my informant had to say, my *personal* interest was tempered and directed by wider *sociological* concerns.

To take that step in this situation would, however, have been self-defeating. I had come to Saint Hill Manor to learn how 'anyman' coming in off the street would be received, not how a visiting sociologist doing a thesis on Scientology would be treated. In some research situations such a distinction would have been of little importance. Everything I knew about Scientology suggested that in *this* instance it would make a good deal of difference.

At the Scientology lodging-house the problem was equally difficult. The other residents with whom I dined and breakfasted were committed Scientologists. In a friendly way they sought to draw me into their conversations. I found it difficult to participate without suggesting a commitment similar to their own, which I did not feel. Returning to the course material, I found as I progressed that I would shortly have to convey — whether aloud, or by my continued presence — assent to claims made by Ron Hubbard the movement's founder, with which I could not agree, and of which I could sometimes make little sense. I indicated my disagreement with some point in the course material to the instructor, and thereby mobilised a series of remedies which Scientology has available to manage disagreement with the 'data'. I was asked to look up all the words in the contentious phrase in a dictionary to ensure that I understood them. When this did not help, I was asked to make some visual configuration out of available bric-à-brac of my disagreement with the phrase. There is not space here to detail all the remedies that were applied. It became clear, however, that were I to proceed with the course I should finally have to convey some agreement with the statement in question. I felt this would have been dishonest and, more pragmatically, my discomfort would have been too great. I therefore quietly slipped away from Saint Hill Manor at a dinner break, rueing perhaps that I was not made of sterner stuff.

Later in 1972, I wrote for the first time to the movement's leaders, indicating that I was a sociologist engaged upon research into Scientology for a thesis. I acknowledged that previous studies of the movement had rarely been models of academic objectivity, and that they had often resulted in bad publicity, and occasionally in intolerant political action against the movement. I therefore suggested with all the pretentiousness of a novice graduate student that they consider the possibility that my own research might be more advantageous than some of the earlier studies. I suggested three reasons why this might be so. First, I point out that I was 'independent'. By this I meant that I had not been commissioned by the State or by any interest group opposed to Scientology (I was at that time a student at Nuffield College, Oxford). Nor could I, I felt, be subjected to pressure by such groups. Secondly, I pointed out that I was 'an academic' and did not therefore have to produce a popular work. I did not have to aim to sensationalise in order to achieve sales. Thirdly, I pointed out that while I was independent, I was also a 'professional sociologist' and had therefore to maintain standards of objectivity, neutrality and ethics to which some other authors do not owe responsibility. I also believed that by providing an objective account of the movement and its history I might be able to refute some of the more extreme claims directed at the movement by interests hostile to it. I stressed, however, that my work would not only involve rebuttals of critical claims. I wrote as follows: 'it would be wrong to suggest that my intention is simply to produce an eulogy of Scientology. Rather my aim is to produce a balanced and reasoned appraisal and since I have no axe to grind I . . . think that with your assistance this might be entirely possible.' I offered to visit East Grinstead to discuss my research with officials of the movement.

In mid 1972 I paid this visit to the headquarters and there discussed my research with a member of its Guardian's Office. (This office is concerned with the movement's external relations.) The official, an Assistant Guardian, was clearly puzzled and concerned about my having spent two days on the Communications Course, and having then left in the middle of it. I attempted to explain the reasons for my departure. He had also received various of the questionnaires which I had sent to names on the list of Scientologists of earlier years, and it was evident that he was suspicious of the fact that the questionnaires seemed to be directed particularly towards apostates and former members rather than towards current members. In subsequent mailings of this questionnaire I modified some of the questions so that they read less as if directed solely at apostates. The Assistant Guardian agreed to provide me with materials of various kinds on the movement although he declined to give me any direct access to its archives. He also agreed to allow me to interview some staff members and students at the headquarters, and to provide me with the names and addresses of people I might visit on a then forthcoming research trip to the United States of America.

I entered into no obligations with this official about the nature of my research. He insisted on laying certain 'ground rules' which were that he would not give me blanket access to materials on Scientology, and that he would pursue legally any publication of 'advanced course' materials. Apart from these stipulations he requested no undertakings from me as to the nature of my research and none were offered. No promises of any kind were made.

I had been formulating some of my early conclusions regarding Scientology in a paper in which I discussed this movement in the context of models of sectarianism that were currently available in the extant literature. The main drift of my discussion was to point to the inadequacy of the prevailing formulations of the concept of sect, and to attempt to produce an argument for those dimensions which seemed to me still to be of utility, employing Scientology in illustration. After my discussions with the Assistant Guardian I sent to him a draft copy of this paper entitled 'The sectarianism of Scientology'. He was altogether unenthusiastic about the paper which I sent. He objected to my use of the terms 'sectarianism' and 'totalitarianism' in this context; to aspects of my characterisation of the movement's founder; and to my account of the movement's development (Wallis, 1973a).

In retrospect, given the degree to which Scientology had in the past suffered from investigation by journalists and agencies of the state, it is not difficult to see why my own behaviour and writings should have led to considerable suspicion and some hostility on the part of the movement. I appeared to be behaving in ways which were reminiscent of earlier investigations of Scientology which had led to persecution of the movement. I had approached apostates and those who were hostile towards it before I had approached the movement's leaders or those who were currently taught by the movement; I had enrolled on one of its courses without declaring my ulterior motive; and then apparently, I had written a paper which its leaders viewed as hostile and which departed to a considerable extent from their own interpretations of the movement's reality.

It was shortly after the Scientology officials had commented unfavourably on my paper 'The sectarianism of Scientology', that a series of events occurred which led me to believe that I was the object of a campaign of harassment designed both to cause me inconvenience, and to discredit me in the eyes of fellow sociologists. The events which transpired are recorded in detail elsewhere (Wallis, 1973b). In brief, they involved the activities of a staff member of the Scientology organisation who visited my University (I had by then become a lecturer at the University of Stirling) presenting himself as a student wishing to undertake some study or research into Scottish religion. He asked to attend my classes and lectures, and inquired whether I could put him up at my home for a few days! This naturally aroused my suspicion and I shortly recalled having seen him in a staff member's uniform when I had taken the Communications Course at the Scientology headquarters. However, I took no action at this stage, not knowing precisely how to react. During his short stay in Stirling he made visits to my home in my absence and, unbeknown to me at that time, presented himself to students and others as a friend of mine in order to make inquiries concerning whether or not I was involved in the 'drug scene'. After a couple of days, I confronted him with my knowledge of his background.

At this point he changed his story, claiming now to be a defector from Scientology come to sell me information. I informed him that I was not buying information and gave him to understand that I believed his story as little as his earlier one. While I checked up on his credentials, he disappeared. I was subsequently able to discover the man's real name, and observed that he was later listed in a Scientology publication as a graduate of one of the movement's many courses.

In the weeks following his visit, a number of forged letters came to light, some of which were supposedly written by me. These letters, sent to my University employers, colleagues and others, implicated me in a variety of acts from a homosexual love affair, to spying for the drug squad. Having few enemies and following so closely upon the receipt of my article by the Scientology organisation, it did not seem too difficult to infer the source of these attempts to inconvenience me.

In fact some of the forged letters *were* a source of considerable inconvenience. One set of letters, containing homosexual declarations of love supposedly written by me were sent to my university employers. They were received during a period in which disciplinary proceedings were being pursued against a number of students for allegedly disruptive activities during the visit by the Queen to the University. My own part in the ensuing debate had not endeared me to the University authorities, whose first action was to show the letters to the University's lawyer, present for the disciplinary hearings, to determine whether or not I had committed any offence against the University's regulations by writing such letters on official notepaper. I should add, however, that they readily accepted that the letters were forgeries and offered the services of the University solicitor to enable me to decide what was to be done about them. Since the police were not able to take any worthwhile steps in locating the culprit, I determined to publicise what had transpired.

Consequently I drafted another article in which I discussed my own experience, and those of several other writers on Scientology, who had suffered either from 'mysterious and unpleasant' happenings, or from extensive litigation. Before publishing it, I visited the movement's East Grinstead headquarters again in April 1973, where I had arranged through the official of the Guardian's Office to interview staff members and students. These interviews I tape-recorded, while a member of the Guardian's staff tape-recorded me conducting them. I was not surprised that a number of my interviewees were engaged upon courses concerned with public relations. This was doubtless a useful practical exercise for them. I also had a lengthy conversation with the Assistant Guardian concerning the research. Towards the end of this conversation, I broached the matter of the spy and the forged letters. The Assistant Guardian did not take this matter up, except to say that he knew nothing about it and would look into it.

I reminded him of this in a subsequent letter, but no admission of any knowledge of, or responsibility for, the events was ever made, and indeed such knowledge and responsibility were subsequently denied. I therefore went ahead with the publication of my article, bravely undertaken by Paul Barker, the editor of *New Society* (Wallis, 1973b). The Scientologists' response was to write to my funding body, the Social Science Research Council complaining of my 'unethical' behaviour in writing this piece and in the conduct of my research, and threatening legal action. The Social Science Research Council acknowledged the Scientologists' letter but took no further steps, accepting my account of the preceding events. *New Society* also published a letter from a Scientology official disputing my account.

In September 1973 the Scientologists themselves published an article concerning my research in a widely-distributed newssheet which they produced (Spittell, 1973). They quoted the Panel on Privacy and Behavioural Research (1967) established by the US President's Office of Science and Technology, whose preliminary report, published in *Science,* had stressed the doctrine of 'informed consent' as an ethical principle which should be adopted by researchers on human subjects. The Scientologists argued that I had not obtained *their* informed consent at the beginning of my study. They also argued that 'an allegedly authoritative paper on the nature of Scientology' (alleged only by the Scientologists I might add) had been based 'on information gained solely from a few people openly hostile to the Church of Scientology'. They also claimed that my completed questionnaires were to go into a data bank, and implied some sinister collection of information on my respondents' political leanings. Further allegations were that I planned to write a popular book on Scientology; that I was conducting a 'campaign' against it; that I aspired 'to make a name and to make money out of sensationalising a non-selling subject'; that I had 'extracted information' under a 'pretence of guaranteed privacy'; that I had distorted the truth; and that I was conducting a 'trial by innuendo'.

Some of these allegations were not totally without foundation. I did hope to 'make a name' out of my study of Scientology, although with a professional rather than a lay audience, and I even hoped I might make the nominal, but none the less useful, royalties that academics usually make from their books. I had never intended to write a popular book, but I can now see the Scientologists' grounds for this claim. I had originally told them I was writing a *doctoral thesis* on Scientology, and I think they had perhaps not realised that doctoral theses are sometimes published, and indeed I had not thought seriously of this myself until my work was some way advanced.

On the issues of 'informed consent' and 'pretended privacy', it is true that I had not informed the *organisation* from the beginning that I was conducting the research, nor do I see why I should have done so, but I did always fully inform interview and questionnaire respondents of the character of my research. I also gave them a guarantee of confidentiality, i.e. an undertaking not to publish their names without their permission. This guarantee has been fully fulfilled. Contrary to the Scientologists' claim, many of my interviews were with individuals openly *favourable* to Scientology. None of my material was appropriate for data-bank purposes. The only 'campaigning' or 'trial by innuendo' that I could be accused of conducting was my *New Society* article, the cautious conclusions of which were, I believe, only what any man on the top of the Clapham omnibus would also have drawn. Finally there is the assertion that I 'distorted the truth'. I claim no privileged access to the truth. I believe all knowledge to conjectural, and it is not impossible that some of my conjectures may prove to be false. 'Distortion' rather implies something stronger, however. It suggests that I recognise as true something other than what I wrote, or that my perceptions were in some way biased by an animus against the Scientologists. Of course, I dispute this. I have at times been irritated, even angered, by the Scientologists' behaviour, but I detect in myself no permanent hostility towards them. I would, indeed, feel impelled to defend them against legislative intolerance such as they had experienced in Australia, where briefly in some states they were banned.

I replied to the article which criticised my research, in a letter which reminded the Scientologists that they had often in the past complained of being allowed no right of reply to hostile articles. They kindly published my letter in their paper.

The year following these events was spent in analysing and writing up my data. This work was completed in the summer of

1974 and my thesis was presented at the end of August. A publisher had exhibited some interest in the manuscript and a contract was signed a month or so before presentation of the thesis. I had for some months thought Scientology's treatment of its critics and commentators was largely directed at the suppression and censorship of works they construed as hostile to their interests. At first, therefore, I planned not to send them my manuscript. The completion of my work led me to reflect on this matter. Suppose some of my 'facts' and interpretations were untrue and were a source of harm to the Scientologists. They surely had a right not to be publicised in a false light. It seemed to me that a sociologist owed his subjects an obligation not to cause them *undeserved* harm. There was, therefore, a major ethical dilemma here, a tension between the obligation to one' subjects, and the possibility of censorship. I reasoned that although Scientologists might sometimes act against commentators in ways that seemed malevolent, perhaps this was because they had been given no prior opportunity to comment. Were they not, after all, reasonable men? Would they not recognise and respect my aspiration to objectivity, and therefore approach my work with an open-mindedness which they were unwilling to exhibit towards more sensationalising, journalistic, or openly hostile works? I decided to send them my manuscript. I should add, however, that this action was not motivated solely by altruism. I thought the manuscript quite a good one, and wanted to see it published. I also wanted to avoid lengthy and astronomically expensive litigation, which I could ill afford. My contract with the publisher stipulated that in the event of a libel action which we lost, I would be responsible for any costs and damages. Perhaps such an action could be avoided by letting the movement's leaders see my manuscript, comment upon it, and provide any further evidence which would support their interpretation. For both ethical and pragmatic reasons, it seemed sensible to allow them an opportunity to comment on the work before it appeared in print.

Early in September 1974 I sent them the manuscript. Later that month I met with an official of the Scientology organisation in London and we discussed in an amicable way the contentious issues which it posed. He provided me with a preliminary list of points which had emerged from his reading of the thesis. These six pages I found heartening. My judgement was vindicated. We could begin to discuss the contentious points, and consider the evidence. Where my view was changed,

I would modify the manuscript. Where it remained unchanged, we could perhaps agree to differ.

I examined the manuscript in the light of these comments, and some of them seemed to me to contain reasonable foundations. For example, I strengthened in various places the sense that some things which had originally read as facts were only various people's *interpretations* of the facts. At one point I changed a statement that people had done something because of Hubbard's authoritarianism to read that they had done it because of 'what some of them viewed as his . . . authoritarianism'. I modified some descriptions which seemed to read more evaluatively than I could justify. At one point for example I had claimed that Hubbard was 'obsessed' by the threat of communism. I now changed this to read that he was 'exercised' by this threat. I added further commentary on Scientology's religious practices and contemporary social reform activities, which I had possibly underemphasised in my original version. I also deleted a section in which I had drawn parallels between Scientology and the Nazi Party. While I continued to believe these parallels were sociologically viable, they were not crucial to my discussion, and I felt that they both lent themselves to sensationalistic interpretation and were *unecessarily* offensive to ordinary Scientologists. In all I made some 27 changes (the exact number depending on how one defines a change).

Early in November the Scientology organisation sent me a more detailed commentary which comprised some 12,000 words. I again turned to the manuscript. This time I found little in my text which I thought I had reason to change. However, I felt the Scientologists' disagreements with my interpretations should be known. I therefore incorporated a number of footnotes setting out their arguments, later transposed into the text, to enable the reader to compare them with my own. My emendations to the manuscript now numbered around forty-six.

I also had what seemed to me to be a bright idea. What the Scientologists wanted I reasoned, was for their version of events to be known. Therefore why should we not let them have some right to reply. Having discussed the idea with my publishers, I wrote to the Scientologists early in November 1974, sending my latest revisions, and offering to include in the book a 5000 word commentary or reply to the book by them, in return for an undertaking to refrain from litigation in connection with its publication.

They replied that they noted my proposal and 'provided

there is no legal barrier and subject to the determination of certain fundamental issues which will result in a partial rewrite' they were prepared to give it favourable consideration. They also sent a further 38 pages of comments and 148 items of supporting documentation. I found the talk of a 'partial rewrite' slightly ominous but, again, turned to the manuscript. I found only a few minor points which I could in good conscience, amend. Once again, however, I inserted a number of additional sentences stating the Scientologists' arguments. I had now made 80 modifications.

I sent these to the organisation and pointed out that: 'If you have further specific commentary and corrections I will be glad to look at these, but there has to be some limit to the length of time this can drag on. The Scientologist' reply contained the following specification of what they had in mind: 'Before we can agree to your proposals all libelous [sic] statements will be corrected, not by footnotes.'

I now suspected that the organisation was in fact determined to see only one interpretation of the matters discussed in my book prevail. A right of reply was not sufficient. The law of libel was to be invoked as a weapon in an attempt to censor my book into a form which rendered it compatible with the Scientologists' views. I naturally protested to the effect that their allegation that certain passages were libellous did not make them so. At this point the Scientologists took the step of submitting the manuscript with the emendations already agreed upon to an eminent Queen's Counsel with considerable experience in libel cases, and of known liberal sympathies. This move was a singularly astute one. Should the lawyer construe the items which they pointed out to him and complained of, as libellous, my publisher and I would not have been able to claim that this was an attempt to suppress freedom of speech, when so notable a civil rights campaigner had found the passages of which they complained, to be defamatory.

In the event, however, only one substantial section was held to be defamatory in the Opinion rendered by the barrister, of which the Scientologists sent me a copy. This section comprised some eight pages of typescript in which instances of the mysterious and unpleasant things which had not infrequently occurred to commentators on Scientology were discussed. In providing an account of these phenomena, I offered an interpretation which, while certainly a plausible, and conceivably a true, explanation for what had transpired, was not in the nature of the case provable. The passages involved were therefore, *prima facie* libellous in content. The circumstances involved in the events in question were often obscure in some respects. The responsibility for their occurrence was always a matter of controversy. Hence while I could satisfy myself that the bulk of the cases cited indicated a particular explanation, it appeared to be a distinct possibility that I would not convince a libel jury that all the cases could thus be accounted for. Moreover, it seemed to me that my responsibilities were more extensive than merely remaining within the bounds of the law. Whatever my personal feelings about Scientology and its organisations, I owed a responsibility as a sociologist toward the subjects of my research. Scientology is viewed with hostility in some quarters, and my responsibility extended to ensuring that I did not impute to the movement and its following behaviour, for which adequate evidence was unavailable, and which might rouse further hostility towards it. At the same time, however, I owed a responsibility to the grantors of my research funds, my colleagues and my readers, not to submit to censorship in the sense of suppressing adequately supported evidence concerning the subjects of my research.

The matter was ultimately resolved in the following manner. Two cases which I felt lacked sufficient substantiation were deleted. In two other instances sentences were included which incorporated statements by the organisation's representatives bearing on the events or persons involved. Throughout the section, any statement attributing responsibility for the events, which I had made in explanation, were removed. Otherwise the pages remained unchanged. The changes which I made, and which after further discussion were agreed by the Scientology organisation, seemed a reasonable and honourable compromise to both parties.

With these changes, negotiations between myself and the Scientologists were all but concluded. A comment on my book was commissioned by them from a sociologist who was also a practising Scientologist. This comment the publishers and I happily incorporated into the book as an appendix. An agreement was drawn up between the Church of Scientology. Heinemann Educational Books, and myself specifying that the Church of Scientology, its officials and its members would refrain from litigation connected with the publication of the book, in consideration of the modifications — ultimately totalling well over one hundred — which I had made, and an undertaking to include the commissioned Scientology comment as an appendix.

Honour had been preserved on all sides and a legal action — which none of the parties concerned seemed eager should take place — had been averted. My book would appear without mutilation or fear of legal consequences (Wallis, 1976) and the Scientologists could confound their enemies by exhibiting our final amicable resolution of the controversy as evidence of their reasonableness and good faith.

Conclusions

The course of this research project appeared to undergo a particular moral career (Goffman, 1968:24), in which both researcher and researched sought to define the behaviour of the other and to locate them within a conceptual framework and theoretical schema thereby rendering their behaviour understandable and predictable, and providing guidelines for reacting to them.

Both parties began with a certain suspicion of the other based on stereotypes which were culturally available. This researcher had much in common with other 'researchers' who turned out to be agents of hostile groups (psychiatrists, the state, the mass media). The researched had features in common with totalitarian groups which do not concede the possibility of a non-member having any valid view on their structure or behaviour. Behaviour by the researcher motivated by what he saw as sensible caution, was interpreted by the researched as underhandedness, prevarication, or spying. Their reaction — whatever its motivation — was construed by the researcher as harassment, and as an attempt to limit investigation or public discussion of their affairs. Hence, relations between researcher and researched escalated to a point of open hostility.

Actions taken to correct the stereotype by one side were viewed as public-relations exercises by the other. However, if that is as true for me as it is for them, what validity can the final work claim to have? My answer to this, I think, has to be that the question cannot be settled in the abstract. It is always possible for someone else to conduct research on Scientology, and to come to different conclusions. At such a time, of course, evidence can be compared and weighed again where necessary. I do not claim absolute objectivity since this seems to me to be an ideal to which we can only try to approximate. I rather claim to have attempted to be objective. I am sure that there are occasions upon which objectivity has eluded me. I note, for example, a recent paper in which I did not, until too late to amend it before publication, find it amiss or even odd to refer to Scientology ministers as wearing 'dog-collars' (Wallis, 1975b). Why did I use that term? Of course, I meant 'clerical collars', but I must have read and reread the paper a dozen times over the course of more than a year, before this struck me as a curious vulgarity. Did this 'amnesia' display a disrespect for ministers of religion in general or Scientology ministers in particular? Without a depth analysis of the researcher, I will probably never know.

The central conclusion to the drawn from this account is that the sociologist's interaction with his subjects forms a part of, and takes part in the context of, the overall interaction between those subjects and the wider society. He may be seen as a potential legitimator and defender of their public image, or as a threat to it. Those groups which are, or have been, in conflict with agencies of the wider society are likely to view a potential threat to their public image with hostility. If they are wealthy and well organised, they have available a powerful weapon with which to defend themselves against the publication of commentary of which they disapprove. The law of libel provides an important protection of individual and corporate character. Its remedies are, however, particularly costly for both plaintiff and defendant. Hence the threat of invoking such remedies is a weighty sanction mobilisable by the wealthy to censor or suppress accounts of themselves which they view as unflattering. As a spokesman for the Scientologists once said: 'Whatever else we may have been called, no one has ever accused us of being poor.'

The law of libel is an arcane mystery to the layman, and a severe, although not perhaps for that reason an unwarranted, constraint on the author of accounts of contemporary individuals and groups. It poses the problem of the relationship between sociological evidence and legal proof. As far as I understand it, the English law of libel requires 'that he who asserts must prove, and the proof required is proof up to the hilt, and the author will fail if he can show only that the defamatory statement was true on the balance of probability based on the evidence before him' (Kimber, 1972:74). Yet, of course, this is precisely the kind of evidential circumstance with which the sociologist is typically faced. In my analysis of the Scientology material, I took every precaution that I thought possible. Interview statements were weighed for the possible bias of the informant and the more extreme and unlikely statements rejected. Information from one interview was checked against information from other interviews, and against documentary sources. Documents for external publication were weighed against documents purely for internal circulation, and where possible against documents from independent sources (e.g. court records). All of this clearly involved selection on the basis of a theory or model of the nature of the information source, and the purpose for which the material was produced. This kind of theoretically based weighing and sifting of evidence is precisely the kind of intuitive skill professional training in research is designed to inculcate. It is unlikely in most research situations, even under the most auspicious circumstances to provide 'proof up to the hilt'.

There are two other problems in relation to the law of libel. First, some features of the background of this movement have been obscured by its officials whose wish it is that only their own version of certain affairs become public knowledge. Information on such matters is hard to come by and the sociologist's account will necessarily rely on a degree of more or less indirect inference. Secondly, the presentation of evidence in court in defending a libel action might require infringing upon the anonymity of respondents. Information was provided by many respondents on the understanding that their names would not be revealed. Probably most of these would have been loath to risk any repercussions by testifying in court to what they told me in private. Sometimes they still had friends or relatives in Scientology. Sometimes they were themselves members and wished to remain so, while none the less having reservations about some of its practices. In other cases, the individuals concerned had found their break with Scientology traumatic, or had begun entirely new lives, and in either case would not have wished to draw attention to themselves in connection with this movement. Hence while my material might be more or less adequate sociologically, there was reason to suspect that it might not be adequate to proving my comments on the movement 'up to the hilt' in every instance.

The problems of a potential libel action do not lie simply in the possibility of losing such an action. My publishers were insured against libel. A requirement of such an insurance policy is that the author undertakes to indemnify the publisher in the event of losses being sustained from a libel claim. The author, typically has no resources adequate to defending, or indemnifying the publisher against, a libel action. Hence if the publishers do not wish to renounce the benefits of their insurance policy, they must be responsive to the wishes of the insurers. A major interest of the insurer must inevitably be that of minimising costs to his company. This interest may often best be secured by an early apology and settlement in favour of the alleged libel victim, and if necessary, the withdrawal of the offending book, rather than undertaking to support the cost of defending the action, *even* when there is a good chance of winning (Kimber, 1972). For even when an award of costs is made, the successful defendant rarely recovers all his expenses. Libel cases are notoriously expensive. Juries are liable to be swayed by a variety of unpredictable circumstances, and the award of damages is subject to so many imponderables as often to defeat prediction.

Hence the weight of pressure in the case of a study such as my own is towards modifying and emasculating the final work, i.e. towards censorship. Publishers and insurers have a common interest in minimising legal conflict, and therefore in the elimination of controversial material. The Scientologists similarly have an interest in the elimination of controversial material. Hence at this point they share an interest with publishers and insurers which may conflict with the interest of the author. Fortunately, as a result of extensive negotiation and some compromise by the parties concerned in the present case, the matter was finally resolved without either litigation, or censorship.

A note on 'censorship'

The notion of 'censorship' is not an easy one to explicate, and I have no space here to explore its manifold possibilities. I have used the term in what seems to me a fairly 'common sense' manner to indicate some form of constraint upon what an author may say, which *runs contrary to his wishes, and/or his conscience*. My satisfaction with the outcome in this case, arises from the fact that none of the changes made to my book violated either my methodological criteria, or my conscience. It may always be said, of course, and indeed almost certainly *will* be said by those who would have wished me to take a more hostile stance *vis-à-vis* Scientology, that this is because my conscience was more malleable than their own would have been under similar circumstances. My own feeling is that my modifications were made precisely in virtue of the fact that in the light of subsequent discussions I could not in good conscience publish material or interpretations of a controversial and potentially damaging character for which I lacked sufficient evidence. Pre-'censorship', or self-'censorship', in the sense of allowing oneself to be persuaded that certain things should not be said, was of course extensive. But this neither seems to me a matter for apology nor for self-recrimination. The exercise of selection is a fundamental component of any scientific or scholarly enterprise. The pursuit of objectivity does not entail that moral criteria should not guide and inform the selection that takes place. They clearly do influence the topics which sociologists study, the aspects of those topics which they choose to discuss, and hence they are inherently involved in both what the sociologist says and what he leaves unsaid. There is no necessary conflict between objectivity and responsibility. An aspiration to objectivity does not require one to say *every-thing*. Rather it requires that as far as possible everything one *does* say should be available to criticism and refutation. Objectivity requires that acceptance of an account does not *depend* upon prior acceptance of a particular set of moral assumptions. There are, however, no simple means of deciding how well an author approximates the ideal of objectivity. The matter is always open to dispute, and this — if I may now venture an explicit value-judgement — appears to me both rational and healthy.

Howard Becker pointed out some years ago, that 'A study that purports to deal with social structure . . . inevitably will reveal that the organisation or community is not all it claims to be, not all it would like to be able to feel itself to be. A good study, therefore, will make somebody angry' (Becker, 1964). The sociologist who undertakes to study the social structure and dynamics of powerful groups firmly committed to some particular view of themselves must expect his revelations to result in hostility and the mobilisation of strategies to censor or even prohibit the publication of his work. He is likely to be drawn into a power struggle over which versions of the move-ments's history, morphology and behaviour are to become publicly available and may indeed be drawn into open conflict with his research subjects. While in the past sociologists have displayed concern, rightly in my view, over the dangers of harming the interests of powerless groups which they have chosen to study, they should not altogether forget the problems of the relatively powerless sociologist faced with the threat of censorship.

It should be mentioned that the present chapter was a source of considerable anxiety to the publishers of the volume in which it originally appeared (Bell & Newby, 1977). They believed that it too contained potentially libellous matter and sought to secure radical changes in content, failing which they subtly suggested that this chapter should not be allowed to endanger the whole volume and could perhaps be omitted entirely. The editors resisted these blandishments, and the publishers were finally convinced, after several months delay, that the Scientologists had no intention of suing a piece in which my research was exhibited as more art than science. Indeed, a Scientology spokesman admitted that in his view this was the best piece I had written about Scientology, and it is not hard to see why.

Bibliography

Aberle, David F. (1966) *The Peyote Religion Among the Navaho*, Chicago: Aldine.

Allan, Graham (1974) 'A theory of millennialism: the Irvingite movement as an illustration', *British Journal of Sociology* 25 (September), pp. 296-311.

Anderson, Kevin V. (1965) *Report of the Board of Inquiry into Scientology*, Melbourne: Government Printer.

Anderson, Nels (1942) *Desert Saints*, Chicago: University of Chicago Press.

Bacon Robert, George Sayer Bain and John Pimlott (1972) 'The economic environment' in A.H. Halsey (editor), *Trends in British Society since 1900*, London: Macmillan, pp. 64-69.

Bain, George Sayer, Robert Bacon and John Pimlott (1972) 'The labour force' in A.H. Halsey (editor) *Trends in British Society since 1900*, London: Macmillan, pp. 97-128.

Bates, Edwin S. and John V. Dittemore (1933) *Mary Baker Eddy: The Truth and the Tradition*, London: Routledge.

Beasley, Norman (1953) *The Cross and the Crown*, London: Allen & Unwin.

Becker, Howard P. (1932) *Systematic Sociology on the Basis of the Bezeihungslehre and Gebildelehre of Leopold von Wiese*, New York: Wiley.

Becker, Howard S. (1963) *Outsiders*, New York: Free Press; (1964) 'Problems in the publication of field studies' in Arthur Vidich, Joseph Bensman and Maurice R. Stein (editors), *Reflections on Community Studies*, New York: Wiley.

217

Beckford, James A. (1975) *The Trumpet of Prophecy: A Sociological Study of Jehovah's Witnesses,* Oxford: Basil Blackwell.

Bell, Colin and Howard Newby (editors) (1977) *Doing Sociological Research,* London: Allen & Unwin.

Berg, David Brandt (Moses David), *Mo Letters* (1970a) 'Colonization not infiltration'; (1970b) 'Dropouts — Part II — Quality or quantity?'; (1971a) 'The gypsies'; (1971b) 'Jesus People or revolution?', (1971c) 'Acts 13:4'; (1971d) 'Details'; (1971e) 'Let my people go'; (1972a) 'Survival'; (1972b) 'Other sheep'; (1972c) 'Dear Ho and Faith'; (1973a) 'Old bottles', (1973b) 'Shiners? — or shamers?'; (1974a) 'Share the know'; (1974b) 'Listening? — Or lamenting?'; (no date a (1970)) 'More about Israel'; (no date b (1970)) 'The rise of the reactionary right'.

Bland, Richard and Roy Wallis (1977) 'Comment on Wilson and Zurcher's "Status inconsistency and participation in social movements"' in *Sociological Quarterly,* 19 (3), pp. 426-429.

Braden, Charles S. (1958) *Christian Science Today,* Dallas: Southern Methodist University Press.

Briggs, Asa (1961) *The History of Broadcasting, Volume 1: The Birth of Broadcasting,* London: Oxford University Press; (1965) *The History of Broadcasting, Volume II: The Golden Age of Wireless,* London: Oxford University Press.

Brill, Harry (1971) *Why Organisers Fail: The Story of a Rent Strike,* Berkeley: University of California Press.

Bruce, Steve (1976) 'The Christian Union: A study of the maintenance of faith and evangelism', unpublished honours dissertation, University of Stirling.

Calley, Malcolm J.C. (1965) *God's People,* London: Oxford University Press.

Campbell, Colin (1972) 'The cult, the cultic milieu, and secularisation' in Michael Hill (editor), *A Sociological Yearbook of Religion in Britain,* No. 5, London: SCM Press.

Capon, John (1972) . . . *And There was Light,* London: Lutterworth.

Caulfield, Max (1976) *Mary Whitehouse,* London: Mowbray.

Cominos, Peter T. (1963) 'Late Victorian sexual respectability and the social system', *International Review of Social History,* 8, pp. 18-48 and 216-50.

Cooper, Paulette (1971) *The Scandal of Scientology,* New York: Tower.

Bibliography

Coser, Lewis A. (1961) 'Introduction' to Max Scheler, *Ressentiment,* Glencoe: Free Press.

Currie, Elliott and Jerome H. Skolnick (1970) 'A critical note on conceptions of collective behaviours' *The Annals of the American Academy of Political and Social Science, 391, pp. 34-45.*

Currie, Robert and Alan Gilbert (1972) 'Religion' in A.H. Halsey (editor), *Trends in British Society since 1900,* London: Macmillan, pp. 407-50.

Curtis, Russell L. and Louis A. Zurcher (1973) 'Stable resources of protest movements: the multi-organisational field', *Social Forces,* 52, pp. 53-61.

Dakin, Edwin Franden (1929) *Mrs. Eddy: The Biography of a Virginal Mind,* London: Charles Scribner's Sons.

Davies, Christie (1975) *Permissive Britain: Social Change in the Sixties and Seventies,* London: Pitman.

Dawson, Christopher (1942) 'What about heretics: An analysis of the causes of schism', *The Commonweal,* 18 September, pp. 513-17.

Dobbie, Flo (1972) *Land Aflame!,* London: Hodder & Stoughton.

Doherty, Robert (1967) *The Hicksite Separation: A Sociological Analysis of Religious Schism in Early Nineteenth-Century America,* New Brunswick: Rutgers University Press.

Durkheim, Emile (1933) *The Division of Labour in Society,* Glencoe: Free Press.

Duster, Troy (1970) *The Legislation of Morality,* New York: Free Press.

Eister, Allan W. (1950) *Drawing-Room Conversion,* Durham, N. Carolina: Duke University Press.

England, R.W. (1954) 'Some aspects of Christian Science as reflected in letters of testimony', *American Journal of Sociology,* 59(5), pp. 448-53.

Enroth, Ronald M., Edward E. Ericson and C. Breckinridge Peters (1972) *The Story of the Jesus People,* Exeter: The Paternoster Press.

Festinger, Leon, Henry W. Reicken and Stanley Schachter (1956) *When Prophecy Fails,* New York: Harper & Row.

Fletcher, Winston (1970) 'Britain's national media pattern' in Jeremy Tunstall (editor), *Media Sociology,* London: Constable.

Fodor, Nandor (1949) *The Search for the Beloved,* New York: Hermitage Press.

Foster, Sir John (1971) *Enquiry into the Practice and Effects of Scientology,* London: Her Majesty's Stationery Office.

Gamson, William A. (1975) *The Strategy of Social Protest,* Homewood, Illinois: Dorsey Press.

Gardner, Martin (1957) *Fads and Fallacies in the Name of Science,* New York: Dover.

Glock, Charles Y. and Rodney Stark (1965) 'On the origin and evolution of religious groups' in their *Religion and Society in Tension,* Chicago: Rand McNally.

Goffman, Erving (1968) *Asylums,* Harmondsworth: Penguin Books.

Greenacre, Phyllis (1941) 'The predisposition to anxiety', *Psychoanalytic Quarterly,* 10, pp. 66-94.

Greenslade, S.L. (1953) *Schism in the Early Church,* London: SCM Press.

Gusfield, Joseph R. (1955) 'Social structure and moral reform: a study of the Woman's Christian Temperance Union', *American Journal of Sociology,* 61 (November), 221-32; (1963) *Symbolic Crusade: Status Politics and the American Temperance Movement,* Urbana, Illinois: University of Illinois Press.

Halsey, A.H. (1972) 'Leisure', in A.H. Halsey (editor), *Trends in British Society since 1900,* London: Macmillan, pp. 538-74.

Hine, Virginia H. (1974) 'The deprivation and disorganisation theories of social movements' in Irving I. Zaretsky and Mark P. Leone, *Religious Movements in Contemporary America,* Princeton, New Jersey: Princeton University Press.

Horowitz, Irving Louis (editor) (1967) *The Rise and Fall of Project Camelot,* Cambridge, Mass.: MIT Press.

Hubbard, L. Ron (1968) *Introduction to Scientology Ethics,* Copenhagen: Scientology Publications Organisation.

Humphreys, Laud (1970) *Tearoom Trade,* London: Duckworth.

Jackson, John (1966) 'Two contemporary cults', *The Advancement of Science,* 23(108), pp. 60-4.

Jackson, John and Ray Jobling (1968) 'Towards an analysis of contemporary cults' in David Martin (editor) *A Sociological Yearbook of Religion in Britain* (No. 1), London: SCM Press.

Jackson, Maurice, Eleanora Petersen, James Bull, Sverre Monsen and Patricia Richmond (1960) 'The failure of an incipient social movement', *Pacific Sociological Review*, 1, pp. 35-40.

Jackson, Michael P. (1974) *The Price of Coal*, London: Croom Helm.

Kanter, Rosabeth Moss (1972) 'Commitment and the internal organisation of millennial movements', *American Behavioral Scientists'*, 16(2), pp. 219-43.

Kaufman, Robert (1972) *Inside Scientology*, New York: Olympia.

Kimber, William (1972) 'Libel — a book publisher's view' in Michael Rubinstein (editor), *Wicked, Wicked Libels*, London: Routledge and Kegan Paul.

Klapp, Orrin E. (1959) 'Vilification as a social process' *Pacific Sociological Review*, 2(2), pp. 71-6; (1969) *Collective Search for Identity*, New York: Holt, Rinehart & Winston.

Kirkpatrick, Robert G. (1971) *The Socio-Sexual Dialectics of Decency Crusades*, University of Texas at Austin: Unpublished PhD Dissertation.

Lee, John A. (1970) *Sectarian Healers and Hypnotherapy*, Toronto: Queen's Printer.

MacIntyre, Alasdair (1971) 'Is a science of comparative politics possible?' in his *Against the Self-Images of the Age*, New York: Schocken Books.

Malko, George (1970) *Scientology: The Now Religion*, New York: Dell.

Mann, W.E. (1955) *Sect, Cult and Church in Alberta*, Toronto: University of Toronto Press.

Messinger, Sheldon (1955) 'Organisational transformation: a case study of a declining social movement in *American Sociological Review*, 20(1), pp. 3-10.

Michels, Robert (1958) *Political Parties*, Glencoe: Free Press (originally published 1911).

Milgram, Stanley (1974) *Obedience and Authority*, London: Tavistock.

Muncy, Raymond Lee (1973) *Sex and Marriage in Utopian Communities*, Indiana University Press: Bloomington, Indiana.

Nelson, Geoffrey (1968) 'The concept of cult', *Sociological Review*, 16(3), pp. 351-62.

221

Niebuhr, H. Richard (1957) *The Social Sources of Denominationalism,* New York: Meridian Books (originally published 1929).

Nyomarkay, Joseph (1967) *Charisma and Factionalism in the Nazi Party,* Minneapolis: University of Minnesota Press.

O'Dea, Thomas F. (1957) *The Mormons,* Chicago: University of Chicago Press.

O'Toole, Roger (1975) 'Sectarianism in politics: case studies of Maoists and De Leonists' in Roy Wallis (editor), *Sectarianism: Analyses of Religious and Non-Religious Sects,* London: Peter Owen, New York: Halsted Press.

Panel on Privacy and Behavioral Research (1967) 'Privacy and behavioral research: preliminary summary of the report of the panel on privacy and behavioral research', *Science,* Vol. 155 (February), pp. 535-8.

Parkin, Frank (1968) *Middle Class Radicalism,* Manchester: Manchester University Press.

Pfautz, Harold W. (1956) 'Christian Science: a case study of the social psychological aspects of secularisation', *Social Forces,* 34, pp.246-51; (1964) 'A case study of an urban religious movement: Christian Science' in E.W. Burgess and D.J. Bogue (editors), *Contributions to Urban Sociology,* Chicago: University of Chicago Press.

Pope, Liston (1942) *Millhands and Preachers,* New Haven: Yale University Press.

Pym, Bridget (1974) *Pressure Groups and the Permissive Society,* Newton Abbott: David and Charles.

Ranulf, Svend (1964) *Moral Indignation and Middle Class Psychology,* New York: Schocken Books.

Scheler, Max (1961) *Ressentiment,* Glencoe: Free Press.

Schneider, Herbert H. and George Lawton (1942) *A Prophet and a Pilgrim,* New York: Columbia University Press.

Smelser, Neil (1962) *Theory of Collective Behaviour,* London: Routledge & Kegan Paul.

Spittal, F. (1973) 'Sociological research: production or destruction', *Freedom* (September), p. 4.

Studdert-Kennedy, Hugh (1947) *Mrs. Eddy: Her Life, Her Work, Her Place in History,* San Francisco: Farallon.

Swihart, Altman (1931) *Since Mrs. Eddy,* New York: Henry Holt.

Trudgill, Eric (1976) *Madonnas and Magdalens: The Origins and Development of Victorian Sexual Attitudes,* London: Heinemann.

Bibliography

Vidich, Arthur and Joseph Bensman (1958) *Small Town in Mass Society,* Princeton, N.J.: Princeton University Press.

Vosper, Cyril (1971) *The Mind Benders,* London: Neville Spearman.

Wallis, Roy (1972) 'Dilemma of a moral crusade', *New Society,* 21 (No. 511, 13 July), pp. 69-72; (1973a) 'The sectarianism of Scientology' in Michael Hill (editor), *A Sociological Yearbook of Religion in Britain,* No. 6, London: SCM Press; (1973b) 'Religious sects and the fear of publicity' *New Society,* 24 (7 June) pp. 545-7; (1974) 'Ideology, authority and the development of cultic movements', *Social Research,* 41, pp. 299-327; (1975a) 'The Aetherius Society: a case study in the formation of a mystagogic congregation', *Sociological Review,* 22(1), pp. 27-44; (1975b) 'Scientology: therapeutic cult to religious sect', *Sociology,* 9, pp. 89-100; (1975c) 'The cult and its transformation' in Roy Wallis (editor), *Sectarianism: Analyses of Religious and Non-Religious Sects,* London: Peter Owen, New York: Halsted Press; (1975d) 'Societal reactions to Scientology: a study in the sociology of deviant religion' in Roy Wallis (editor), *Sectarianism: Analyses of Religious and Non-Religious Sects,* London: Peter Owen, New York: Halsted Press; (1976) *The Road to Total Freedom: A Sociological Analysis of Scientology,* London: Heinemann Educational Books; New York: Columbia University Press.

Weber, Max (1970) *From Max Weber* (edited by H.H. Gerth and C. Wright Mills), London: Routledge & Kegan Paul.

Whitehead, Harriet (1974) 'Reasonably fantastic: some perspectives on Scientology, science fiction and occultism' in Irving I. Zaretsky and Mark Leone (editors), *Religious Movements in Contemporary America,* Princeton, New Jersey: Princeton University Press.

Whitehouse, Mary (1967) *Cleaning-Up TV: From Protest to Participation,* London: Blandford Press; (1972) *Who Does She Think She Is?,* London: New English Library (revised paperback edition).

Whitworth, John McKelvie (1976) 'Communitarian movements and the world', in Roy Wallis (editor), *Sectarianism: Analyses of Religious and Non-Religious Sects,* Peter Owen Ltd: London.

Willems, Emilio (1967a) *Followers of the New Faith,* Nashville: Vanderbilt University Press; (1967b) 'Validation of authority in Pentecostal sects of Chile and Brazil', *Journal for the Scientific Study of Religion,* 6, pp. 253-8.

Wilson, Bryan R. (1959a) 'An analysis of sect development', *American Sociological Review,* 24, pp. 3-15; (1959b) 'The origins of Christian Science: a survey', *The Hibbert Journal,* 57, pp. 161-70; (1960) *Sects and Society,* London: Heinemann; (1967a) (editor) *Patterns of Sectarianism,* London: Heinemann; (1967b) 'Analytical studies of social institutions' in A.T. Welford *et al.* (editors), *Society: Problems and Methods of Study,* London: Routledge & Kegan Paul; (1970a) *Youth Culture and the Universities,* London: Faber & Faber; (1970b) *Religious Sects,* London: Weidenfeld & Nicolson; (1975) *The Noble Savages: The Primitive Origins of Charisma and its Contemporary Survival,* Berkeley and London: University of California Press.

Wilson, John (1971) 'The sociology of schism', Michael Hill (editor), *A Sociological Yearbook of Religion in Britain,* No. 4, London: SCM Press.

Wilson, Kenneth L. and Louis A. Zurcher (1976) 'Status inconsistency and participation in social movements: an application of Goodman's hierarchical modelling', *Sociological Quarterly,* 17 (Autumn), pp. 520-33.

Yinger, J. Milton (1970) *The Scientific Study of Religion,* New York: Macmillan.

Young, Jock (1971) *The Drug Takers,* London: McGibbon & Kee.

Zald, Mayer (1970) *Organisational Change: The Political Economy of the YMCA,* Chicago: University of Chicago Press.

Zald, Mayer and Roberta Ash (1966) 'Social movement organisations: growth, decay and change', *Social Forces,* 44, pp. 327-40.

Zurcher, Louis and R. George Kirkpatrick (1976) *Citizens for Decency: Anti-Pornography Crusades as Status Defence,* Austin: University of Texas Press.

Zurcher, Louis A., R. George Kirkpatrick, Robert G. Cushing and Charles K. Bowman (1971) 'The anti-pornography campaign: a symbolic crusade', *Social Problems,* 19 (No. 2, Fall), pp. 217-38; (1973) 'Ad hoc anti-pornography organisations and their active members: a research summary', *Journal of Social Issues,* 29 (No. 3), pp. 69-94.

Zweig, Stefan (1933) *Mental Healers,* London: Cassell.

37 Eastwood Road
South Woodford
London E18 1BN
Telephone 01-989 7073

Nationwide Festival of Light

25th September 1976

Dear Friend,

      I do hope you can spend a few moments filling in the attached questionnaire. In doing so you will assist the cause of scientific research and also be of help to the Nationwide Festival of Light who have organised this great gathering. There has never been any thorough investigation into who our supporters are and where they come from. In responding to this survey, which the Executive Committee of the Festival of Light have been informed of and are happy to sanction, you will be assisting the cause of pure knowledge and also helping us to see how good our communications are and to discover a little about what sort of people have at heart the values for which we are standing.

Thank you for so much for your help.

Yours sincerely,

O. R. Johnston *Director*

STIRLING UNIVERSITY SURVEY
OF PARTICIPANTS IN NFOL RALLY TRAFALGAR SQUARE

This questionnaire has been prepared by sociologists at the University of Stirling, Scotland, at the suggestion of the Director of the Nationwide Festival of Light. As you will see from the covering letter, it has the approval of NFOL's Executive Committee, who will receive a full report of our findings. The survey team and the Executive of NFOL have a common interest in two main areas — first, in discovering what sorts of people are participating in today's rally; and secondly, what are their main interests and objectives. We all, therefore, hope that you will be prepared to assist us by answering the questions below and on the attached sheet. WOULD YOU PLEASE TAKE THIS QUESTIONNAIRE HOME WITH YOU AND COMPLETE IT THERE. A stamped, addressed envelope is provided in which the completed questionnaire can be returned to us. You will note that your name is not required, since all the information gathered will be quite anonymous.

Thank you for assisting us in this project.

Roy Wallis, D. PHIL.
Richard Bland, M.A.
University of Stirling

1. Would you please tick any of the following activities connected with the Festival of Light in which you have previously taken part:

   (i) The 1971 rally in Trafalgar Square/Hyde Park   . . . . .
   (ii) The 1972 'Dunkirk Miracle' or the London Festival for Jesus   . . . . .
   (iii) Collecting signatures for the Petition for Public Decency

   . . . . .
   (iv) Operation Newsagent   . . . . .
   (v) Spree 73   . . . . .
   (vi) An NFOL activity other than the above   . . . . .
   (vii) No previous activity in connection with NFOL   . . . . .

2. How did you first hear about this rally?

   (i) From your minister   . . . . .
   (ii) Through a church organisation   . . . . .
   (iii) Through an inter-denominational organisation   . . . . .
   (iv) From a friend   . . . . .
   (v) From a leaflet   . . . . .
   (vi) Some other way (describe)

   . . . .

   . . . .

3. How far did you travel approximately to get to the rally? (i.e. one way only) (miles) . . . .

226

4. Listed in the next column are a number of reasons which people might have for participating in today's rally. Could you rank these in the order in which they reflect your own feelings. Put '1' by the reason most important, '2' by the next most important, and so on. If any of the statements has no relationship to your own feelings, would you put '0' by it.

(i) To witness publicly to my Christian faith in the hope of bringing others to Christ   . . . . .

(ii) To protest against the continuing moral decline of Britain   . . . . .

(iii) To secure more effective legislation against immorality   . . . . .

(iv) To protest against the loss of respect and esteem shown to people who live a respectable life   . . . . .

(v) To join with others in showing that there are still many Christians in Britain, and that they have a voice   . . . . .

5. Would you feel that your participation in today's rally will have been wasted if no concrete changes in our society come about as a result of it?

     Yes . . . .
     No . . . .

If 'No', could you say briefly in the space below what you think will have been gained.

. . . .

. . . .

. . . .

. . . .

6. Many Christians feel that in order to reverse the moral decline of Britain pressure for more effective legislation on moral issues and more active evangelism are both needed. If you had to put a priority on one rather than the other for immediate action, which would you place first?

   More active evangelism . . . . .
   More effective legislation   . . . . .

We should now like to ask a few question which will help us to get a clearer picture of supporters of NFOL attending this rally.

7. Sex: Male   . . . . .
     Female   . . . . .

8. What is your age?   . . . . .

9. Marital Status: Single   . . . . .
      Married   . . . . .
      Widowed . . . . .
      Separated/
      Divorced . . . . .

10. If you are, or have ever been married, how many children do you have? . . . . .

11. What denomination are you connected with? . . . .

12. How often would you say that you attended church?
At least once a week . . . . .
At least once a month . . . . .
Less than once a month . . . . .
Rarely . . . . .
Never . . . . .

13. We would now like some information about your occupation.
13a. Are you
In a full-time job . . . . .
A full-time student . . . . .
A Housewife . . . . .
Retired . . . . .
In some other category (please describe for us)

. . . .

. . . .

. . . .

Full-time occupation or retired
13b. If you are in a *full-time job* could you please give us a job name and a short description of the work actually done. If you are *retired*, please answer as for your last full-time job.

. . . .

. . . .

. . . .

Student or housewife
13c. If you are a *student,* could you please tell us about your *father's* job; if you are a *housewife,* could you please tell us about your *husband's* job. We would like a name for the job and a short description of the work actually done.

. . . .

. . . .

. . . .

Student
13d. If you are a *student,* could you please tell us what sort of educational institution you are in (school, teacher training college, secretarial college, university, or whatever).

. . . .

14. At what age did your *full-time* education end? . . . . .

15. Are or were your parents regular church attenders?
Mother: Yes . . . No . . .
Father: Yes . . . No . . .

Thank you for your help. Attached to the questionnaire is a stamped envelope addressed to Dr. Roy Wallis, Department of Sociology, University of Stirling, Stirling FK9 4LA. After completing the questionnaire would you please put it in the envelope and post it. No further stamps are necessary.

228

Index

TF D